10/20

D0447138

Patron Saints

Michael Freze, S.F.O.

Our Sunday Visitor Publishing Division
Our Sunday Visitor, Inc.
Huntington, Indiana 46750

Our Sunday Visitor Publishing Division
Our Sunday Visitor, Inc.
200 Noll Plaza
Huntington, Indiana 46750

International Standard Book Number: 0-87973-464-7
Library of Congress Catalog Card Number: 92-80498

Cover design by Monica Watts

PUBLISHED IN THE UNITED STATES OF AMERICA

464

DEDICATION

This book is dedicated to all the faithful who employ the guidance, protection, and intercession of the patron saints. May you always find comfort and assurance from these intermediaries of God's grace, and may they guide and strengthen you in your faith.

CONTENTS

Teachers, Telecommunications Workers, Television Workers, Theologians, Travelers, Travel Hostesses, Watchmen, Weavers, Wine Merchants, Women's Army Corps, Workingmen, Writers, Yachtsmen.

III. SPECIAL NEEDS AND CONDITIONS / 119

Abandoned, Adopted Children, Alcoholism, Bachelors, Blindness, Bodily Ills, Cancer Patients, Charitable Societies, Child Abuse, Childless, Children, Converts, Convulsive Children, Deafness, Death of Children, Desperate Situations, Difficult Marriages, Divorced, Dying, Emigrants, Epilepsy, Expectant Mothers, Eye Diseases, Falsely Accused, Fathers, Fire Protection, Guardians, Handicapped, Happy Meetings, Headache Sufferers, Heart Patients, Homeless, Invalids, Jealousy, Kidnap Victims, Learning, Lost Vocations, Mental Illness, Mothers, Murderers, Orphans, Parents of Large Families, Plague Patients, Possessed, Poverty, Prisoners, Protectors of Crops, Rejected by Religious Order, Retreats, Rheumatism, Runaways, Schools, Searchers for Lost Items, Second Marriages, Separated Spouses, Sickness, Single Laywomen, Stepparents, Tertiaries, Throat Disease, Travelers, Unattractive People, Victims of Betrayal, Victims of Child Abuse, Victims of Jealousy, Victims of Physical Abuse, Victims of Rape, Victims of Torture, Victims of Unfaithfulness, Widows, Widowers, Women in Labor, Young Brides, Young Grooms, Youth.

IV. OUR LADY / 195

Basilica of Saint Mary Major, Holy Mountain of Our Lady, Immaculate Heart of Mary, Madonna of St. Luke, Mary (Queen of Africa), Notre Dame Cathedral of Paris, Notre Dame de Chartres, Our Lady Help of Christians, Our Lady in America, Our Lady Mediatrix of All Grace, Our Lady of Africa, Our Lady of Altötting, Our Lady of Bandel, Our Lady of Bandra, Our Lady of Banneux, Our Lady of Beauraing, Our Lady of Copacabaña, Our Lady of Czestochowa, Our Lady of Europe, Our Lady of Fátima, Our Lady of Grace, Our Lady of Guadalupe, Our Lady of Guadalupe of Estremadura, Our Lady of High Grace, Our Lady of Hungary, Our Lady of Japan, Our Lady of Kevelaer, Our Lady of Knock, Our Lady of La Salette, Our Lady of La Vang, Our Lady of Limerick, Our Lady of Loreto, Our Lady of Lourdes, Our Lady of Love, Our Lady of Lujan, Our Lady of Madhu, Our Lady of Mariazell, Our Lady of Montserrat, Our Lady of Mount Carmel, Our Lady of Mount Carmel at Aylesford, Our Lady of Nazareth, Our Lady of Peace, Our Lady of Perpetual Help, Our Lady of Pompeii, Our Lady of Pontmain, Our Lady of Ransom, Our Lady of Safe Travel, Our Lady of Shongweni, Our Lady of Sorrows, Our Lady of Tears, Our Lady of the Assumption, Our Lady of the Cape, Our Lady of the Hermits, Our Lady of the Immaculate Conception, Our Lady of the Milk and Happy Delivery, Our Lady of the Miraculous Medal, Our Lady of the Pillar of Saragossa, Our Lady of the Rosary, Our Lady of the Snow, Our Lady of the Turumba, Our Lady of Victory, Our Lady of Walsingham, Our Lady Who Appeared, St. Mary of the Hurons, Sacred Heart of Mary, Virgin of Charity, Titles of the Blessed Virgin Mary.

V. APPENDIX A: SYMBOLS OF THE PATRON SAINTS / 217

CONTENTS
(continued)

AUTHOR'S PREFACE

The idea for *Patron Saints* evolved out of a cooperative effort between myself and my current publisher. This is my third book in a series on saints and spirituality (the others being *They Bore the Wounds of Christ: The Mystery of the Sacred Stigmata*, 1989, and *The Making of a Saint*, 1991, both published by Our Sunday Visitor).

Originally, I had suggested to Bob Lockwood that we make my last work on sainthood and sanctity a bit longer, since such a topic is so broad and comprehensive in nature. It was suggested to me that I break down my work into several different books in a series, as I have consented to do. We are now planning a fourth in the area of saints and spirituality: *Voices, Visions, and Apparitions: Supernatural Manifestations in the Life of the Church*, which will be released after this current work is published.

The justification for a book on patron saints is quite obvious to me. For one thing, there are few (if any) books in print which deal extensively and exclusively with such a topic. I had to spend a great deal of time researching dozens of sources for information on patron saints just to accumulate the material presented in this book. Secondly, there are no sources available which give a comprehensive treatment on patron saints from every walk of life and for every type of circumstance imaginable: countries and nations, occupations and vocations, special needs and conditions, etc.

In this book, you will find an additional feature which should prove helpful to any serious student of the lives of the saints. I have chosen to present this material as a resource guide, using alphabetized categories for all entries. In this way, one has the convenience of locating any particular patron saint and his or her intercessory role quickly and efficiently.

Furthermore, all entries include brief biographical profiles for those who want a background on the life of the particular saint.

Following each biographical entry is a brief summary of what that saint is a patron of and how he or she came to be invoked for particular favors: as protectors from various illnesses or dangers, as intercessors for favors or blessings, etc.

This work is also different because it includes a breakdown of the various roles of the Blessed Virgin Mary as patron of many places and causes. To my knowledge, no other work in print offers this variety of perspectives on the lives, deeds, and roles of the patron saints, both ancient and modern.

It is hoped by this author that the reader will be able to use this work as a standard resource guide whenever confronting the issue of patron saints and their intercessory roles. There are many "lives of the saints" books on the market, usually in a dictionary or encyclopedia-type format. This book goes beyond the A-Z listing of saints, for everything is placed according to appropriate categories.

Another convenience is provided for the reader at the end of each entry. If there are other patron saints of a particular theme or category not profiled, I have included these additional names for further reference in case one wants to research other saints on their own (space does not permit every patron saint who ever lived to be profiled in detail; this would made the book prohibitive in price).

To aid the reader in quickly finding relevant information about the nature or background of the saint's particular patronage, I have placed the information in a brief second paragraph immediately following the biographical profile. In that way, if the reader wants to disregard the life history of a saint, he or she can skip to the second paragraph for specific details about why the saint is a patron. This breakdown should benefit those who need to locate particular information without weeding through an entire profile.

When a biographical profile has already been done once in the text, to avoid repetition I have given references where to look for the complete profile should a saint reappear many times under different categories. This was important to do, for many saints are patrons for several different causes. In this case, I do give a brief description of why that saint is a patron for a certain place, occupation, vocation, or need. Then I refer the reader to the proper location of the detailed biographical profile.

One weakness in a book of this nature concerns the basis for many of the saints' patronages. There are a number of patrons whose intercessory role is based upon myth or legend. There are those who are known as patrons of particular needs or occupations, for example, without a clear understanding of why they are associated with this intercessory role. A good example is found with the category "Grocer" under the unit "Occupations and Vocations." Saint Michael the Archangel is invoked as the patron of grocers. But there is no strong foundation to justify that Michael helps grocery workers in particular ways. Perhaps at some point in history a certain store owner received a favor because of his invocation of the Archangel; perhaps the story is legendary. Under these circumstances where sufficient proof or justification is lacking in the historical records, one must take an educated guess as to why the association exists in the first place. Fortunately, this is an exception to the rule, but it does exist.

In order to provide a quick and easy guide for locating any particular saint or category, I have broken down all the terms and names for this very purpose. The Table of Contents includes an alphabetical list of all the categories and subsequent terms for easy reference. The Index is assembled according to all the saints' names used in this book. Behind each of these names is a breakdown of every category in which they appear. In fact, the indexing system is really composed of five separate sections or sub-indexes. For further information, see the introduction to the Index of Patron Saints found at the end of the book.

It is my sincere desire that you the reader find in this material a meaningful contribution to the study of the saints. It certainly has enriched my understanding and appreciation for those special holy people whom God continues to provide in our midst.

Michael Freze, S.F.O.
Deer Lodge, Montana

INTRODUCTION

In my last book on saints and sanctity — *The Making of a Saint* — I focused upon two aspects of sainthood: 1) the lives, deeds, virtues, charisms, spirituality, and imperfections of these chosen souls; and 2) the Catholic Church's official investigative processes and procedures concerning the Servant of God in question (known as a *Cause of Canonization*). The former aspect emphasized the actual lives of the saints as they were lived out in particular states and circumstances — in other words, the day-to-day realities of saints in our midst. The other consideration dealt with the Church's response to the reputation of sanctity of the Servant of God. In this case, authorities use particular methods and criteria for evaluating and judging which souls are worthy to be considered models of our faith and intercessors before the people of God. This is done through the lengthy and complex *beatification* and *canonization* processes.

This current work focuses upon a particular kind of saint — the patron — and the intercessory power that person enjoys among the faithful. As with any *Servant of God* whose Cause has been introduced, there must be authentic proof that the patron saint has interceded for the faithful by bringing them a miracle from God. This miracle can take the form of many different types of intercession: physical, spiritual, or mental healings; protection from physical or spiritual danger, invasion, accidents, physical ailments, fires, etc.; protection from death; the finding of lost items; and particular charisms which increase one's faith, patience, understanding, wisdom, knowledge, strength, talents, or skills.

In a Cause of Canonization, one authentic miracle is required for beatification and one more separate miracle for canonization. The only exception is with martyrs, where the requirement for the beatification miracle is normally dispensed with. In either case, the miracle required is quite exact: it must be a physical healing, period. This rule was established because physical healings are most likely to be "proven" or authenticated since they can be observed through science and medicine in the hospitals and laboratories; furthermore, Church officials, theological and psychological experts, and other people of authority can use their talents and judgments through objective studies involving the alleged miracle at hand. Thus, the physical healing is the most observable and reliable miracle that science and religion can offer judgments about in the world of the supernatural order.

Patron saints must also pass the physical miracle test as well, otherwise they cannot be beatified or canonized. Indeed, many of the patrons mentioned in this book are solely the instruments of physical healings. However, I have gone far beyond the study of miraculous healings in this work by including other ways in which our saints have interceded on our behalf. Whenever we talk about other types of intercession (such as those mentioned above), miraculous healings are already presumed because of the patrons' status as canonized saints.

It is true, however, that many famous saints of the ancient or medieval Church were canonized without the norms of today's rigorous demands. Often a saint would be canonized by a Pope because of a lengthy tradition surrounding the Servant of God: a reputation of sanctity, a life of heroic virtue, miraculous intercessions, etc.

When the public spontaneously claims a Servant of God to be holy and virtuous — and especially if that reputation has continued unbroken for years or centuries — the Church would often bypass the normal lengthy canonization procedures to canonize the saint. There were many of these *equivalent* or *equipollent* canonizations between the twelfth and sixteenth centuries.

Traditional values (such as reputations of sanctity) have always influenced the Church throughout her history; indeed, our teaching body of the Church — the Magisterium — considers both Sacred Scripture and Sacred Tradition as the foundations of our faith. When the Church Magisterium understands both of these sacred deposits in light of an ongoing guidance from the Holy Spirit, she formulates her doctrines, dogmas, and practices for each and every generation of believers.

In light of these facts, it is easy to see why many earlier saints were canonized at a later period when living witnesses were no longer present to give credible testimony about the Servant of God in question. Spontaneous acclamation of the faithful, a long-standing tradition, and the approval and encouragement of the local bishop were in many cases enough justification to quickly proceed with the Cause.

Today, of course, it is quite different. Years of extensive investigations are needed to gather information, question witnesses, and to evaluate and judge the credibility of a particular Servant of God as a model for the faithful and as an intercessor before God. These years of study are designed to provide credible answers about a candidate's reputation of sanctity, virtues, deeds, and intercessory powers.

With these facts in mind, let us remember that many patron saints included in this book are known for specific intercessory powers strictly through a long, unbroken tradition (St. Augustine or St. Jerome), through myth or legend (St. Christopher), or just through answered prayers in the modern world. Because nearly every patron in my book has been formally canonized at some point in the past (I do not include more than a few "beatifieds" in this work), then we must respect all miracles or intercessory powers these saints possess.

It might be said that certain patron saints who are known for different types of intercession — St. Augustine of Hippo (354-430), for example, who is patron of brewers and theologians — may never have interceded for anyone's physical healing during the course of their lives. But we cannot be sure they did not, either.

What may be lacking is historical records or testimonies, but those alone do not prove whether or not a saint interceded for someone's cure at some point in time. It may be the case that this particular saint was better known for a certain type of intercession, or perhaps that intercessory power was more prevalent than a single healing.

This point must be addressed so that the reader understands why many of these patron saints are not involved in physical healings in this book. These could have occurred as well, but we lack solid evidence to prove this is so. With the types of intercession mentioned in this book, there is at least one case on record where sufficient proof or tradition has supported the case in question. For those singular cases where an intercessory power may be the product of legend or myth (such as Nicholas of Myra's "magical ways" with children), I decided to include them anyway, for we cannot disprove their authenticity, either.

Let us use caution and discernment when reading about these saints, careful to avoid both extremes of credulosity and unhealthy skepticism. There should be no danger in readily believing particular legendary accounts of patron saints, for it is usually the case where at least one serious witness or recipient of a patron's intercession in the past has sworn to his or her authenticity.

In the end, who are we to judge whether or not a particular story is true if we aren't there to witness it firsthand? Let us remember that lacking eyewitness testimony or historical accounts does *not* give any definite proof for or against anything in this world.

Perhaps at this point we should talk a bit about the nature of signs or wonders which frequently occur in the lives of the patron saints. These are often the only pieces of evidence we have for verifying the authenticity of a particular intercession or healing which the faithful experience. An example might be appropriate here.

How long has it been since one single person on our planet has seen God in a physical expression? Even Moses did not have a true visual experience of God with the so-called theophany of the burning bush some 1,290 years before Christ (see Ex 3:1-6). There, we see that Moses "hid his face, for he was afraid to look at God" (v. 6). Indeed, we know that "no one has ever seen God" (1 Jn 4:12) and one cannot see God's face and live (Ex 33:20). Why is this so? We know that God is Spirit (Jn 4:24), and that we must as human beings worship him in spirit and in truth (v. 24).

If we cannot see God as He really is with our physical eyes, does this prove the point that God does not exist? Of course not. We believe many things we cannot physically see but nevertheless experience in some profound and moving way. Such is the case with many intercessory powers of the saints where we have little or no eyewitness testimonies or historical records to back up the claims.

We must use caution when drawing conclusions based upon other people's testimonies. Sometimes we just don't have them, and at other times we as humans cannot interpret them correctly. The world of extraordinary grace and miracles is well beyond the finite mind to grasp in its entirety. We must leave room for God to act without demanding to know every motive for His actions. If we don't, then presumption will take over and we'll get nowhere in a hurry.

On the other hand, let us not be too gullible or too quick to believe everything we see or hear, either! The devil has often taken advantage of overly credulous souls, even appearing at times as an angel of light to deceive the faithful (2 Cor 11:14). Jesus once warned us not to follow every person who claims to be a prophet without careful discernment (Mt 24:24).

I have always felt that the best road to take is a middle approach, being cautious but not blind to the possibility of God's direct action in our midst. This attitude may be considered "riding the fence" or "indecisiveness" by some people, but so what? One *should* be both careful and open at the same time; trusting no one is certainly giving everyone the benefit of the doubt. This should be considered a wise approach to the discernment of the supernatural. It is balance that must be sought: not prejudgment or an overwillingness to react prematurely to a claim at hand. Because our world is subject to both light and darkness, taking the safe middle road is the only protection we as Christians continue to have; it is the only safeguard available in doing our best to discern legitimate and authentic cases of sanctity, heroic virtues, and miracles which we can be reasonably confident are of God.

Few things of the supernatural order can really be proven by human standards. However, in many cases we are given signs that our judgments are correct and favorable with God. We must continue to look for these signs whenever they occur, but not to the point of disregarding every claim without them. Jesus warned us about being so insistent upon signs in His Gospel (Mt 12:38-39). Yet we also know that to disregard them altogether is not healthy, either: "You know how to interpret the appearance of the sky, but you cannot interpret the signs of the times" (Mt 16:3).

Again, we must remind ourselves that we have to approach these issues with a proper balance between credulity on one hand and extreme skepticism on the other. This must be true for any theological study involving spiritual or supernatural issues. It is no different for a serious study on the lives and intercessory powers of the patron saints.

Editor's note: *About the Author.* Michael Freze, S.F.O., is the Catholic author of many nationally and internationally published books and articles. He has contributed regularly to *The Voice of Padre Pio* (San Giovanni Rotoldo, Italy) , *The Shroud of Turin News Letter* (St. Louis, Mo.), *The Franciscan Forum* (Chicago, Ill.), *Catholic Twin Circle* (Los Angeles, C alif.). and *The Montana Catholic* (Helena, Mont.).

Freze has published the following books: *Questions and Answers: The Gospel of Matthew* (Baker Book House, 1986, reprinted in Tokyo, Japan, in 1987); *Questions and Answers: The Gospel of Mark* (Baker Book House, 1987); *They Bore the Wounds of Christ: The Mystery of the Sacred Stigmata* (Our Sunday Visitor, 1988), and *The Making of Saints* (Our Sunday Visitor, 1991). Future books include *Voices, Visions , and Apparitions* and *Demonology: A Catholic View,* both tentatively planned for publication by Our Sunday Visitor in 1993.

A best-selling author for OSV (*They Bore the Wounds of Christ*), Freze is a member of the Anaconda Catholic Community in Anaconda, Montana. A graduate of the University of Montana at Missoula, he has a secondary teaching degree with majors in English, history , and religious studies. He has taught English and religion at a Catholic school in Butte, Mont., and has tutored throughout the Anaconda School District.

I. Countries and Nations

AFRICA
See unit on "Our Lady."

ALSACE
Odilia (d. c. 720): Born at Obernheim in the Vosges Mountains; blind from birth; abandoned by parents and adopted by a convent; entered convent at Baume; became abbess of her convent at Hohenburg; known for miracles and visions; founded a monastery at Niedermunster, where she died on December 13.

Odilia was miraculously healed of blindness at her baptism, conducted by St. Erhard of Regensburg, Bavaria, Germany. Because of this, she is also considered patroness of the blind. Feast day December 13.

AMERICAS
Our Lady of Guadalupe (see unit on "Our Lady").

Rose of Lima (1586-1617): Born at Lima, Peru; known for her beauty; resisted parents' efforts for her to marry; lived as a recluse in a garden shack at her home, where she practiced great penance and mortification; joined the Dominicans as a tertiary; experienced many mystical gifts and visions; received invisible stigmata (five sacred wounds in her heart and possibly the crown-of-thorn wounds); died at home in Lima on August 24; canonized by Pope Clement X in 1671 as the first native-born saint of the New World.

It is claimed that many of the intercessions of Rose allegedly spared Lima from nearby earthquakes. Feast day celebrated August 23.

ANGOLA
Immaculate Heart of Mary (see unit on "Our Lady").

ARGENTINA
Our Lady of Lujan (see unit on "Our Lady").

ARMENIA
Gregory the Illuminator (257-332): Also known as "The Enlightener"; son of Anak, who killed King Khosrov I of Armenia; taken to

Caesarea to avoid orders to kill his family by followers of the slain king; later married and had two sons; became Bishop of Ashtishat (Armenia), where he evangelized with great success; helped free Armenia from Persians; many miracles attributed to him; considered the apostle and patron saint of Armenia.

Helped free the Armenians from Persia. Feast day celebrated September 30.

ASIA MINOR

John the Apostle (first century): Popularly thought to be "the beloved disciple" (Jn 20:2) who stood by the cross with Mary (Jn 19:25-27) and was first of the Twelve to reach the tomb of Jesus (Jn 20:3-4); one of the Twelve Apostles, a Galilean fisherman who was the son of Zebedee and brother to James the Greater; Jesus gave both brothers the nickname "Boanerges," meaning "sons of thunder"; along with Peter and James, John saw our Lord transfigured (Mt 17:1-8) and was witness to other events; tradition claims that he was eventually taken prisoner to Rome under Emperor Diocletian; his miraculous survival of an attempt to put him to death led the authorities to banish him to the island of Patmos, where he allegedly wrote the book called *Revelation* or *The Apocalypse*; tradition also claims that after Diocletian died (A.D. 96), John was allowed to return to Ephesus, and that it was here that he wrote the fourth Gospel between 90-100; also the author of 1 John and possibly 2-3 John (his authorship of the Gospels and Epistles is disputed).

Patron of Asia Minor because St. Irenaeus claimed that John settled in Ephesus with the Blessed Virgin Mary after Jesus' resurrection (probably immediately following the martyrdom of Peter and Paul). An ancient tradition suggests that after John died his body was never found; hence, he may have been miraculously assumed into heaven without tasting death. The rumor is supported by the reference in Jn 21:20-23, which indeed suggests that many believed "the beloved disciple" could not die a natural death. Catholics believe that Mary was assumed into heaven in this way, possibly from her last residence in Ephesus or Jerusalem. Feast day, December 27.

AUSTRALIA

Our Lady Help of Christians (see unit on "Our Lady").

BELGIUM

Joseph (first century): Of royal lineage from David; came from Bethlehem but moved to Nazareth, where he took up carpentry work; all we know of Joseph is recorded in Matthew 1-2 and Luke 1-2; betrothed to

Mary, but reluctant to marry her after he assumed she was pregnant by another; the angel Gabriel told him in a dream that the power of the Holy Spirit had made Mary pregnant, convinced, he married her and became foster father to Jesus of Nazareth; according to Matthew, Joseph took Mary and Jesus to Egypt after hearing Gabriel say that Herod was going to try to kill the child; after Herod died, Joseph brought the family back to Nazareth; Joseph and Mary took Jesus to Jerusalem but temporarily lost him when they were returning to Nazareth (the story of Jesus in the Temple is based upon this incident); he probably died before Jesus' Passion, for the Gospels do not mention him again during the later part of Jesus' life.

Joseph was declared a model for all families by Pope Leo XIII in 1889. The May 1 feast of St. Joseph the Worker was established by Pope Pius XII in 1955. He was also declared patron of the Universal Church by Pope Pius IX in 1870, patron of social justice by Pope Pius XI, and patron and protector of workingmen by Pope Benedict XV. Joseph has since been named patron of Belgium. Feast day March 19. (Also patron of *Canada*, *Carpenters*, the *Dying*, and *Peru*.)

BOHEMIA

Ludmila (860-921): Daughter of a Slavic prince; married the Duke of Bohemia, Borivoj, who was baptized by St. Methodius; she was strangled to death by anti-Christian forces; buried in St. George's church at Prague; venerated to this day in Czechoslovakia.

Built the first Christian Church in Bohemia slightly north of Prague. Feast day September 16.

Wenceslaus (907-929): Born near Prague; son of Duke Ratislav of Bohemia; educated by grandmother (St. Ludmila); learned Latin at a young age; became ruler of Bohemia in 922 after his father died; married and had a son; murdered on his way to Mass by his brother Boleslaus because Wenceslaus' son was now heir to the throne (thus denying Boleslaus the honor).

Spread Christianity throughout Bohemia. Many miracles were reported at his tomb. Patron of modern *Czechoslovakia*. Feast day, September 28.

BORNEO

Francis Xavier (see "Missions, Foreign").

BRAZIL

Peter of Alcántara (1499-1562): Born at Alcántara, Estremadura, Spain; studied law at Salamanca University; joined the Observant Franciscans at age 16; known for great penances; founded a friary at

Babajoz at age 22; ordained in 1524; renowned preacher; superior of many religious houses; great mystic; initiated Franciscan reform; confessor of St. Teresa of Avila; encouraged her to reform the Carmelites; wrote *Treatise on Prayer and Meditation*, which was used by St. Francis de Sales; died at convent in Estremadura (October 18); canonized by Pope Clement IX in 1669. Declared patron of Brazil in 1862; feast day, October 19.

Other Patron: *Immaculate Conception* (see unit on "Our Lady").

CANADA

Anne (first century B.C.): Legendary figure who was the wife of Joachim and mother of the Blessed Virgin Mary (according to the apocryphal *Protevangelium of James*); as tradition claims, Anne was barren but received word from an angel that she would have a child, which she promised to dedicate to God (very similar to the infancy narrative of Luke's Gospel concerning the Incarnation of Jesus through Mary); a legend reports that Anne was from Nazareth, the daughter of the nomad Akar; she had married Joachim at age 20 and gave birth to Mary at age 40; apparently, Joachim died just before Jesus' birth.

Anne is the patroness of Canada. Her feast day is July 26. (Also patron of *Cabinetmakers* and *Women in Labor*, "Occupations and Vocations.")

Joseph (see also *Belgium*, or *Carpenters* under "Occupations and Vocations").

CHILE

James the Greater (see *Pilgrims* under "Occupations and Vocations").
Our Lady of Guadalupe (see unit on "Our Lady").

CHINA

Joseph (see *Belgium*, or *Carpenters* under "Occupations and Vocations").

COLOMBIA

Louis Bertran (1526-81): Born at Valencia, Spain; joined Dominicans at age 18; ordained in 1547; master of novices for thirty years; known for his preaching; influenced St. Teresa of Ávila to reform her order (they first met in 1557); helped plague victims in Valencia; engaged in missionary work throughout the Caribbean, converting thousands of Indians; eventually came back to Valencia (1569), where he trained preachers; died from an illness at 55 years of age; canonized by Pope Clement X in 1671.

In 1562, Louis went to Cartagena in New Granada (Colombia) as a missionary. It is reported that in the first three years he converted thousands of Indians to the faith, and eventually baptized some fifteen thousand people. Many miracles and prophecies occurred during his stay there. Some of the places he traveled to were Panama, the Leeward Islands, St. Thomas in the Virgin Islands, and St. Vincent in the Windwards. Feast day, October 9.

Peter Claver (1581-1654): Born at Verdu in Catalonia, Spain; studied at University of Barcelona; began Jesuit novitiate at age 20; continued studies at college of Montesione at Palma in Majorca; sent on missionary work to New Granada (Colombia) in 1610; studied at Jesuit house of Santa Fe, where he later worked as cook, porter, sacristan, and infirmarian; ordained a priest at Cartagena in 1615; died in his cell after a long illness; canonized by Pope Leo XIII in 1888.

Peter Claver was declared patron of all missionary activities among Negroes (Blacks) by Pope Leo XIII. While in Columbia, Claver was dedicated to serving the imported slaves of his region. He taught the Christian faith to the Blacks and baptized over three hundred thousand slaves. He was also known for many prophecies and miracles. Peter Claver ministered to the Blacks with food and medicine, caring for the sick and lepers. Feast day, September 9.

CORSICA

Immaculate Conception (see unit on "Our Lady").
Devota (see *Monaco*).

CUBA

Virgin of Charity (see unit on "Our Lady").

CZECHOSLOVAKIA

John Nepomucene (1340-93): Born at Nepomuk, Bohemia; studied at the University of Prague; vicar general of Archbishop John of Genzenstein at Prague; murdered on March 20 at Prague; canonized by Pope Benedict XIII in 1729.

Patron of Czechoslovakia, where he is invoked against floods and against slander. Nepomucene was thrown into the river Moldau in 1393. The body had washed ashore in the morning, and loyal followers buried it in the cathedral of St. Vitus. There is an old bridge over the place where he was thrown in the river. It is marked with a plate containing seven stars, recalling the story that on the night he died seven stars shone brightly over the water. For the invocation against slander, see *Confessors* under "Occupations and Vocations." Feast day, May 16.

Other Patrons: *Wenceslaus, Procopius.*

DENMARK

Ansgar (801-65): Born near Amiens, France; became a monk at Old Corbie monastery in Picardy; became abbot of New Corbie and first Archbishop of Hamburg in 831; great missionary work; appointed first Archbishop of Bremen in 848; gift of preaching and miracles; known as the "Apostle of the North" and first Christian missionary of Scandinavia; died at Bremen on February 3.

Ansgar built the first Christian church in Sweden. He became legate to the Scandinavian countries through Pope Gregory IV. Engaged in great missionary work throughout Denmark. Feast day, February 3.

Canute (d. c. 1086): Born the illegitimate son of King Sweyn Estrithson of Denmark; he was also the nephew of King Canute of England; became King of Denmark as Canute IV (succeeding his brother in 1081): married Adela, sister of Count Roberts of Flanders; known for his missionary work and building of churches; tried to take over England because of his claim to the throne, but failed; fled to the island of Funen; he was murdered there along with his brother Benedict and seventeen followers; miracles reported at his tomb; canonized by Pope Pascal II in 1101.

The miracles attributed to Canute — as well as the fact that he was killed while kneeling at the altar when he finished his confession — led Pope Paschal II to canonize him at the request of King Eric III of Denmark. Feast day January 19.

DOMINICAN REPUBLIC

Dominic (1170-1221): Born at Calaruega, Spain; studied at University of Palencia (1184-94); ordained a priest there; preached against Albigensians; reformed Cistercians; founded the Order of Preachers with six companions in France (Dominicans); order approved by Pope Honorius III in 1216; traveled and preached all over Italy, Spain, France, and Hungary; died at Bologna on August 6, 1221; canonized by Pope Gregory IX in 1234.

The patron saint of astronomers. Dominic reportedly received a sign from heaven in 1206 which led to his founding of a monastery to shelter nine nuns at Prouille near Fanjeaux. These nuns had been former Albigensian heretics. Feast day celebrated October 8.

Our Lady of High Grace (see unit on "Our Lady").

EAST INDIES

Thomas the Apostle (first century): A Galilean Jew who became one of the Twelve Apostles; His Syriac name means "twin," and the Greek version of his name is Didymus; Thomas is best known for his doubting that Jesus had risen (Jn 20:24-25); he later believed when Jesus appeared to him and allowed him to touch his wounds and flesh (Jn 20:26-29); tradition claims that he missionized in India and was martyred there in A.D. 72

Some legends claim that Thomas did missionary work in Parthia, Malabar, Edessa, and parts of the East Indies. Feast day celebrated on July 3.

ECUADOR

Sacred Heart: The devotion and adoration given to Jesus Christ in memory of his blood sacrifice for the salvation of all believers. Specifically, the Sacred Heart is adored because it represents the heart of the crucified Lord which was pierced by a Roman soldier (Jn 19:34), causing blood and water to issue forth. Devotion to the Sacred Heart began with the revelations and apparitions of Jesus to St. Margaret Mary Alacoque (1647-90) before the Blessed Sacrament. Later, Claude de la Columbière (1641-82), Margaret Mary's spiritual director, adopted devotion to the Sacred Heart in his Jesuit Order (including the Apostleship of Prayer). Prior to the actual revelations of St. Margaret Mary Alacoque, many saints had developed the idea of devotion to the Sacred Heart: Bernard of Clairvaux (1090-1153), Bonaventure (1221-74), Mechtilde (1210-80), Gertrude (1256-1302), Frances of Rome (1384-1440), Francis de Sales (1567-1622), and John Eudes (1601-80). This is a movable feast day held on the Friday after the second Sunday after Pentecost solemnity. Pope Clement XIII approved of a Mass and Office for this feast in 1765. In 1856, Pope Pius IX extended the observance of this feast throughout the Roman Rite.

EL SALVADOR

Our Lady of Peace (see unit on "Our Lady").

ENGLAND

George (see *Portugal*, or *Boy Scouts* under "Occupations and Vocations").

EQUATORIAL GUINEA

Immaculate Conception (see unit on "Our Lady").

EUROPE

Benedict of Nursia, Father of Western monasticism, brother of Scholastica, also considered patron of speliologists (cave explorers), perhaps because some institutions were in caves and grottoes.

Cyril and Methodius (ninth century): Greek missionaries, brothers venerated as apostles of the Slavs; Cyril (d. 869) and Methodius (d. 885) began their missionary work in Moravia in 863; developed a Slavonic alphabet; used the vernacular in the liturgy, a practice which was approved; canonized in 1880 by Pope Leo XIII.

Declared patrons of Europe along with St. Benedict in 1980. They were given this honor because of their enormous influence upon the Church throughout the continent, especially in Eastern Europe where they were responsible for converting many Slavs and getting the Slavonic tongue approved for the liturgy in such places as Russia, Serbia, The Ukraine, and Bulgaria: a fact which holds true to this day. Because of this, they are also known as "Apostles of the Slavs." Feast day celebrated February 14.

FINLAND

Henry of Uppsala (d. c. 1156): Originally from England, Henry ended up in Rome; in 1151, he left for Scandinavia with the papal legate, Nicholas Cardinal Breakspear (the future Pope Adrian IV); became Bishop of Uppsala, Sweden, in 1152.

Henry invaded Finland with King Eric of Sweden in order to defeat the pirates of that country; Henry stayed on in Finland when the king returned home; he was eventually killed by a convert named Lalli, who sought revenge upon Henry because he imposed a severe penance on him for another murder he had committed. Feast day, January 19 (although he probably was never formally canonized).

FRANCE

Joan of Arc (1412-1431): Born to a farm family on January 6 at Domremy, France, youngest of five children; experienced supernatural visions at age 13 (such as St. Michael, St. Catherine, and St. Margaret); told in these voices to save France by aiding the Dauphin; canonized by Pope Benedict XIV in 1920.

Joan led the French army in 1429 against the English invaders besieging Orléans. They were captured by Burgundians the following year and turned over to an ecclesiastical court on charge of heresy. Joan was found guilty and was burned at the stake. Her innocence was eventually declared in 1456. Joan of Arc was declared patroness of France; she is also known as the Maid of Orléans; feast day on May 30.

Our Lady (Notre Dame) of Lourdes, La Salette, the Miraculous Medal, Pontmain, etc. (see unit on "Our Lady").

Thérèse of Lisieux (1873-97): Born at Alençon, France, on January 2; youngest of nine children; after mother's death when Thérèse was 5, family moved to Lisieux; raised by older sisters and aunt; professed into Carmelite

Order in 1890, taking the name Thérèse of the Child Jesus; lived a hidden, cloistered life; suffered from tuberculosis, dying nine years later; her "little way" of spiritual perfection became widely known through her autobiography, *The Story of a Soul*; died on September 30 at Lisieux; canonized by Pope Pius XI in 1925; declared patron of foreign missions (with Francis Xavier) in 1927; patroness of aviators.

In 1944, Therese was declared co-patroness of France with Joan of Arc. Her feast day is celebrated on October 1.

GERMANY

Boniface (Winfrid): (c. 680-754): Thought born at Crediton, Devonshire, England, and baptized with the name Winfrid; ordained in 715; famous teacher and preacher; martyred near Dukkum in Holland on June 5; canonized by Pope Pius IX in 1874.

Boniface was sent by Pope Gregory II to evangelize in Germany. He was known as the "Apostle of Germany." Boniface established a monastery at Fulda and became Archbishop of Mainz in 747. He also was made metropolitan of Germany beyond the Rhine and became the apostolic delegate for Germany. He reformed the Frankish church. Feast day, June 5.

George (see *Portugal).*

Michael the Archangel (see *Grocers* under "Occupations and Vocations."

GIBRALTAR

Our Lady of Europe (see unit on "Our Lady").

GREECE

Andrew the Apostle (first century): Born in Bethsaida of Galilee near the lake of Genesareth (Sea of Galilee); son of Jonah and brother to Peter, who with Andrew became the first of Jesus' Apostles (Mt 3:18-20); Eusebius tells us that Andrew preached in Scythia; Theodoret claims that he also went to Greece, as do St. Gregory Nazianzen, St. Jerome, and St. Philastrius; other traditions state that Andrew settled in Byzantium and in time he died a martyr at Patras, Achaia (Greece); that his remains were later moved to Constantinople and his relics were transferred to the cathedral of Amalfi in Italy after the invasion of Constantinople by the Crusaders. Because it was claimed that Andrew also preached as far away as Kiev in *Russia*, he is also considered patron of that country. (See also *Scotland*.)

Nicholas of Myra (see *Russia*).

HOLLAND

Willibrord (658-739): Born in Northumbria, England, he was sent by St. Wilfrid to Ripon Monastery at age 7; later spent twelve years studying at Irish monasteries with Sts. Egbert and Wigbert; ordained in 688; did missionary work in Friesland (690); ordained bishop of the Frisians at Utrecht by Pope Sergius I; founded the Echternach Monastery in Luxembourg; baptized Pepin the Short (Charles Martel's son) in 714; died during a retreat at Echternach in Luxembourg.

Willibrord's missionary work was so successful that he became known as "the Apostle of the Frisians." Feast day November 7.

HUNGARY

Our Lady of Hungary (see unit on "Our Lady").

King Stephen (975-1038): Born at Esztergom in Hungary; baptized in 985 at age 10; married Gisela, sister of Henry III, Duke of Bavaria, at age 22; became ruler of the Magyars after his father's death in 977; died at Szekesfehervar, Hungary, on August 15; canonized by Pope Gregory VII in 1083.

Stephen was crowned first King of Hungary in 1001 with the blessings of Pope Sylvester II. He later appointed St. Astrik (Anastasius) as first archbishop of Hungary; Stephen is remembered for numerous contributions to the Church and government of Hungary: he built many churches and St. Martin's Monastery; he united the Magyars, instituted legal reforms, reorganized the government, established various episcopal sees, and was famous for his charitable actions toward the poor. Feast day celebrated August 16.

ICELAND

Thorlac Thorhallsson (1133-93): Born in Iceland; deacon at age 15; ordained at age 18; studied abroad; founded monastery at Thykkviboer; named Bishop of Skalholt (1178); reformed his church; cult never officially approved; canonized five years after his death by Pope Innocent III in 1198.

Thorlac was declared patron of Iceland in 1984. His feast day is December 23.

INDIA

Our Lady of the Assumption: A title and role given to Mary and especially honored in the countries of *India* and *Paraguay* (q.v.). In 1950, Pope Pius XII declared as dogma that Mary was spared physical death and taken up to heaven both body and soul immediately at the end of her earthly life. This belief centers around the fact that Mary was immaculately conceived and lived a life free from all sin. If this is the case, then a sinless body should not be subjected to the sting of physical death and corruption. The dogma of the Assumption is only fitting, for the Mother of God, who, like her Son, was preserved from sin her entire life, should be exempt from normal human corruption. Devotion to Our Lady of the Assumption gives hope for all believers that one day we too will overcome death, be created anew, and have eternal life with God in heaven. Then there will be no more sorrow, tears, suffering, or corruption, but only everlasting happiness and peace in the Lord.

IRELAND

Bridget (Brigit): (c. 450-525): Possibly from Faughart near Dundalk, Louth, Ireland; parents baptized by St. Patrick; became a nun and lived the contemplative life with seven other nuns at Croghan Hill; died at Kildare on February 1.

Bridget founded the monastery at Kildare and became the abbess of the first convent in Ireland. Along with Sts. *Patrick* and *Columba*, she is considered the patron of Ireland. Feast day, February 1. (See *Dairy Workers* under "Occupations and Vocations.")

Columba (c. 521-97): Born Colum (Colm, Columcille) of royal parents at Gartan, Donegal, Ireland; became a deacon at Moville; ordained to priesthood in Clonard; moved to Glasnevin, later returning to Ulster, where he preached, taught, became a monk and founded monasteries; as a missionary in Scotland, founded a monastery at Iona which was a center for converting Scots, Picts, and northern English; died at Iona on June 9 with a reputation for holiness and miracles.

Columba founded many monasteries all over Ireland, including Derry, Durrow, and Kells. He also preached throughout the country. Columba gave Ireland its first copy of St. Jerome's psalter. Feast day, June 9.

Patrick (389-461): Born in Roman Britain or at Kilpatrick near Dunbarton, Scotland; legend and myth surround his life; carried off in slavery at age 16 to Ireland; escaped to Gaul; ordained in 417; made bishop by St. Germanus and returned to Ireland in 432; converted Ireland to Christianity; founded cathedral at Armagh; wrote *Confessio* and *Letter to the Soldiers of Coroticus*.

Patrick is patron of Ireland along with Sts. *Bridget* and *Columba*. Many legendary miracles are attributed to him (such as driving the snakes out of Ireland). His cult began in Downpatrick after his death. His feast day is celebrated on March 17.

ITALY

Catherine of Siena (1347-80): Born March 25 at Siena, Italy, one of twenty-five children; mystical experiences began at age six; resisted efforts of parents to have her marry; lived a life of prayer, penance, and contemplation; visions of Jesus, Mary, and the saints; care for the sick and poor; Bl. Raymond of Capua her confessor and biographer; received the visible stigmata at Pisa in 1375 (became invisible through most of her life, but reappeared at her death); supported crusades against the Turks; wrote the *Dialogue*, her mystical experiences with God; died of stroke on April 21 in Rome; canonized in 1939; declared Doctor of the Church by Pope Paul VI in 1970.

Catherine was declared patroness of Italy by Pope Pius XII in 1939. She helped encourage Pope Gregory XI to return to Rome in 1376, thus ending the Avignon Papacy which plagued the Church for many years (1305-76). Her feast day is April 29.

Francis of Assisi (1182-1226): Born to a wealthy merchant family in Assisi, Italy; spent youth seeking pleasure and worldly things; a soldier, imprisoned in 1202; returned to wars in 1205; vision of Christ at Spoleto caused conversion; went on pilgrimage to Rome in 1206; lived a life of poverty and simplicity; denounced his worldly father as he embraced the faith; repaired churches in Assisi area; worshiped at the Portiuncula, a little chapel outside of Assisi; founded the Franciscan Order in 1209; verbal approval for rule by Pope Innocent III in 1210; after several revisions, final approval of rule by Pope Honorius III in 1223; built first Nativity crèche at Grecchia in 1223; received the visible stigmata (the first known) on Mount Alverna in 1224; known for his love of animals and nature; wrote the famous *Canticle of the Sun*; died on October 3, 1226; canonized in 1228.

Francis is patron of *Italy, Catholic Action,* and *ecologists*. He preached all over central and southern Italy, gaining thousands of converts along the way. Francis helped promote concern and respect for the land and animals of his native region. His feast day is celebrated on October 4. (See *Ecologists* under "Occupations and Vocations.")

JAPAN

Peter Baptist (1545-97): Born near Ávila, Spain; joined Franciscans in 1567; worked as a missionary in Mexico; sent to Philippines in 1583; assigned to Japan in 1593 as a commissary to the Franciscans; died a martyr in Japan; canonized by Pope Pius IX in 1862.

Peter Baptist was proclaimed patron of Japan because he was crucified there along with twenty-five other Christians under the Emperor Toyotomi Hideyoshi. This occurred on February 5 near Nagasaki. Known as one of the Martyrs of Japan. Feast day, February 6.

KOREA

Joseph (see *Carpenters* under "Occupations and Vocations").

Mary (1st century): A Jewish maiden from the lineage of the house of

David and the tribe of Judah; tradition claims that her parents Anne and Joachim — both legendary figures — were from Nazareth; according to Catholic teaching, Mary was conceived without the stain of Original Sin (the doctrine of the Immaculate Conception, declared by Pope Pius IX in 1854, which is celebrated on December 8); the Church celebrates her birthday on September 8, although there is no historical evidence to prove exactly when she was born; because she was believed to be a chosen child of God, a feast of her presentation in the Temple is celebrated on November 21; according to tradition, she was engaged to Joseph at age 14; when she conceived Jesus by the power of the Holy Spirit (the Feast of the Annunciation, March 25), Gabriel visited her in Nazareth to confirm the miraculous Incarnation; assured that she remained faithful, Joseph married her thereafter; Mary visited her cousin Elizabeth in her third month of pregnancy (and Elizabeth's sixth with John the Baptizer), a celebration we acknowledge with the Feast of the Visitation (July 2); Mary gave birth to Jesus in a cave near Bethlehem after the family was required to appear there for the Roman census; the Church has celebrated this birthday on December 25 (Christmas), although there is no evidence that this date is accurate; the celebration of Christ's birthday on December 25 only dates back to the fourth century, coinciding with the Roman celebration called Saturnalia, the feast of the winter solstice; Mary presented her new child in the temple (the Feast of the Purification, February 2); according to Matthew's Gospel, Joseph took the family to Egypt after the angel Gabriel warned him in a dream that Herod was going to kill all infants under the age of two in order to destroy the new Messiah; the Holy Family relocated in Nazareth, where Jesus was raised; Mary was present at Jesus' first miracle at Cana, where he turned the water into wine (Jn 2:1-11); she was also present at the foot of the cross (Jn 19:25-27) and in the Upper Room with the Apostles for prayer and Eucharist after Jesus' death (Acts 1:12-14); tradition claims that she lived with John the Apostle in Ephesus after Jesus' resurrection; the Church states that she was assumed into heaven body and soul without undergoing corruption (the doctrine of the Assumption as declared by Pope Pius XII in 1950). (See various roles of Mary under the section "Our Lady.")

LESOTHO

Immaculate Heart of Mary (See unit on "Our Lady").

LITHUANIA

Casimir of Poland (1458-84): Born on October 13 in Krakow, the third child of thirteen to King Casimir IV of Poland and Elizabeth of Austria (daughter of Emperor Albert II of Germany); known for holiness and charitable deeds at an early age; refused his father's command to go against King Matthias Corvinus of Hungary in order to take over the

Hungarian empire; imprisoned in a castle at Dobzki for disobeying his father; died on March 4 at the court of Grodno while visiting Lithuania; many miracles reported at his tomb in Vilna; known as the "Peace Maker"; canonized by Pope Adrian VI in 1522.

Declared the patron saint of Poland and Lithuania. His feast day is March 4.

LUXEMBOURG

Willibrord (see *Holland*).

MALTA

Paul (d. c. 67): A Jew from the tribe of Benjamin; born Saul in Tarsus, thus a citizen of Rome; studied under Gamaliel in Jerusalem; a tentmaker by trade; became a strict Pharisee in his early years; notorious persecutor of Christians (he was present at the killing of the first martyr, Stephen); while traveling to Damascus to arrest some Christians, Jesus' voice called to him and he was instantly blinded; after the voice asked him why he persecuted His Church, Paul was converted (c. A.D. 34-36); spent three years in solitude in Arabia; returned to Damascus to preach; local Jews turned on him, and he was forced to go to Jerusalem around 36-39, meeting the Apostles; Barnabas befriended him and helped him to be accepted by the Christian community there; returned to Tarsus for a few years; in A.D. 43, Barnabas brought him to Antioch, where he became a teacher in the local church; sent on three missionary journeys: 45-49, he and Barnabas went to Cyprus, Perga, Antioch in Pisidia, and cities in Lycaonia (it was during this journey that he changed his name to Paul); on the second journey, 49-52, he and Silas visited such places as Philippi, Thessalonica, Berea, Athens, and Corinth; on his third journey, 53-58, he spent two years in Ephesus; after returning to Jerusalem, he was arrested by Roman Governor Felix at Caesarea; his successor, Festus, arranged for his trial in Rome; there he was kept prisoner 61-62; arrested again at Troas, returned to Rome for another imprisonment; according to tradition, he was martyred there as was St. Peter about A.D. 67 under Emperor Nero; stories claim he was beheaded and Peter was crucified upside down; Paul's writing output was enormous; he is the biggest contributing author to the books of the Bible: Romans (57-58), 1 Corinthians (54); 2 Corinthians (57); Galatians (54); Colossians, Philemon, Ephesians, and Philippians (61-63); 1 and 2 Thessalonians (51-52); 1-2 Timothy and Titus; authorship of Hebrews is disputed. Feast day of Paul's conversion is celebrated on January 25.

Paul is considered the patron of Malta because of a shipwreck in a storm off that island on his way to be tried in Rome (A.D. 61 or 62).

Courageously, Paul carried on with another ship headed for Rome, where he would die under Emperor Nero a few years later.

Our Lady of the Assumption (see unit on "Our Lady").

MEXICO

Our Lady of Guadalupe (see unit on "Our Lady").

MONACO

Devota (d. 303): Born in Corsica; martyred for her faith during Diocletian's persecutions of Christians.

Devota's remains are preserved at the Riviera de Ponenta in Monaco. She is patron of both Monaco and Corsica. Feast day January 17.

MORAVIA

Cyril and Methodius (see *Europe*).

NEW ZEALAND

Our Lady Help of Christians (see unit on "Our Lady").

NORWAY

Olaf II (d. 1030): Born in Norway; pirate as a youth; served King Ethelred of England fighting against the Danes; captured Norway from the Swedes and Danes and was proclaimed king; helped to Christianize Norway; killed at the Battle of Stiklestad on July 29; miracles surrounding his shrine; canonized by Pope Alexander III in 1164.

Not too popular during his lifetime, Olaf became one of the great heroes of Norway. A chapel built at his shrine became the Cathedral of Trondheim, pilgrimage center for all Scandinavia. Feast day, July 29.

PAPUA NEW GUINEA

Michael the Archangel (see *Grocers* under "Occupations and Vocations").

PARAGUAY

Our Lady of the Assumption (see *India* or "Our Lady").

PERU

Joseph (see *Belgium,* or *Carpenters* under "Occupations and Vocations").

PHILIPPINES

Sacred Heart of Mary (see unit on "Our Lady").

POLAND

Casimir (see *Lithuania*).

Stanislaus (1030-79): Born of noble family at Szczepanow near Krakow, Poland, on July 26; famous preacher and spiritual adviser; ordained Bishop of Krakow (1072); martyred by Boleslaus for denouncing cruelties; canonized by Pope Innocent IV in 1253; patron of Cracow; feast day, April 11.

Our Lady of Czestochowa: A miraculous icon brought to Czestochowa by Prince Ladislaus Opolczyk to the monks of Saint Paul in 1384, probably made between the fifth and eighth centuries. After it suffered damage by raiders in 1430, King Ladislas Jagiello had the icon restored by Austrian artists. Also known as the "Madonna of Czestochowa," this image shows Mary pointing her right hand to the Child Jesus held in her left arm. Many kings and high-ranking officials the world over came and paid tribute to the Madonna of Czestochowa. Miracles surrounding this icon began in 1402, and later the people identified this Marian image as the "Healer of the Sick, Mother of Mercy, and the Queen of Poland." By 1957, over fifteen hundred healings were on record. The first public coronation of the icon occurred in 1717 with Pope Clement XI. By 1979, over two million pilgrims visited Our Lady of Czestochowa. Today, more than 10,000 altars around the world have duplicate images of this famous and miraculous icon.

PORTUGAL

Immaculate Conception (see unit on "Our Lady").

Anthony of Padua (1195-1231): Born in Lisbon, Portugal; joined the Canons Regular of St. Augustine in 1210; ordained in 1220; became a Franciscan and changed his name to Anthony in 1221; preached to Moors in Morocco; a successful preacher throughout Italy; came to Padua in 1226; famous as confessor; known for work with prisoners, the poor, and the heretics; died from dropsy en route from Camposanpiero to Padua, at a Poor Clare convent at Arcella on June 13; canonized only one year later (fastest on record) in 1232; declared Doctor of the Church by Pope Pius XII in 1946; famous for his miracles and wonder works; nicknamed "Hammer of the Heretics," "Living Ark of the Covenant," and "Wonder Worker."

Anthony is patron of Portugal because he was born and raised there, receiving his early formation in Lisbon. He became a Franciscan while still in Portugal (1221). Feast day, June 13.

Francis Borgia (1510-1572): Born at Gandia near Valencia, Spain; son of the Duke of Gandia; mother reportedly granddaughter of King

Ferdinand V of Aragon; married Eleanor de Castro in 1529 and had eight children; widowed in 1546; joined the Jesuits in 1548; appointed commissary general of the order in Spain by St. Ignatius (1554); appointed Father General in 1565; expanded the Jesuits; instrumental in the Catholic Counter Reformation; encouraged missionary work; founded colleges and universities; revised Jesuit rule in 1567; called second founder of the Jesuits; died in Rome on September 20; canonized by Pope Clement X in 1671.

Francis spent time in Portugal working against the Inquisition under King Philip II. He spread the work of the Jesuits in this country as well as in Spain and France. Feast day, October 18.

George (d. 303): Legendary figure who is patron of England, Portugal, Germany, Aragon, Genoa, and Venice; venerated in the East as one of the Fourteen Holy Helpers; martyred in Lydda, Palestine; legend claims he slew a dragon in Libya (*Golden Legend*); "St. George's Arms" became a part of the British uniforms of soldiers and sailors; patron of knights, soldiers, and Boy Scouts; feast day April 23. (See also *Boy Scouts* under "Occupations and Vocations.")

Vincent of Zaragoza (d. 304): Ordained a deacon by Bishop Valerius of Zaragoza; engaged in preaching and teaching throughout Spain; imprisoned at Valencia because of the persecutions of Dacian, governor of Spain; tortured but remained steadfast in the faith; burned on a gridiron; thrown in a dungeon thereafter, where he eventually died.

Tradition claims that some of Vincent's relics were transferred to Lisbon, Portugal. Devotion to him soon spread rapidly. He is also considered patron of vinedressers, probably because his name suggests some connection with wine. Feast day, January 22.

RUSSIA

Andrew the Apostle (see *Greece*).

Nicholas of Myra (d. c. 350): Born at Patara, Lycia, Asia Minor; legendary aspects of life; ordained Bishop of Myra; known for holiness and miracles; imprisoned for faith under Emperor Diocletian; participated at Council of Nicaea (325); opponent of Arianism; according to legend, gave money and gifts to the poor; saved three girls from prostitution by throwing bags of gold in their home, causing all three to eventually marry; this and other traditions (such as his restoring the dead girls to life) started the practice of giving children Christmas gifts in his name for good luck; Nicholas became Sint Klaes to the Dutch, then Santa Claus; in 1087, relics brought to Bari, Italy, where they remain in the St. Nicholas Basilica;

patron of Russia, Greece, Apulia, Sicily, Lorraine; of storm-beset sailors, coopers, and children; feast day, December 6.

Thérèse of Lisieux (see *France*).

SCANDINAVIA

Ansgar (see *Denmark*).

SCOTLAND

Andrew the Apostle (first century): A legend claims that part of his relics were transferred to Scotland by St. Rule (Regulus) in the fourth century. This occurred after an angel warned him to take the relics to a safe place "toward the ends of the earth" in a northerly direction. He stopped at Saint Andrews, Scotland, preserved the relics there, and became its first bishop. Feast day, November 30. (See *Greece*.)

Columba (see *Ireland*).

SILESIA

Hedwig (Jadwiga): (1174-1243): Eighth child of Count Berthold IV; two brothers became bishops: Eckbert of Bamberg and Berthold of Aquileia; sister Getrude became mother of St. Elizabeth of Hungary; educated at convent in Kitzingen; married Henry I of Silesia in 1186; had seven children (three died in childhood); known for her fair administration and justice toward all; helped to found several monasteries throughout her territory; founded a number of houses for religious and encouraged Cistercians, Franciscans, and Dominicans to come to Poland; built Hospital of the Holy Ghost at Breslau; charitable to lepers; the first convent for women in Silesia was founded by her husband Henry in 1202 (Cistercian convent at Trebnitz); moved to that convent after her husband died, becoming a tertiary there; many miracles reported through her intercession; canonized by Pope Clement IV in 1267 (only twenty-four years after her death).

Hedwig became Duchess of Silesia, Poland, when her husband became Duke of Silesia upon his father's death in 1202. She was only twelve years old at the time of the marriage, and he was only eighteen. Feast day, October 16.

SLOVAKIA

Our Lady of Sorrows (see unit on "Our Lady").

SOUTH AFRICA

Our Lady of the Assumption (see unit on "Our Lady").

SOUTH AMERICA

Rose of Lima (scc *Americas*).

SPAIN

Teresa of Ávila (1515-82): Born at Ávila, Castile, Spain, March 28; educated by Augustinians, but had to leave their convent when illness struck; became a Carmelite at Ávila in 1536; professed in 1537; left for several years because of illness, but returned in 1540; experienced many voices and apparitions 1555-56; founded a stricter rule for her nuns at St. Joseph Convent, Ávila (1562); founded second convent at Medino del Campo, where she first met St. John of the Cross (Juan Yepes); founded first Carmelite monastery for men at Duruelo (1568); gave John of the Cross authority to found reformed convents for men thereafter; traveled throughout Spain reforming her order; after much resistance from many quarters, was restricted by the Carmelite Prior General in spreading her new reforms; finally received official approval for her Discalced Reform of the Carmelite Order by Pope Gregory XIII in 1580; famous writer of many spiritual classics, including her *Autobiography* (1565), *The Way of Perfection* (1573), and *Interior Castle* (1577); died at Alba de Tormes, Spain, on October 4; canonized by Pope Gregory XV in 1622; declared Doctor of the Church by Pope Paul VI in 1970, the first woman to be so honored and one of only two (St. Catherine of Siena was also declared a Doctor in 1970).

Teresa was declared patron saint of Spain because of her extraordinary work founding convents throughout the land, as well as her successful efforts at reform (see profile above). Feast day, October 15.

SRI LANKA (CEYLON)

Lawrence (d. 258): Born at Huesca, Spain; one of seven deacons of Rome; widely venerated martyr who suffered death, according to legend, by being fried on a gridiron; feast day on August 10.

Known for his ability to inspire great devotion even in the face of death, Lawrence has often been prayed to for increased faith and courage in the midst of trial and suffering. (See *Cooks* under "Occupations and Vocations.")

SWEDEN

Bridget (Birgitta): (1303-73): Daughter of a noble Swedish family, her mother died when she was twelve; raised by her aunt at Aspenas, married and later widowed; went to Rome and reformed monasteries there; famed for mystical gifts and prophecies; criticized such popes as Urban V (who later approved her new order, called Brigittines, founded in 1370); known for her visions as noted in her own writing called *Revelations*; died in Rome on July 23; canonized in 1391; patron saint of Sweden (feast, Feb. 1).

Eric (d. 1161): Great Christianizer of Upper Sweden; built the first large church in his country at Old Uppsala; codified Swedish law (King Eric's Law or the Law of the Uppland); victorious against invading Finns; martyred May 18, 1161 at the hands of Danish invaders; never formally canonized, but recognized as Sweden's patron from his death until the Protestant Reformation.

Because of his zeal for spreading Christianity and protecting his country, Eric's banner has been carried in battle by many Swedes throughout the centuries. To carry his banner was thought to bring good luck.

TANZANIA
Immaculate Conception (see unit on "Our Lady").

UNITED STATES
Immaculate Conception (see unit on "Our Lady").

WALES
David (fifth or sixth century): Legendary figure; possible son of King Sant of South Wales and St. Non; became a priest; missionized throughout Wales; died at Mynyw monastery; canonized by Pope Callistus II in 1220.

David founded a dozen monasteries throughout Wales, including the famous one at Menevia in the southwestern part of the country. His feast is celebrated on March 1.

WEST INDIES
Gertrude (the Great): (c. 1256-1302): Parents unknown; placed in the care of the Benedictine nuns at Helfta, Saxony, at age five; friend of St. Mechtilde; mystic who experienced many apparitions of Christ; spread devotion to the Sacred Heart; famous for spiritual writings (*Revelation of St. Gertrude*); died at Helfta on November 17; never formally canonized, but a universal feast day of November 16 was approved in 1677 by Pope Clement XII.

It is unclear why Gertrude was named patron of the West Indies. Perhaps it came about because of the devotion displayed to her there. Feast day November 16.

Gregory the Great (see *Musicians* under "Occupations and Vocations").

II. Occupations and Vocations

ACCOUNTANTS

Matthew the Apostle (first century): A Levite, son of Alpheus, born in Galilee; later worked as a tax collector (Mt. 9:9-13; 10:3); because of his tribal background, was also known as Levi; called by Christ to be His follower at Capernaum (Mk 2:14; Lk 5:27-32); became one of the Twelve Apostles; traditionally revered as author of the first Gospel (c.a. 80-85), supposedly based on a lost original in Aramaic, though the Gospel is in Greek; evidence from the Gospel reveals that it was written by a Jewish Christian of Palestine (probably in Antioch, Syria) for a Jewish-Christian audience; this Gospel stressed the importance of Jewish law and prophecy; tradition claims Matthew preached throughout Judea, then went to the East; that he died a martyr's death in Ethiopia (some legends say he died in Persia); also a patron of bankers and bookkeepers.

Patron saint of accountants and bookkeepers because of his writing skills and his role as Roman tax collector, which required an ability with numbers. Feast day, September 21.

ACTORS

Genesius (d. c. 300): Legendary figure whose story is known through the accounts of St. Gelasius of Heliopolis; according to legend, Genesius performed a Christian play in front of Emperor Diocletian; this play was about baptism and conversion in the faith; because of Diocletian's paganistic background and his anger at this public demonstration, he had Genesius tortured with iron hooks and fire; even then, Genesius continued to proclaim the Lord; he eventually was beheaded.

Genesius used the following lines during the course of his play before the pagan Emperor Diocletian: "I am resolved to die a Christian. . . . I desire to receive the grace of Jesus Christ and to be born again, that I may be delivered from my sins." The power of his acting ability so enraged the emperor that he was martyred for his faith. Thus Genesius is considered a powerful patron of all actors, actresses, and comedians. He is to be invoked for strength, courage, and the ability to persuade and influence others in their faith. Traditional feast celebrated on August 25.

ADVERTISERS

Bernardine of Siena (1380-1444): Born in Massa Marittima, Italy, the son of the local governor; orphaned at age seven and raised by his aunt; began schooling in Siena at age twelve; enrolled at age seventeen in a confraternity of Our Lady where he helped the poor and sick; worked at a hospital in Siena during the plague (1400); later joined the Franciscans; professed and ordained in 1403; engaged in some preaching, but lived a life of retirement and prayer; became known as a great apostle and reformer; in 1417 his preaching in Milan began his fame as a public speaker; eventually preached all over Italy and encouraged devotion to the Holy Name; elected Vicar General of the Friars of the Strict Observance (1430) after turning down the offer to become Bishop of Siena (Pope Martin V, 1427); died at Aquila during a mission in 1444; many miracles reported at his tomb; canonized by Pope Nicholas V in 1450, only six years after his death.

Patron of advertisers and communications personnel because of his evangelization and conversions of thousands to his beloved Franciscan Order. Bernardine founded many convents and reformed the rules of the Observance. Through preaching and teaching, his influence was felt throughout his country. Feast day, May 20.

ALPINISTS

Bernard of Montjoux (996-1081): Born in Italy; became a priest; elected Vicar General of Aosta; built schools and churches in his diocese; missions in the Alps; declared patron saint of both alpinists and mountaineers by Pope Pius XI in 1923.

Became patron and protector of alpinists because of his four decades spent in missionary work throughout the Alps. He also founded two hospices there for the benefit of lost travelers in the mountain passes of Great and Little Bernard (appropriately named after him). Feast day, May 28.

ALTAR BOYS

John Berchmans (1599-1621): Born at Driest, Brabant (Belgium), the oldest son of a shoemaker; early vocation to the priesthood; at age thirteen became a servant in the home of a priest in the cathedral at Malines, where he entered Jesuit school in 1615, becoming a novice in 1616; studied in Rome during 1618, where he died three years later; miracles reported at his tomb; beatified in 1865; canonized in 1888.

John Berchmans was to die as one of the youngest saints of the Jesuit Order (he was only 22). Because of his reputation for holiness and simple, childlike dedication to his vocation and ministry, he is invoked as a patron for young altar boys. John Berchmans performed his tasks with admirable humility, wishing to continue in his "little way" by letting himself be ruled "like a baby a day old." Feast day, August 13.

ANESTHETISTS (ANESTHESIOLOGISTS)

René Goupil (1606-42): Born at Anjou, France; joined Jesuits but forced to leave because of illness; later became a surgeon; sent to Quebec as a Jesuit lay missionary (1638); worked with the Huron Indians in 1640; captured and tortured by Iroquois (bitter enemies of the Hurons) in 1642 while traveling with Isaac Jogues; killed on September 29 by tomahawk mutilation near Albany, New York: the first North American martyr; canonized by Pope Pius XI in 1930.

Patron of anesthetists because of his heroic ability to overcome excruciating pain with undying faith. Feast day, October 19.

ARCHERS

Sebastian (d. c. 288): Born at Narbonne in Gaul, but raised in Milan; many legends surround his life; joined the army at Rome in 283; converted many in the face of persecution; cures reported through his intercession: gout, deafness, etc.; elected captain of guards of both Emperor Diocletian and Maximian; when Maximian found out that he was a Christian, he ordered him killed; eventually beaten to death; venerated as a martyr in Milan as early as the time of St. Ambrose (340-97); buried on the Appian Way.

Considered the patron of archers because, when first ordered to death, he was shot with arrows by one of Diocletian's soldiers; although he was left for dead, the widow of St. Castulus (Irene) found him still alive and nurtured him back to health. Sebastian later proclaimed the Christian faith even more vigorously and denounced the emperor's paganism. Feast day, January 20. (See also *Athletes, Soldiers*.)

ARCHITECTS

Thomas the Apostle (first century): Born in Galilee and nicknamed Didymus, a Greek word meaning "twin"; became one of the Twelve Apostles; famous for doubting Jesus' resurrection, but later converted when he saw the risen Christ and touched his wounds (Jn 20: 24-31); one legend claims that he preached in India; others say he went to Parthia, Persia. Mesopotamia, and Edessa; tradition alleges that he was martyred in India and that his remains were transferred first to Edessa, then to the island of Khios in the Aegean, and finally to Ortona in the Abruzzi, where they are still venerated; an ancient account puts his death on July 3, A.D. 72; the Syrian tradition proclaims Thomas's feast day on July 3 as well, the date when they claim his remains were transferred to Edessa from Mylapore, a city in the region of Malabar; today his universal feast is celebrated on December 21.

Considered the patron of architects because of the tradition that he built or founded so many churches during his missionary journeys, including seven in Malabar.

ARMORERS

Dunstan (910-88): Born of nobility at Baltonsborough near Glastonbury, England; educated by monks; served in the court of King Athelstan while still a youth; became a Benedictine monk in 934; ordained in 939 by his uncle, St. Alphege, Bishop of Winchester; made abbot of Glastonbury by King Edmund in 943; became famous for his monastic reforms and establishing centers of learning; adviser to King Edred after Edmund was murdered; became Bishop of Worcester in 957 and of London in 958; appointed Archbishop of Canterbury in 959 by King Edgar; remained Edgar's adviser for sixteen years; appointed legate by Pope John XII; restored ecclesiastical discipline and continued to reform Church and state in England; died in Canterbury after a brief time of teaching school there; famous musician, hymnist, metalworker, and illuminator of manuscripts.

Dunstan is patron of armorers, goldsmiths, blacksmiths, locksmiths, and jewelers because of his fame and talent in these areas. There was also a popular legend claiming that he once grabbed the nose of the devil with his pair of blacksmith's pincers after a long period of temptation. Feast day, May 19.

ARTISTS

Catherine of Bologna (1413-63): Daughter of a lawyer and diplomat; became a Franciscan tertiary at Ferrara, noted for efforts to reach perfection even at that tender age; known for visions and apparitions, as well as assaults by the evil spirit; vision of Mary with infant Jesus in her arms; appointed superior of a strict convent at Bologna, approved by Pope Nicholas V; established a convent of Corpus Christi; became sick in 1463 and never recovered; died on March 9; reports of a heavenly aroma from her body after death; incorrupt body still preserved at church convent in Bologna; canonized by Pope Clement XI in 1712.

Patron of artists because of her beautifully painted miniatures, still preserved at the convent of Corpo di Cristo in Bologna. Feast day, March 9.

Other Patrons: *Luke* (first century), *Blessed Angelico* (February 21, 1984).

ASTRONOMERS

Dominic (1170-1221): Born at Calaruega, Spain; studied at University of Palencia (1184-94); ordained a priest there; preached against Albigensians; reformed Cistercians; founded a women's institute at Prouille (1206); founded the Order of Preachers (Dominicans) with six companions in France, primarily to convert the Albigensians; order approved by Pope Honorius III in 1216; by 1221, had established sixty friaries in eight provinces; friend of Pope Gregory IX and St. Francis of Assisi; fought the Albigensian heresy; order known for preaching and Bible study; traveled and preached all over Italy, Spain, France, and Hungary; raised a cardinal's nephew from the dead after he was killed in a riding accident; died at Bologna in great poverty on August 6, 1221; canonized by Pope Gregory IX in 1234.

Patronage of astronomers: On the feast of St. Mary Magdalen in 1206, Dominic had a sign from heaven encouraging him to found a convent at Prouille for nine women who had converted from Albigensianism. Thus began the concern for heretics which eventually led to his founding of the Dominican Order (1216). Feast celebrated on October 8.

ATHLETES

Sebastian (d. c. 288) Patron saint of athletes because of his physical endurance and his energetic way of spreading and defending the faith, Sebastian is also patron to all soldiers. He entered the Roman army under Emperor Carinus (283) in order to defend the confessors and martyrs of his day without drawing attention to himself. His efforts kept the faith of Marcus and Marcellian firm during their persecutions, right up through the time of their martyrdom. He was declared patron of plague sufferers because of his reported cures of those afflicted with many diseases. (See also *Archers, Soldiers.*)

AUTHORS

Francis de Sales (1567-1622): Born at Thorens in Savoy, France, August 21; studied at Jesuit college of Clermont in Paris (1580-88); took law and theology at University of Padua; received doctorate at age twenty-four; ordained in 1593; spent five years as a missionary in the Chablais; converted thousands to Catholicism; became bishop of Geneva in

1602; famous preacher, teacher, and intellect; founded many schools and taught catechetics; spiritual director of St. Frances de Chantal; founded the Order of the Visitation (the Visitandines) with Frances in 1610; beatified the year of his death—1622—by Pope Gregory XV, the first formal beatification and one of the fastest ever; canonized by Pope Alexander VII in 1665. Patron of authors and the Catholic press.

Francis de Sales was declared a Doctor of the Church by Pope Leo XIII (1877) because of the many spiritual classics he wrote, including *Introduction to the Devout Life* (1609) and *Treatise on the Love of God* (1616). These works stressed that sanctity and perfection are possible for every Christian, and showed the ways to achieve these goals. Feast day January 24.

AVIATORS

Joseph of Cupertino (1603-63): Born of a poor family on June 17 at Cupertino, Italy; refused entrance to Conventual Capuchins; became a Capuchin lay brother; dismissed because of clumsiness and low intelligence, but later accepted as a tertiary by the Franciscan Conventuals at Grottela; remained at Grottela for seventeen years; finally ordained in 1628; famous for ecstasies, miracles, and levitations; died on September 18 at Osimo; canonized by Pope Clement XIII in 1767; patron saint of air travelers and pilots.

Joseph allegedly experienced some seventy levitations during the course of his life, many of which were verified by eyewitnesses. Pope Urban VIII was impressed by his holiness, and his lofty experiences became known around the world. Feast day, September 18.

Thérèse of Lisieux (1873-97): Born at Alençon, France, on January 2; youngest of nine children; after mother's death, family moved to Lisieux; raised by older sisters and aunt; professed into Carmelite Order in 1890, taking the name Thérèse of the Child Jesus; lived a hidden, cloistered life, suffering from tuberculosis until death nine years later; her "little way" of spiritual perfection became widely known through her autobiography, *The Story of a Soul*; died on September 30 at Lisieux; canonized by Pope Pius XI in 1925.

Declared patroness of aviators and co-patron (along with St. Francis Xavier) of foreign missions by Pope Pius XI in 1927. Also proclaimed co-patroness (along with St. Joan of Arc) of France by Pope Pius XII in 1944. Thérèse had once wanted to serve the Carmelites at Hanoi in Indo-China (who also wished to have her), but tuberculosis got the best of her, causing great pain and suffering the last eighteen months of her life. God's will led her to a life of prayer and vicarious suffering in her convent.

Her good intentions and prayers for foreign missions gave her a special place as patroness of faraway countries. It was a "hidden life" of heroic virtue, the "little way" to perfection, which made her widely known. Feast day October 1.

Other Patrons: *Our Lady of Loreto* (see unit on "Our Lady").

BAKERS

Elizabeth of Hungary (1207-31): Born at Pressburg, Hungary, daughter of Andrew II of Hungary; married Ludwig (son of Landgrave Herman I of Thuringia); bore four children; known for charity; built several hospitals; became a Secular Franciscan after the death of her husband (1228); died at Marburg at age twenty-three; miracles reported at her tomb; canonized by Pope Gregory IX in 1235.

Patroness of bakers and the Secular Franciscan Order. Became a Franciscan tertiary (Secular or lay Franciscan) in 1228, caring for the aged, sick, and the poor at a hospice in Marburg. Because of her earlier vocation as wife and mother of 4 children, Elizabeth served as a model of heroic virtue in fulfilling her duties in that particular state of life. She is also invoked as patron of bakers because of her reputation for feeding the sick and poor at the hospital she built in Wartburg. In 1225, she distributed her entire supply of grain to the needy after a famine hit Germany in that same year. Feast day, November 17.

Other Patrons: *Nicholas* (see *Russia* under "Countries and Nations").

BANKERS

Matthew the Apostle (first century): The Gospel of Matthew tells us that St. Matthew was a tax collector for the Roman government in Palestine at the time when Jesus chose him to be one of His Apostles (Mt 9:9); indeed, he became known as "Matthew the tax collector" whenever he was referred to with the other Apostles (see Mt 10:1-4). Feast day, September 21. (See *Accountants*.)

BARBERS

Cosmas and Damian (d. c. 303): Arabian twin brothers, physicians; studied medicine in Syria; charitable to the poor; defied death by water, fire, and crucifixion before they were finally beheaded with their three brothers during Diocletian's persecution.

Patrons of barbers and physicians. Both Cosmas and Damian studied medicine and became famous for their skills. They offered their services free of charge. Many healings from their intercessions have been claimed throughout the centuries. It is not clear how they became patrons of barbers, except for the fact that barbers were often surgeons as well. Maybe they are invoked because the method of their martyrdom — beheading — involves the same bodily part that a barber must work with. Feast on September 26.

BASKETMAKERS

Antony (Anthony) of Egypt (251-356): Born south of Memphis in Upper Egypt; raised his sister when parents both died; early model of piety and charity; eventually entered his sister in a convent; gave away all of his inheritance to the needy; became a hermit near Koman in 272; lived on bread and water; tempted by the devil; left Koman and moved to Mount Pispir (now Der el Memun) in 285, a solitary fort on top of a hill; lived there in complete isolation for twenty years, dedicated to prayer, penance, and fasting; in 305, he came out of hiding and formed ascetical groups at Fayum (the first Christian monastery); went to Alexandria to support the Christians being persecuted there under Emperor Maximin; returned to Pispir and founded another monastery; later returned to Alexandria to help fight the Arian controversy; retired at Mount Kolzim near the Red Sea with his friend Macarius; founder of Christian monasticism; famous for holiness and wisdom; friend of Emperor Constantine and St. Athanasius; died at the age of 105.

Invoked as a patron of basket-makers: Antony's monastic rule required acts of prayer and manual labor throughout the day, for his were self-sustaining colonies. Included in this labor were such necessities as tilling the soil, weaving baskets and clothing, raising their own crops, etc. He is also the protector against "St. Antony's Fire" (the contagious burning disease of erysipelas, cause of past epidemics). Many cures of this disease have been reported through Antony's intercession. Feast day, January 17.

BEGGARS

Martin of Tours (316-97): Born at Sabaria, Pannonia, Hungary; early army career; ordained Bishop of Tours, France (371); opposed Arianism and Priscillianism; friend of St. Hilary (with whom he founded a monastery); established monastery at Marmoutier; known for visions, revelations, and prophecy; one of the greatest proponents of Western monasticism before the time of St. Benedict; died at Candes in Touraine on November 8.

Patron saint of beggars and of France: In 337 at Amiens, Martin cut his cloak in half and gave one half to a beggar in the freezing cold. Later that night he had a vision of Christ being the one he served disguised as the beggar. This incident led to his conversion. He is invoked as patron of France because of his role as Bishop of Tours and his role in founding the monastery at Poitiers, the first one in Gaul. He also founded a great monastery at Marmoutier. Feast celebrated on November 11.

BLACKSMITHS

Dunstan (910-88): Besides having been a Benedictine monk, abbot of Glastonbury Abbey, and Archbishop of Canterbury, Dunstan was known as a fine composer and metalworker. Feast day May 19. (See *Armorers*.)

BOOKKEEPERS

Matthew the Apostle (first century): Traditionally, the author of the Gospel written in his name. The book was put together sometime around A.D. 80-90, most likely at Antioch in Syria. Matthew was apparently an educated Jew who taught in Greek and Aramaic for Jewish converts to Christianity. Feast day, September 21. (See also *Accountants*.)

BOOKSELLERS

John of God (1495-1550): Born at Montemoro Novo, Portugal on March 8; soldier in wars between France and Spain, as well as against the Turks in Hungary; at age forty, moved to Africa to help rescue Christian slaves; returned to Granada (where he died) promoting the faith; canonized by Pope Alexander VIII in 1690.

Patron of the sick, nurses, hospitals, and booksellers: When returning to Gibraltar, John opened a store and sold religious books and articles (1538). John of God was known for helping the sick and the poor. He started a house for this purpose, which was the beginnings of the founding of the Order of Brothers Hospitalers, or the Brothers of St. John of God. Feast day, March 8.

BOY SCOUTS

George (d. c. 303): Legendary figure; suffered martyrdom at Lydda, Palestine, during the reign of Emperor Constantine; possibly a soldier in the imperial army; legend (twelfth century) suggests that he slew a dragon as a Christian knight in Sylene, Libya; the dragon was attacking the city and a princess, and George rescued them from this foe; after the local princess had led the dragon to the city, all the inhabitants agreed to be baptized if George would kill this beast (which legend claims he did); George later married the princess; this legend is found in the *Golden Legend* (thirteenth century).

Patron of knights, soldiers, and the Boy Scouts: George was invoked by knights and soldiers as early as the Middle Ages, especially among the Crusaders. Later on, "St. George's Arms" (a red cross on a white background) became a symbol on all uniforms of British soldiers and sailors. He is patron of Boy Scouts because of his heroic call to help the innocent in the face of danger and injustice. George exemplifies the strength and heroic character which the Boy Scouts are trained to possess. Feast day, April 23.

BREWERS

Augustine of Hippo (354-430): Patron of brewers because of his conversion from a former life of loose living, which included parties, entertainment, and worldly ambitions. Augustine also lived for fifteen years with a mistress and had a child out of wedlock, named Adeodatus (372). His complete turnaround and conversion has been an inspiration to many who struggle with a particular vice or habit they long to break. Feast day, August 28. (See *Theologians*.)

Other Patrons: *Luke the Evangelist, Nicholas of Myra*

BRICKLAYERS

Stephen of Hungary (975-1038): Born at Esztergom in Hungary; baptized in 985 at the age of ten; married Gisela, the half-sister of Duke Henry III of Bavaria (who became Emperor Henry II in 1002); ruled the Magyars beginning in 997; in 1001, became first King of Hungary (the crown came from Pope Sylvester II); Stephen elected Hungary's first archbishop and established many sees in his country; united the Magyars; died in Szekesfehervar, Hungary, on August 15; canonized by Pope Gregory VII in 1083.

Patron saint of bricklayers: He built many churches during his reign as Hungary's first king. Stephen also completed the building of St. Martin's Monastery, which had been started by his father. Feast day, August 16.

BRIDES

Nicholas of Myra (d. c. 350): Legend records that a citizen of Patara lost all of his money and could not afford to support his three daughters, nor could he find them husbands because of their poverty. When he contemplated prostitution for his daughters, Nicholas intervened by throwing bags of gold at the man's window in order to pay for their dowries. Feast day, December 6. (See *Russia* under "Countries and Nations.")

BRUSHMAKERS

Antony of Egypt (251-356): Antony was a hermit who lived in the desert of Egypt and practiced a life of extreme penance and mortification.

He may be the patron of brushmakers because of his daily work habits, which included manual labor. Feast day January 17. (See *Basketmakers.*)

BUILDERS

Vincent Ferrer (1350-1419): Born at Valencia, Spain, on January 23; joined Dominicans in 1367; taught philosophy; commanded to preach through a vision of Christ, St. Dominic, and St. Francis (1398); helped to end the Western Schism; defender of Avignon Popes; converted Bernardine of Siena and Mary of Savoy; preached throughout Western Europe; died at Vannes, Brittany; canonized by Pope Callistus III in 1455.

He is the patron of builders because of his fame for "building up" and strengthening the Church: through his preaching, missionary work, in his teachings, as confessor and adviser. Feast day, April 5.

BUSINESSWOMEN

Margaret Clitherow (1556-86): Born in the City of York; married John Clitherow at age fifteen; bore three children (Henry, William, and Anne); originally a Protestant, but converted several years into her marriage; imprisoned many times between 1577-84 at York Castle for failure to support the Protestant Church in England; in prison, she studied, prayed, and fasted; eventually hid priests in her home as the government of Queen Elizabeth sought to abolish Catholicism in her country; tortured for her faith; a board was placed over her back and weights were thrown on top of her, crushing her bones as the burden increased; she prevailed in her faith, even in the midst of this martyrdom; died at the age of thirty; canonized by Pope Paul VI on October 25, 1970; also known as St. Margaret of York.

Margaret was a capable businesswoman who assisted her husband in their butcher shop. She was known for her fair prices and honesty with customers. Feast celebrated on March 25.

BUTCHERS

Antony of Egypt (251-356): It is unclear why Antony is patron of butchers. Perhaps it is because of the sheepskin cloaks he continually wore as a sign of his simplicity and poverty. It may have something to do with Antony's famous association with the pig. He was continually bothered by the evil spirit, who was often depicted in the symbolic form of a pig (reminiscent of Mt 8:28-32, whereby Jesus commanded the demons to enter the herd of swine in the area of the Gadarenes). Antony is also considered the patron of domestic animals and farm stock. Feast day, January 17. (See *Basketmakers.*)

Luke the Evangelist (first century): Revered by tradition as author of the third Gospel and the Acts of the Apostles; most likely a Greek who came from Antioch, Luke emphasizes the universal salvation of all believers, Jew and Gentile alike; his is the "Gospel of mercy;" he was a companion to Paul on his second missionary journey (51-54) as well as the third journey (54-58); Luke was with Paul during the latter's imprisonment in Rome (61-63); left for Greece after Paul's death; wrote his Gospel around A.D. 90; the Acts were written in Rome; tradition claims he died at Boethia at the age of eighty-four, possibly martyred.

Patron of butchers, painters, physicians, and surgeons: Luke was a physician by trade (Col 4:14). A tradition claims that he painted several beautiful portraits of the Blessed Virgin Mary, as it is possible he visited her many times in Jerusalem. It is unclear why Luke is a patron of butchers. Perhaps his symbol — the ox — closely resembles a butcher's vocation of sacrificing life in order to sustain life through food, or it may imply a sacrificial offering to the Lord. Feast celebrated on October 18.

CABDRIVERS

Fiacre (or Fiachra) (d. c. 670): Born in Ireland; a hermit at Kilfiachra; went to France and lived as a solitary at Breuil, Brie; built a hospice for travelers; known for his aid to the poor; famous spiritual advisor; many miraculous healings attributed to his intercession.

Patron saint of cabdrivers because in Paris the cab cars are known as *fiacres*, after his name. The first coach for hire in Paris was near the Hotel Saint-Fiacre. Also the patron of gardeners: It is reported that Fiacre built himself a cell out of land given to him in order to live a life of prayer and contemplation; St. Faro, Bishop of Meaux, offered him as much land as he could dig up with his staff in a day. Fiacre miraculously pointed his staff to the ground and sufficient land was cleared of brush and trees without any digging or plowing; Feast day, September 1.

CABINETMAKERS

Anne (first century B.C.): Legendary figure who was the wife of Joachim and mother of the Blessed Virgin Mary (according to the apocryphal *Protevangelium of James*); as tradition claims, Anne was barren but received word from an angel that she would have a child, which she promised to dedicate to God (very similar to the infancy narrative of Luke's Gospel concerning the Incarnation of Jesus through Mary); a legend reports that Anne was from Nazareth, the daughter of the nomad Akar; she had married Joachim at age twenty and gave birth to Mary at age forty. Apparently, Joachim died just before Jesus' birth.

Patron of cabinetmakers: It is unclear how Anne came to be invoked by these craftsmen, especially since the story of her existence is based upon legend to begin with (the apocryphal *Protevangelium of James*). If the legend is really true, then perhaps Anne was a remarkable wife and homemaker, even attending to the building and upkeep of her place. Feast day July 26.

CANONISTS

Raymond of Peñafort (1175-1275): Born at Peñafort, Catalonia, Spain; taught philosophy at Barcelona by age twenty; studied law at Bologna in 1210; received a doctorate in 1216; became archdeacon of Barcelona in 1219; joined Dominicans in 1222; famous for his preaching, especially to the Moors and Christians in Spain; confessor to Pope Gregory IX in Rome; elected Archbishop of Tarragona in 1235, but resigned later because of a serious illness; came back to Spain in 1236, where he continued preaching and serving as confessor; elected master general of Dominicans in 1238; revised Dominican rule; established friaries at Tunis and Murcia; started the Inquisition in Catalonia; convinced St. Thomas Aquinas to write his *Summa Contra Gentiles*; influential writer in his own right, having penned the *Summa de poenitentia (Summa Cassuam)* between 1223-38; died at Barcelona on January 6; canonized by Pope Clement VIII in 1601.

Patron of canon lawyers: He codified papal decrees of 1150, which formed the basis for canon law until the 1917 Code went into effect. Feast day, January 7.

CARPENTERS

Joseph (first century): Of royal lineage from David; came from Bethlehem but moved to Nazareth, where he took up carpentry work; all we know of Joseph is recorded in Matthew 1-2 and Luke 1-2; betrothed to Mary, but refused to marry her after he learned she was pregnant from another source; the angel Gabriel told him in a dream that it was the power of the Holy Spirit which had made Mary pregnant; convinced by his dream, he later married and became foster father to Jesus of Nazareth; according to Matthew, Joseph took Mary and Jesus to Egypt after hearing Gabriel say that Herod was going to try to kill the child; after Herod died, Joseph brought the family back to Nazareth; Joseph and Mary took Jesus to Jerusalem but temporarily lost him when they were returning to Nazareth (the story of Jesus in the Temple is based upon this incident); he probably died before Jesus' Passion, for the Gospels do not mention him again during the later part of Jesus' life; declared a model for all families by Pope Leo

XIII in 1889; the May 1 feast of St. Joseph the Worker established by Pope Pius XII in 1955; declared patron of the Universal Church by Pope Pius IX in 1870; called patron of social justice by Pope Pius XI. Declared patron and protector of workingmen by Pope Benedict XV.

Invoked as patron of carpenters because of the biblical story which identifies him by trade: "Is not this the carpenter's son?" (Mt 13:55). Feast day, March 19.

CARVERS

Olaf II (995-1030): A talented worker with wood from his early years onward. In a later incident, as King of Norway, Olaf was carving a piece of wood, but a servant reminded him that it was a Sunday (when no manual labor was allowed). He then gathered the chips of wood and lit them in the palm of his hand. It was his way to give example to others that he would practice the laws which he himself imposed upon others. Feast day, July 29. (See *Norway* under "Countries and Nations.")

CATECHISTS

Charles Borromeo (1538-84): Born to a noble family at Lake Maggiore, Italy; studied at Benedictine abbey, as well as at Milan and Pavia, where he received his doctorate in canon law in 1552; his uncle was Pope Pius IV, who made him Secretary of State and then Cardinal of Milan; convinced Pope Pius to reconvene the once-suspended Council of Trent (1562); promotor of clerical education; known for his compassion to the poor; founded a society for secular priests, the Oblates of St. Ambrose (now the Oblates of St. Charles) in 1578; resisted Protestantism; died in Milan on November 4; canonized by Pope Paul V in 1610.

Patron saint of learning, catechists, and the arts: Charles established the Confraternity of Christian Doctrine, which contained 740 schools, 3,000 catechists, and 40,000 pupils. He was the originator of "Sunday schools" 200 years before the Protestants began theirs. He promoted learning among the clergy and instituted a literary academy in the Vatican. Feast day, November 4.

Robert Bellarmine (1542-1621): Born at Montepulciano, Tuscany, Italy, on October 4; against his father's wishes, he became a Jesuit in 1560; studied at Florence, Mondovi, Padua, and Louvain; ordained at Ghent in 1570; named professor at Louvain; well-known for his teaching and preaching; became professor of controversial theology at the Roman College (where he remained for eleven years); became rector of Roman College in 1592; elected provincial of the Naples Jesuits in 1594; theological adviser to Pope Clement VIII (beginning in 1597); named

Cardinal by the same Pope in 1599; appointed Archbishop of Capua in 1602 but was called back to Rome three years later by Pope Paul V; great defender of the faith against the Protestants; lived the last days of his life in Rome, where he died on September 17; canonized by Pope Pius XI in 1930; declared a Doctor of the Church by the same Pope in 1931.

Patron saint of catechists because of his great teaching and defense of the Catholic faith. He is the author of many influential works which helped to shape Catholic theology in a profound way: *De potestate papae*, *Art of Dying Well*, etc. He is also famous for his Catholic defense and teaching of the faith in an apologetic work against Protestantism called *Disputationes de controversiis Christianae Fidei adversus hujus temporis Haereticos*. Feast day, September 17.

CHANDLERS (CANDLEMAKERS)

Ambrose (340-97): Born at Trier, Germany; sent to Rome after his father's death; eventually became a lawyer; famous for his rhetoric and learning; named governor of Liguria and Aemilia by Emperor Valentinian, with his capital at Milan; declared Bishop of Milan by popular acclaim after the former bishop (who promoted Arianism) died; although he refused the episcopacy at first, he was forced to take it by order of Emperor Valentinian; after his baptism, Ambrose was ordained Bishop of Milan in 374; changed his life to one of prayer, study, and simplicity; known for his preaching; opponent of Arianism; friend and mentor of St. Augustine, whom he converted to Christianity after a public sermon; he baptized Augustine in 387; adviser to Emperor Gratian; refused to support Arianism in spite of pressure from the Emperors Valentinian II and Theodosius; forced Theodosius to do public penance before he could receive the sacraments (his troops murdered 7,000 people in Thessalonica to revenge the death of governor Butheric); Theodosius publicly confessed his sin, converted, and eventually died in the arms of Ambrose; Ambrose died on March 4 in Milan; one of the Church's greatest writers and leaders; best-known works are *De officiis ministrorum*, *De virginibus*, and *De fide*; declared Doctor of the Church.

Patron saint of chandlers: Although the origin of this patronage is uncertain, perhaps it has to do with the fact that a bright light or halo was seen around Ambrose by his scribe Paulinus while Ambrose was writing a commentary on the Forty-third Psalm. Paulinus described his face as white as snow. Feast day, December 7.

Bernard of Clairvaux (1090-1153): Born at Fontaines les Dijon in Burgundy, third of seven children; studied at Chatillon; left for the first Cistercian monastery at Citeaux in 1112 with friends and relatives; founded the Cistercian house of Clairvaux at Langres (1115); Clairvaux became the motherhouse of sixty-eight Cistercian monasteries, and Bernard was elected its abbot; considered the second founder of the Cistercians; famous for his preaching and miracles; fought against the heresies of Abélard and the Albigensians; known for many writings such as *Diligendo Deo* and *De consideratione*; also wrote 300 sermons, 500 letters, commentaries on Scripture, and many discourses on mysticism; died at Clairvaux on August 20; canonized by Pope Alexander III in 1174; declared a Doctor of the Church by Pope Pius VIII in 1830; the last Father of the Church.

It is unclear why Bernard is proclaimed patron of chandlers. Perhaps it is because he was known as "the oracle of the Church" and "the light of prelates." Since candles surround the altar of the Mass, Bernard once exclaimed that "one who serves by the altar should live by the altar." Another possible connection rests with the fact that the name of the valley of his new Cistercian monastery was changed to Clairvaux because it was situated "right in the eye of the sun." Since blessed candles reflect Christ as the Light of the World, any of these possibilities would explain Bernard's role as patron of chandlers. Feast day, August 20.

CHOIRBOYS

Dominic Savio (1842-57): Born at Riva, Italy; student of St. John Bosco in Turin at the age of twelve; formed the Company of the Immaculate Conception to help Don Bosco in his work; known for prophecies, spiritual wisdom, and heavenly visions; died before his fifteenth birthday; canonized by Pope Pius XII in 1954.

Dominic Savio became a student at the Oratory of St. Francis de Sales in Turin, Italy. He had formed a group there called the Company of the Immaculate Conception, which was devoted to taking care of the church grounds and helping young boys who were misfits of society. He attracted many young people to the Church. Feast day, March 9.

CHURCH CLEANERS

Theobaldus (d. 1150): Born at Vico in the Piedmont, Italy, but grew up at Alba; learned the trade of shoemaker; turned down the offer of his boss to marry his daughter and take over his business after he died; instead, he chose a life of poverty and celibacy; known for giving away his food and earnings to the poor.

Theobaldus spent his last years as a sweeper and cleaner of the cathedral church of St. Lawrence. Many miracles were attributed to his intercession after death. Feast day, June 1.

CLERICS

Gabriel of the Sorrowful Mother (1832-62): Born Gabriel Possenti, the eleventh child of thirteen in Assisi, Italy; educated at the Jesuit school in Spoleto; began formation for the Jesuit Order at age seventeen; kept his promise to become a Religious after being miraculously cured of a disease; entered the Passionist Order at Morroville in 1856; changed his name to Gabriel of the Sorrowful Mother (or Gabriel of Our Lady of Sorrows); known for his penances and personal holiness; helper of the poor; died of tuberculosis at Isola di Gran Sasso in the Abruzzi at age twenty-four; canonized by Pope Benedict XV in 1920.

Patron of clerics because of his exemplary life and faithfulness to his vocation. Gabriel's obedience to God and the Church, his compassion for all people, and his efforts to achieve perfection in the everyday circumstances of life make this saint a model of virtue for all clerics everywhere. Feast day, February 27.

COMEDIANS

Genesius (d. c. 300): The favorite comedian of his day. He once performed in a play which ridiculed the beliefs of the Catholic Church. One day, while mocking the Sacrament of Baptism during a skit performed before the emperor, a fellow player approached him and said, "Well, my child, why hast thou sent for me?" Suddenly, Genesius received an inspiration from the Holy Spirit and converted. From then on, he was a strong defender of the faith. Feast day, August 25. (See *Actors.*)

COMMUNICATIONS PERSONNEL

Bernardine of Siena (1380-1444): Bernardine was noted for his fine preaching and sermons. His fame spread throughout Italy, and eventually he was promoted to vicar general of the Friars of the Strict Observance in 1430. His communicative skills and influence over others were such that he helped to increase the membership of his reformed order from 300 to over 4,000. Bernardine is considered the order's second founder after Francis of Assisi. Feast day, May 20. (See *Advertisers.*)

CONFESSORS

Alphonsus de Liguori (1696-1787): Born at Marianelli near Naples, Italy, on September 21; received doctorate in canon and civil law at the University of Naples at age sixteen; practiced law for eight years; became an Oratorian priest in 1726; involved in missionary work around Naples for two years; founded the Redemptorines in 1731 after being convinced of a vision of Sister Mary Celeste which called for a new order; at Scala in

1732, founded the Congregation of the Most Holy Redeemer (the Redemptorists), which was devoted to missionary work; elected Superior of the Redemptorists in 1743; rule approved for men by Pope Benedict XIV in 1749 and for women in 1750; famous for his many spiritual writings, including *Moral Theology* (1748) and *Glories of Mary* (1750); experienced the dark night of the soul; retired in Nocera after a series of illnesses; died on August 1; canonized by Pope Gregory XVI in 1839; declared a Doctor of the Church by Pope Pius IX in 1871.

Patron saint of confessors because of the hours spent daily in the confessional serving the people of God. Great crowds would come for his direction and absolution, and thousands were converted through his extraordinary gift. Alphonsus was a model of Christian sanctity and perfection. Feast day celebrated August 1.

John Nepomucene (1340-93): This saint refused to tell Emperor Wenceslaus IV what his young wife (the Queen of Bohemia) had revealed to him during confession. The emperor was extremely jealous and suspicious of his wife's faithfulness to him. When John Nepomucene refused to reveal those confessions, it is alleged that Wenceslaus had him put to death. Feast day May 16. (See *Czechoslovakia* under "Countries and Nations.")

COOKS

Lawrence the Martyr (d. c. 258): One of seven deacons of Rome; cared for the goods of the Church, distributed alms to the poor, and helped the sick; sold all he owned, proclaiming the poor people of the Church as the real treasure of this world; this angered the emperor, for Lawrence was mocking the value Rome placed upon money, power, and possessions; he ordered that Lawrence be put to death; died a martyr through the hands of Emperor Valerian (as did Pope Sixtus).

Lawrence refused to renounce the faith, even while being slowly burned on a gridiron. According to St. Ambrose, the divine fire in Lawrence's heart was so aflame that he did not feel the fire of his martyrdom. It is reported that during his agonizing death, Lawrence blurted out, "Let my body be turned; one side is broiled enough." After his executioner had turned him, he said, "It is cooked enough, you may eat." Lawrence then prayed for the conversion of Rome and died. Thus, he is named the patron and protector of all cooks. Feast day celebrated August 10.

Martha (first century): Sister of Mary and Lazarus, who all lived in Bethany; according to tradition, Jesus frequently visited these three at their home during the course of his ministry; Martha (who was the eldest) took care of the house whenever guests were present; she prepared the food and service for Jesus during one of his stays, while Mary gazed at him in contemplation; Jesus replied, "Martha, Martha, you are anxious and troubled about many things; one thing is needful. Mary has chosen the good portion, which shall not be taken away from her" (Lk 10:41-42).

Patron of cooks not only because she was faithful to serving others in her home (and thus fulfilling her Christian duties according to her state and circumstance in life); also, she serves as a reminder from our Lord that one's busy work should always be accompanied by an awareness of the presence of God and by contemplation of His love and goodness throughout each living day. We must "make room for God" in our hearts and direct all our actions according to His will. We must offer up as a loving sacrifice all our works to Him. Feast day, July 29.

COOPERS

Nicholas of Myra (fourth century): Although it is not quite clear why Nicholas is patron of coopers, there is a legendary story whereby it is claimed that he brought three children back to life who had been pickled by an innkeeper and kept in a brine tub. Since coopers are repairers of barrels, the miraculous story of the children's association with the brine tub or barrel gives hope and good fortune to all coopers everywhere! Feast day, December 6. (See also *Russia* under "Countries and Nations.")

COPPERSMITHS

Maurus (sixth century): Given to the care of St. Benedict by his father at age twelve; made assistant to the government of Subiaco by Benedict; miraculously saved a drowning boy (Placid) from a lake by walking over to him on the water; eventually became superior of the monastery at Subiaco; according to an unreliable legend, he left for France and became leader of the abbey of Glanfeuil (Saint-Maur-sur-Loire); died after an illness; buried near the altar in the church of St. Martin.

It is not clear why Maurus is patron of coppersmiths. Feast day, January 15.

COUNCILMEN

Nicholas of Flüe (1417-87): Born of a wealthy family near Sachseln, Obwalden Canton, Switzerland, on March 21; married Dorothy Wissling and had ten children; fought a war with Zurich (1439) and later served as captain in the Thurgau War (1453); became magistrate and councillor for Obwalden; in 1467, became a hermit with his wife's consent and settled at Ranft near Sachseln; he spent his last nineteen years there, existing on only the Holy Eucharist for his food; known as "Bruder Klaus," he was respected for his piety and wisdom and became Switzerland's most famous saint (although he never became her patron); died in his cell at Ranft; canonized by Pope Pius XII in 1947.

After returning from the Thurgàu War (1453), Nicholas was appointed magistrate and councillor by his fellow countrymen of Obwalden. His role as judge and councillor was known to be respected, for he was a man of great fairness and justice to all. Nicholas was responsible for the Edict of Stans, which resulted in the inclusion of Fribourg and Soleure in the Swiss Confederation (1481) after independence had been won from Charles the Bold of Burgundy. Feast day, March 22.

COUNTESSES

Elizabeth of Hungary (1207-31): Elizabeth was the daughter of Andrew II of Hungary and Gertrude of Andechs-Meran. She married Ludwig, the son of Herman I of Thuringia, in 1221. The couple had four children and a happy marriage. During her term as countess, Elizabeth was known for her charity toward the sick and poor. She even built a hospital near the family castle to aid the sick. Feast day, November 19. (See *Bakers*.)

COUNTS

Charles the Good (1083-1127): Raised in the court of his mother's father (Robert de Frison), the Count of Flanders; eventually became a knight; participated in crusade to Palestine; later succeeded to the throne; married Margaret, daughter of Renault, Count of Clermont; devoted to the Flemish people; reformed the laws of his land; fed the hungry after a great drought; attended Mass every morning, walking the way barefoot each day; beheaded by the conspirator Borchard after having one arm cut off; died on March 2; relics kept in Cathedral of Bruges; devotion to this martyr approved by Pope Leo XIII in 1882.

Known as "Charles the Good" because of his reputation for being a just and friendly ruler while he was Count of Flanders and Amiens. He observed the fasts of the Church and helped the plight of the poor. Feast day, March 2.

Gerald of Aurillac (855-909): Known for his prayers, studies, and meditations at an early age; early illness kept him at home for several years; became Count of Aurillac, France; recited Divine Office each day at 2:00 A.M.; made pilgrimage to Rome; dedicated a church at Aurillac to St. Peter; added an abbey to the church; blind for his last seven years; died at Cenezac; buried at his abbey in Aurillac.

Gerald was known for giving all of his wealth to the poor as Count of Aurillac. His modest dress was a reflection of his deep humility. Feast day, October 13.

COURTIERS

Gummarus (Gommaire) (d. 744): Son of the lord of Emblem, near Lièrre in Brabant (Belgium); raised without an education; served in the court of Pepin; married Guinimaria, who was well-to-do, stubborn, and a great source of trial for Gummarus; left for eight years with King Pepin to serve in the war in Lombardy, Saxony, and Aquitaine; returned and found his wife unbearable as before; during his absence, Guinimaria had treated their servants cruel and refused to pay them their just due; Gummarus later made full restitution to them; after an unsuccessful attempt to covert his wife over many years, he finally left her and became a recluse; left on pilgrimage for Rome and set up a hermitage at Nivesdonck; founded the abbey at Lièrre with St. Rumold.

Gummarus showed great patience during his term of office under King Pepin. He was humble, honest, and hard-working. Perhaps the greatest test of Gummarus's life was the burden placed upon him by his wife (see above). Nevertheless, he bore his trials and served his countrymen well. Feast day, October 11.

CRUSADERS

Charles the Good (1083-1127): Charles joined the crusade to Palestine, where he earned the reputation of being a good soldier. He fought alongside his uncle, Robert II. Feast day, March 2. (See *Counts*.)

Louis IX, King of France (1214-70): Born at Poissy, France on April 25; son of King Louis VIII and Blanche of Castile; married Margaret, daughter of Count Raymund Berenger of Provence, in 1234; had eleven children; became King of France in 1234; defeated rebels of southern France (1242-43) and King Henry III of England (1242); founded many religious institutions and schools; rebuilt the Sainte-Chapelle in Paris (1245-48); protected the rights of vassals; brought France to a period of peace and prosperity; built the first French navy; reformed lax laws; canonized by Pope Boniface VIII in 1297.

Louis was involved in two different crusades. The first one was in 1248, when he captured Damietta (1249) but tasted defeat with the Saracens at El Mansura (1250). He was taken prisoner, but upon his release he went to the Holy Land and stayed there until 1254. At that time, his mother died and he returned to France. Another crusade (1270) took Louis to Tunisia. On his way there, he came down with typhoid fever. He died shortly thereafter in Tunis. Feast day, August 25.

Other Patrons: *Bl. Ferdinand of Portugal; Bl. Louis of Thuringia.*

DAIRY WORKERS

Bridget (Brigid): (c. 450-525): Possibly from Faughart near Dundalk, Louth, Ireland; parents baptized by St. Patrick; became a nun and lived the contemplative life with seven other nuns at Croghan Hill; founded the monastery at Kildare and became the abbess of the first convent in Ireland; died in Kildare on February 1; along with Sts. Patrick and Columba, patron of Ireland.

Patron of dairy workers. Legend reports that when she was sent to collect butter made from the milk of her family's cows, she gave it all to the poor. Later, when she begged God to supply her with more butter, her prayers were answered. Another time, when there was no milk to give to a begging leper, Brigid gave her water instead. Miraculously, the water turned to milk. After taking a drink, the leprous woman was instantly healed. Feast day, February 1.

DANCERS

Philemon (d. 305): A popular musician and entertainer during the reign of the Emperor Diocletian; martyred near Alexandria, Egypt, after refusing to sacrifice to the gods.

Philemon was a well-known dancer and piper who offered to take the place of Apollonius in a sacrificial dance to the pagan gods. This he did for four gold coins. Although he hid his face from Diocletian's persecutors (Christians were punished and tortured in those days), before the dance he had a powerful conversion by the Holy Spirit. Philemon secretly received Baptism by desire and refused to dance. He was arrested for his "crime" and martyred with Apollonius in 305 by being sewn up in sacks and cast into the sea. Feast day celebrated on March 8.

DEACONS

Marinus (Marino) (fourth century): Born in San Marino near Urbino, Italy; many legends surround his life; a stonemason by trade; worked with St. Leo (also a stonemason); helped quarrymen who were sentenced to hard labor because of their faith; falsely accused by a madwoman from Rimini of being her estranged husband; panicking, Marius fled to Monte Titano and hid until the woman could no longer find him; he later retreated further into the mountains and became a hermit; on the side of this mountain he formed a new monastery, which became the basis for San Marino today.

Marinus was ordained a deacon in the Church by St. Gaudentius, Bishop of Rimini. For the next twelve years, he remained a hard-working mason, known for his kindness. Feast day, September 4.

DENTISTS

Apollonia (d. 249): Deaconess martyred for not renouncing her faith during the reign of Emperor Philip; the account of the life of Apollonia was written by St. Dionysius to Fabian, Bishop of Antioch.

Apollonia had all her teeth knocked out after being hit in the face by a Christian persecutor under the reign of Emperor Philip. After she was threatened with fire unless she renounced her faith, Apollonia jumped into the flames voluntarily. She is considered the patron of dental diseases and is often invoked by those with toothaches. Ancient art depicts her with a golden tooth at the end of her necklace. Also in art, she is seen with a pair of pincers holding a tooth. Feast day, February 9.

DIETICIANS

Martha (first century): Martha was the sister of Mary and Lazarus and lived in Bethany. It was Martha who took care of the cooking and waiting on guests when Jesus paid a visit to her home (Lk 10:38-42). Feast day, July 29. (See *Cooks*.)

DUKES

Henry II (973-1024): Born to Henry, Duke of Bavaria, and Gisella of Burgundy; born at Hildesheim, Bavaria, on May 6; educated at the cathedral school in Hildesheim and by Bishop Wolfgang of Regensburg; later married Cunegunda, but remained childless; succeeded his father in 995 as Duke of Bavaria; became emperor of consolidated Germany in 1002 and King of Italy in 1004; his brother (by then Duke of Bavaria) jealously turned against him; they fought, but Henry was victorious; he later forgave all who engaged in war against him; crowned Holy Roman Emperor in 1014 by Pope Benedict VIII; miraculously cured by St. Benedict after an illness at Monte Cassino; became one of the greatest rulers of the Roman Empire; his wife was canonized in 1200; died in his palace of Grona near Gottingen, Germany; Henry was canonized by Pope Eugenius III in 1146.

In his role as Duke of Bavaria (and later as King of Germany), Henry was known for Church reforms, building schools, repairing churches, forming dioceses, appointing bishops, opening synods, and supporting monasteries. His feast day is July 15.

DUCHESSES

Hedwig, Queen of Poland (1374-99): Youngest daughter of King Louis I of Hungary; after the king's death in 1382, Hedwig became his successor; charitable to all; passed laws to help the poor; died after a difficult childbirth at age of twenty-eight; miracles reported at her tomb.

Under political pressure and against her will, Hedwig obediently married Jagiello, Prince of Lithuania. Once engaged to William, Duke of Austria and the real love of her life, she had been pressured to forfeit the marriage for political reasons. Hedwig offered her marriage to Jagiello as a sacrifice, uniting her cross to that of the Savior. Her husband eventually converted and baptized through Hedwig's influence. Honored in Poland on February 28.

Ludmila (860-921): Born the daughter of a Slav prince between the Elbe and the Moldau; married Borivoj, Duke of Bohemia (who was baptized by St. Methodius); helped build the first Christian church in Bohemia, slightly north of Prague; known for her gentleness and charity; one of their children was Wenceslaus, whom she raised to be a faithful and pious Christian; strangled to death by rivals at the castle of Tetin; also venerated in Czechoslovakia; feast day, September 16. (See *Bohemia* under "Countries and Nations.")

DYERS

Lydia Pupuraria (first century): Famous because she was Paul's first Christian convert at Philippi; baptized after Paul came to know her and stayed in her home (Acts 16:12-15).

Lydia was born in a town in Asia Minor called Thyatira (Ak-Hissar) which was famous for its dye products. Lydia's name means "purple-seller," and she was working in the dye trade when Paul first met her at Philippi. Feast day unknown.

Maurice (d. c. 287): Served in the Theban Legion of Upper Egypt; refused Maximian's orders to worship the pagan gods; martyred at Agaunum, possibly with the entire Legion of six thousand soldiers; relics preserved at the abbey of Agaunum.

It is unclear why Maurice is a patron of dyers. He is also considered patron of Savoy, Sardinia, infantry soldiers, swordsmiths, and weavers. Feast celebrated September 22.

ECOLOGISTS

Francis of Assisi (1182-1226): Born to a wealthy merchant family in Assisi, Italy; spent youth in pleasure-seeking and worldly things; went to war, imprisoned in 1202; returned to wars in 1205; vision of Christ at Spoleto cause of conversion; went on pilgrimage to Rome in 1206; lived a life of poverty and simplicity; denounced his worldly father as he embraced the faith; repaired churches in Assisi; worshiped at the Portiuncula, a little chapel outside of Assisi; founded the Franciscan Order in 1209; verbal approval for rule by Pope Innocent III in 1210; after several revisions, final approval of rule by Pope Honorius III in 1223; built first Nativity scene at Grecchia in 1223; received the visible stigmata (first known) on Mount Alverna in 1224; canonized in 1228; patron of Italy, Catholic Action, and ecologists.

Francis was well-known for his love of nature and animals. As a tribute, he wrote the famous "Canticle of the Sun" (1225). In this beautiful poem, Francis praises the Creator and all of creation: Brother Sun, Sister Moon, Brother Wind, Sister Water, etc. Feast day, October 4.

EDITORS

John (Don) Bosco (1815-1888): Born of a poor family at Becchi, Piedmont, Italy; ordained in Turin; worked with abused and orphaned boys there; co-founded the Daughters of Mary Help of Christians (for girls); built many churches; died in Turin on January 31; canonized by Pope Pius XI in 1934.

John Bosco founded the Salesians in 1859 (for the education of boys). In 1863, there were 39 Salesians. When he died, there were 768. Today, there are thousands across the world. Salesian accomplishments include schools from primary grades through colleges and seminaries, adult schools, technical schools, agricultural schools, hospitals, foreign missions, and pastoral work. In addition, they are known for their printing and bookbinding shops. Feast day, January 31.

EMPRESSES

Adelaide (931-99): Daughter of Rudolph II of Upper Burgundy; married the son of Hugh of Provence (Lothair); he eventually became King of Italy; the couple had one child named Emma, who ended up marrying Lothair II of France; Lothair died in 950; Adelaide refused to marry Berengarius's son and was imprisoned in a castle on Lake Garda; released by Otto the Great of Germany after he came into Italy and conquered Berengarius's army; Otto married Adelaide on Christmas in Pavia (951), thus combining his German Empire with Italy; they had five children; Otto was crowned emperor at Rome in 962; in 973, Otto died and was succeeded by his eldest son, Otto II; Adelaide founded monasteries for monks and nuns; she died at her monastery at Seltz on the Rhine near Cologne; canonized by Pope Urban II in 1097.

Adelaide was known for her kind treatment of the poor during her reign as empress. She brought about a reconciliation between the wife of her son Otto II (Theophania), her servants, and herself. Adelaide helped to convert many pagans in her country and forgave her enemies. Her feast day is December 16.

Helena (250-330): Born at Drepanum, Bithynia; daughter of an innkeeper; married Roman General Constantius Chlorus in 270; her son Constantine was born between 274-88; the couple was divorced after Constantius was named Caesar under Emperor Maximian (293); Constantine was declared emperor in 312 after his battle at the Milvian bridge; he gave Helena the title "Augusta"; her face appeared on the Roman coins which were struck; died in the East (probably at Nicomedia) and buried at Constantinople.

Helena was converted to Christianity at age sixty-three about the time that her son, Emperor Constantine, enforced the Edict of Milan. Afterwards, she converted many through her promotion of the faith. She was known for her work with the poor and the building of churches. Legend claims that she discovered the True Cross of Jesus while on pilgrimage to the Holy Land. She was kind to soldiers and the poor in Palestine. Feast day, August 18.

Pulcheria (399-453): Born on January 19, the daughter of Emperor Arcadius and Empress Euxodia; her brother Theodosius was declared emperor and she was named "Augusta" in 414; supported Pope St. Leo the Great in his defense of Christian orthodox teachings; became empress when her brother died in 450; vowed to a life of chastity and virginity; married General Marcian and remained a virgin; helped to form the Council of Chalcedon (451) condemning monophysitism; helped to fight the Nestorian and Euthychian heresies of her day; brought the relics of St. John Chrysostom to the Church of the Apostles in Constantinople; died in Constantinople in July of 453.

Pulcheria was known for building many churches and hospitals during her reign. She was also responsible for the building of a university at Constantinople. She gave away her wealth to charity. Pulcheria is venerated throughout the Latin Church, as well as in Greece. Feast celebrated September 10.

ENGINEERS

Ferdinand III of Castile (d. 1253): Son of Alfonso IX, King of León, and Berengaria, daughter of Alfonso III, King of Castile (Spain); declared King of Castile at age eighteen; born near Salamanca; proclaimed King of Palencia, Valladolid, and Burgos; his mother advised and assisted him during his young reign; married Princess Beatrice, daughter of Philip of Suabia, King of Germany; they had seven sons and three daughters; his father (the King of León) turned against him and tried to take over his rule; the two reconciled later; fought successfully against the Moors; in 1225, he held back Islamic invaders; prayed and fasted to prepare for war; extremely devoted to the Blessed Virgin; between 1234-36, conquered the city of Córdoba from the Moors; Queen Beatrice died in 1236; Ferdinand overtook

Seville shortly thereafter; founded the Cathedral of Burgos and the University of Salamanca; married Joan of Ponthieu after the death of Beatrice; died on May 30 after a prolonged illness; buried in the habit of his Secular Franciscan Order; his remains are preserved in the Cathedral of Seville; canonized by Pope Clement X in 1671.

Ferdinand was a great administrator and a man of deep faith. he founded hospitals, bishoprics, monasteries, churches, and cathedrals during his reign. He also reformed and compiled a code of laws which were used until the modern era. Ferdinand rebuilt the Cathedral of Burgos and changed the mosque in Seville into a cathedral. He was a just ruler, frequently pardoning former offenders to his throne. Feast day, May 30.

FARMERS

Isidore the Farmer (1070-1130): Born in poverty at Madrid, Spain; hired farmhand; known for miracles, piety, and charity toward the poor; married Maria Torribia (Maria de la Cabeza), who also became a saint; known for his charity towards the poor; canonized in 1622; miracles reported at shrine; patron of farmers.

Isidore remained a hired farmhand all his life for a wealthy merchant from Madrid. During each workday he prayed faithfully and communicated with his guardian angel and the saints. It is reported that Isidore went to Mass early each day before work. Whenever he was late for plowing, the angels assisted him and did his work in his place. Tradition records that angel-like oxen were seen in his master's field helping Isidore with his daily chores. Numerous miracles were attributed to this saint, such as multiplication of food for the poor whenever a shortage occurred. Feast day, May 15 (U.S.).

Other Patron: *George* (see *Boy Scouts*).

FARRIERS

John the Baptist (first century): Son of the priest Zechariah (Zachary) and Elizabeth, the cousin of Jesus; John was a descendant of the house of Aaron; Zachary received a vision of the archangel Gabriel while serving at the altar; the messenger told him that Elizabeth — though far past childbearing age — would conceive and bear a son; because of his unbelief at first, Zachary's speech was taken away until the birth and circumcision of his son; when he wrote down that his name was to be John, his speech returned (Lk 1:57-64); because of his great joy and under the inspiration of the Spirit, Zachary composed the famous *Benedictus* (Lk 1:67-79), a canticle of love and thanksgiving to God; according to the Gospels, John jumped in Elizabeth's womb when the Blessed Virgin greeted her (1:41);

John grew up to be a great preacher and prophet, living in the desert region of Judea near the Dead Sea (Mt 3:1); his preaching began by the Jordan River around A.D. 27 (when he was about thirty); he called for repentance and conversion of heart, proclaiming that the kingdom of God was at hand (Mt 3:2); John baptized Jesus in the Jordan River, which began the Lord's public ministry (Mt 3:13-17); Herod Agrippa had him imprisoned at Machaerus Fortress on the Dead Sea when John condemned Herod for having an affair with his half-brother Philip's wife, Herodias; later, Salome (daughter of Herodias) asked King Herod for John's head on a platter after she danced for the king and he promised any gift she wanted; John was the last of the Old Testament prophets and one of the greatest from the New; he was the "precursor" of the Messiah (Mt 3:3).

It is not clear why John the Baptist is patron of farriers (blacksmiths). Perhaps it is because he was so close to the earth and labored so hard for the kingdom. It may have to do with the association of his strength and support for the coming kingdom and the iron of a blacksmith's trade. Feast day, June 24 (August 29 for his beheading).

FERRYMEN

Julian the Hospitaler (date unknown): Legendary figure who reportedly married a wealthy widow as a gift from the king; when his wife put his parents up for a night while he was gone, Julian returned home, thought there was a man in bed with his wife, and killed them both; remorseful, he engaged in great acts of penance; later built an inn for travelers and a hospital for the poor.

A leper once visited Julian, who gave him his own bed as an act of charity. Legend claims that the leper was an angel sent to test his faith. Julian left his home after killing his parents (see above) because of his great restlessness and guilt. He was determined to do penance for the rest of his life. Once on a journey he came upon a wide river where people would cross. In a dream, he heard a voice ask him to cross the river and help the people to the other side. When he went to them, he found one nearly dead from the cold. He started a fire, bedded him down, and nursed him back to health. Suddenly this sickly man became bright like sun and ascended into heaven. Julian understood this miracle as a sign that God accepted his penance. He is the patron of hotelkeepers, travelers, and boatmen. His feast is celebrated on February 12.

FIELDWORKERS

Notburga (1264-1313): Born in Rattenberg, Austria; worked as a humble servant; at age eighteen was employed by Count Henry of

Rothenburg, Germany, as a servant in the kitchen; known for giving food away to the poor (including at times her own); later served as a housekeeper for the Count of Tirol; miracles reported at her tomb; buried at the Church of St. Rupert at Eben.

Notburga was employed as a fieldworker at Eben after her service to Count Henry of Rothenburg. Her boss ordered her to continue reaping the fields after discovering that she suddenly quit one Saturday afternoon. Notburga refused, claiming that she must go to church for Saturday Vespers and would continue to pray until Sunday. She claimed that a good Christian should not reap on Sunday with good weather anyway. When her boss argued that the weather might change and ruin his crops, Notburga threw her sickle into the air, where it remained suspended. Feast day, September 14.

FIREMEN

Florian (d. 304): Born in Austria; an officer in the Roman army in Noricum, Austria; surrendered to Aquilinus at Lorsch during the Christian persecutions of Diocletian; he would not renounce his Christian faith; scourged and thrown into the River Enns with a rock around his neck; his body was found and placed in the Augustinian abbey of St. Florian near Linz.

After being beaten for his profession of faith, Florian was set on fire before being thrown into the River Enns. Many miraculous healings have been reported through his intercession. Florian is patron of Poland, Austria, and firemen. He is a powerful protector against all dangers caused by fire or water. His feast day is May 4.

FISHERMEN

Andrew the Apostle (first century): Born at Bethsaida in Galilee near the Lake of Gennesareth; son of Jonah the fisherman and brother to St. Peter the Apostle; grew up in Capernaum; converted after hearing John the Baptist preach; became John's disciple; he became the first of Jesus' disciples; encouraged his brother Peter to follow Jesus as well; Andrew was present at the Feeding of the Five Thousand (Jn 6:8-9); tradition claims that Andrew preached in Scythia, Greece, and Byzantium; legend claims that he was crucified at Patras in Achaia; tradition says his relics were transferred to the Church of the Apostles in Constantinople; they were stolen in 1204 by the Crusaders and brought to the cathedral of Amalfi in Italy. (See also *Scotland*.)

Andrew and Peter were fishing at the Sea of Galilee when Jesus called them to be His first Apostles: "Follow me, and I will make you fishers of men" (Mt 3:19). The Gospel claims that Andrew left his fishing job and became our Lord's disciple. Andrew is also the patron of Greece. Feast day, November 30. (See *Greece* under "Countries and Nations.")

FLORISTS

Thérèse of Lisieux (1873-97): Born at Alençon, France, on January 2; youngest of nine children; after mother's death when Thérèse was five, family moved to Lisieux; raised by older sisters and aunt; professed into Carmelite Order in 1890, taking the name Thérèse of the Child Jesus; lived a hidden, cloistered life; suffered from tuberculosis and died seven years later; became widely known through her autobiography, *The Story of a Soul*; died on September 30 at Lisieux; canonized by Pope Pius XI in 1925; declared patron of foreign missions (with Francis Xavier) in 1927; patroness of aviators; in 1944, declared co-patroness of France with Joan of Arc.

Considered patron of florists because of her spirituality known as the "little way" of holiness and perfection. Thérèse believed in living faith to the fullest in each moment of the day, regardless of what state or circumstance one found himself in during his earthly life. This required a self-abandonment to God, acceptance of all suffering, and an attempt to live out the Christian faith in simplicity and humility. When Thérèse was close to death, she told one of her followers that she will spend her life in heaven doing good for those on earth. She also said that when she died, a shower of roses would fall on her followers, bringing God's graces to many of the faithful; thus her nickname, the "Little Flower." Feast day, October 1.

FOREST WORKERS

John Gualbert (d. 1073): Born at Florence, Italy, son of the noble Visdomini family; converted to the faith while searching for the killer of his brother Hugh; when he met up with the murderer, he was given the supernatural grace to forgive him on the spot; became a Benedictine monk at San Miniato del Monte Monastery; founded his own monastery at Vallombrosa near Fiesole; known for his charity, poverty, and aid for the poor; many mystical experiences; many claims of miracles through his intercession; received the gifts of prophecy and wisdom; died at Passignamo near Florence; canonized by Pope Celestine III in 1193.

John Gualbert and several companions built a monastery at Vallombrosa out of timber and mud from the surrounding country near Fiesole. This small community formed the basis of what was to become the beginning of the Vallombrosan Benedictines. Feast day, July 12.

FULLERS

Anastasius the Fuller (d. 304): Anastasius was born to a noble family at Aquileia. After reading the words of St. Paul to the Thessalonians, which say that it is wise to work with one's own hands, Anastasius became a fuller and practiced his trade at Salona (Split) in Yugoslavia. He died a martyr's death during the persecutions of Emperor Diocletian. Feast day, September 7. (See *Weavers*.)

James the Less (d. 62): The son of Alphaeus and one of the Twelve Apostles listed in the synoptic Gospels. A fuller is one who shrinks and thickens cloth. It is unclear why James is a patron of this occupation. Perhaps a fuller has received favors from his intercession in the past. Feast day May 3. (See *Hatters*.)

FUNERAL DIRECTORS

Joseph of Arimathea (first century): A secret follower of Jesus because he feared the reaction of the Jewish leaders; present at the Crucifixion (Jn 19:30; Lk 23:50-52); legend claims that Joseph accompanied Paul to Gaul; later, he went to England with twelve other missionaries; the archangel Gabriel told them to build a church there in honor of the Blessed Virgin (Glastonbury Abbey); Joseph is reported to have died there; another legend claims that he caught the blood of Jesus while he died upon the Cross; one story claims that Joseph was made custodian of the chalice used at the Last Supper.

It was Joseph who persuaded Pontius Pilate to give him the Lord's body so that it could have a proper burial (Mt 27:57-60). He gave Him a fine burial, wrapping Jesus' body in linen and laying it in his own tomb near Calvary in the side of a hill (Mt 27:57-60). His feast is celebrated on March 17.

Dismas (d. c. 29): Name from tradition, also known as "the Good Thief"; what we know of him is found in the Gospel of St. Luke; he was one of the two thieves crucified with Jesus (Lk 23:32); after one of the criminals mocked Jesus and exclaimed, "Are you not the Christ? Save yourself and us!" (v. 39), the good thief Dismas remarked, "Do you not fear God, since you are under the same sentence of condemnation? And we indeed justly; for we are receiving the due reward of our deeds; but this man has done nothing wrong" (vs. 40-41); when Dismas asked Jesus to remember him in his kingdom (v. 42), Jesus replied: "Truly, I say to you, today you will be with me in Paradise" (v. 43); many scholars claim this story was a fabrication; St. Porphyrius (d. c. 400) once had a vision of the Gospel story, reaffirming to him that the incident did indeed occur.

Dismas is the patron of prisoners because it was reported that he was a converted criminal who was once confined, having been accused of murder or acts against the Roman state. He is also the patron of funeral directors. Perhaps this association exists because of his conversion at the moment of death. There may have been claims of funeral directors receiving favors from praying to Dismas, but this is mere conjecture. The feast is celebrated on March 25 because of a tradition that Jesus died on the Cross this day (Easter, of course, falls at different times each year).

GARDENERS

Adelard (Adalhard) (d. 827): Grandson of Charles Martel, nephew of King Pepin and first cousin to Charlemagne; became a monk at Corbie in Picardy in 773; eventually chosen abbot; became Charlemagne's counselor; forced by the king to quit the monastery and work for him as chief minister for his son Pepin; accused of supporting a rival power (Bernard) against Emperor Louis the Debonair; banished to a monastery on the island of Heri; recalled to the king's court five years later (821); later retired to the abbey at Corbie; died January 2 after an illness; miracles reported after his death.

When Adelard first became a monk at Corbie in Picardy (773), his first assignment was gardener of the monastery. He did his job humbly and piously, praying throughout the day. His great virtues eventually helped him to become abbot. Feast day, January 2.

Fiacre (d. c. 670): Fiacre was a hermit from Kilfiachra, Ireland. He eventually migrated to France, where he took up quarters on land given to him by St. Faro. There he was known for his kindness toward travelers. Fiacre built a cell in the garden of his property, as well as an oratory in honor of the Blessed Virgin Mary. Many miracles were claimed through his working the land and interceding for others. Feast day September 1. (See *Cabdrivers.*)

Phocas (date unknown): A gardener from Sinope, Paphlagonia, on the Black Sea; performed his duties with care and purpose; gave food and lodging to any stranger in need; lived as an anchorite pursuing prayer and contemplation; suffered martyrdom for being a Christian; beheaded by soldiers who were given orders to look for Phocas in order to try him for his faith; inadvertently, the soldiers stayed at Phocas's house when they asked him for a place to sleep; when they told Phocas their mission and asked his whereabouts, he prepared himself for death by digging his own grave; in the morning, he admitted to the soldiers that he himself was Phocas and calmly faced his death.

Gardener by trade, Phocas led a life of simplicity, oneness with nature, and a purity recalling God's creation of the first human gardeners, Adam and Eve. Feast day September 22.

GLASSWORKERS

Luke the Evangelist (first century): It is unclear why Luke is patron of glassworkers. Perhaps the tradition comes from the story that Luke once painted a beautiful picture of the Blessed Virgin which was sent by Empress Eudokia in the fifth century to St. Pulcheria in Jerusalem. Because glass has been used by the Church for centuries depicting the various saints (such as with stained-glass windows), the connection with Luke is easily seen. Feast day, October 18. (See *Butchers.*)

GOLDSMITHS

Dunstan (910-88): Dunstan was appointed abbot of the Glastonbury Abbey in 943. He was later made Archbishop of Canterbury (959). He was a well-known metalworker of his day, and also produced beautifully illuminated manuscripts. Feast day, May 19. (See *Armorers.*)

GRAVEDIGGERS

Antony of Egypt (251-356): Antony was a hermit of the Egyptian desert. He founded a monastery of ascetics at Fayum in 305. Daily prayer and manual labor were required of his companions. Antony predicted the time of his death and requested that he be buried in the earth beside his mountain cell. He refused to allow his companions to embalm his body (a common practice by that time in Religious communities), predicting that upon his death Christ would receive his body in an incorrupt state. Feast day, January 17. (See *Basketmakers.*)

GROCERS

Michael: One of the three archangels mentioned in the Bible (the others being Gabriel and Raphael); he is mentioned twice in the Old Testament (Dn 10:13ff.; 12:1), where he is depicted as the protector of the Chosen People; Michael appears twice in the New Testament: in Jude 9, where he argues with the devil over Moses' body; and in Revelation 12:7-9, where he throws the devil and his demons out of heaven; the "captain of the heavenly host"; found in much apocryphal literature of the early Christian centuries; a special helper for those at the moment of death. Michael's role as patron of grocers is unclear. He is also invoked as protector against evil forces. Feast celebrated on September 29 (Michaelmas Day), a day chosen in the sixth century to honor the founding of a basilica in his name on the

Salerian Way in Rome. Since 1970, Raphael and Gabriel are joined
together with Michael on September 29 as the feast of the archangels.

GUARDIANS

Joseph of Palestine (d. 356): Joseph was an assistant to Rabbi Hillel
(not to be confused with the Rabbi Hillel of whom the Talmud speaks)
during the days of the Roman persecutions. Hillel hid the fact that he was a
Christian. Several days before his death, he requested that a bishop visit
him disguised as a physician. Then he ordered his bath filled, claiming it
was for health reasons but secretly planning to be baptized by the bishop
before his death. Joseph was witness to all this, and it would eventually be
the cause of his religious conversion. Rabbi Hillel entrusted the care of his
son and his prized religious books to Joseph; hence the latter is considered
the patron of guardians. Later on, Joseph was to establish churches
throughout Palestine. He also hid other Christians from the hands of the
persecutors (such as St. Epiphanius). Feast day, July 22. (See *Converts*
under "Special Needs.")

HAIRDRESSERS

Martin de Porres (1579-1639): Born November 9 at Lima, Peru;
illegitimate son of Spanish knight John de Porres and Anna, a freed
Panamanian; became a lay-brother Dominican in Lima; founded an
orphanage and hospital; gave away food to the poor; desired to become a
foreign missioner but was refused; instead, he practiced great penances and
advanced in the interior life; recipient of many mystical graces, including
bilocation and transportation; compassionate to animals of all kinds; served
the African slaves in Peru; a dear friend of St. Rose of Lima; died at Rosary
Convent; canonized by Pope John XXIII in 1962.

When Martin was twelve years old, his mother sent him to apprentice
with a barber-surgeon. After three years of training, he left and became a
Third Order Dominican at Rosary Convent. However, Martin continued his
trade as a lay-brother, being barber, surgeon, wardrobe-keeper, and
infirmarian for his fellow Dominicans at Lima. Also the patron of
interracial justice. Feast day, November 5.

HATTERS

James the Lesser (d. 62): Son of Alpheus; one of the Twelve Apostles
listed in the synoptic Gospels; one of eleven Apostles in the upper room in
Jerusalem after Christ's Ascension (see Acts 1:13); one of the "brothers" of
the Lord (Mt 13:55; Mk 6:3) along with Joseph, Simon, and Jude; Peter
asked James to spread the good news about his escape (Acts 12:17);

traditionally thought of as the head of the primitive Church in Jerusalem; known as "James the Less" through the reference in Mt 15:40 in the King James and Douay Versions of the Bible; the *New English Bible*, the *Living Bible*, and the *New International Version* of the Bible refer to him as "James the Younger"; thrown from the top of the Jerusalem Temple by the Pharisees; later stoned to death.

It is not clear why James the Lesser is patron of hatters. Perhaps it is due to the fact that he wore the symbolic crown as head of the Church in Jerusalem — just as the Pope today wears a unique cap which symbolizes his role as Supreme Shepherd over the universal Church. Feast day, May 1.

HOSPITAL ADMINISTRATORS

Basil the Great (329-79): One of ten children born to St. Basil the Elder and St. Emmelia in Caesarea, Cappodocia, Asia Minor; taught by his father and grandmother, St. Macrina the Elder; later studied at Constantinople and Athens; classmates of St. Gregory Nazianzen and the future Emperor Julian the Apostate; taught rhetoric at Caesarea; after baptism, lived as a hermit by the Iris River at Pontus; ordained in 363; there he founded the first monastery in Asia Minor; his rule became the basis for monasticism in the East; fought Arianism; known for his help to the sick and the poor; responsible for the victory of orthodoxy over Arianism at the Council of Constantinople (381-82); wrote 400 letters and many doctrinal pieces; famous for *On the Holy Spirit* and *Philocalia*; proclaimed Doctor of the Church and patriarch of Eastern monks.

Basil had great experience and success as an organizer and administrator within his monastic environment. He was also the founder of a hospital at Caesarea, called the Basiliad, which became well-known. Feast day, June 14.

Frances Xavier Cabrini (1850-1917): Born to a farm family on July 15 at Sant' Angelo Lodigiano, Italy, one of thirteen children; foundress of the Missionary Sisters of the Sacred Heart (1877); came to New York in 1889 to work with Italian immigrants; founded numerous orphanages, schools, and hospitals in the U.S., Nicaragua, Italy, Costa Rica, Panama, Chile, and Brazil; died at her convent in Chicago; became an American citizen in Seattle in 1909; canonized as America's first citizen saint by Pope Pius XII (1946); declared patroness of immigrants by Pope Pius XII (1950).

Frances established more than 50 foundations, which helped to build schools, orphanages, and hospitals the world over. She helped to found the Columbus Hospital at Chicago (1892). Feast day, November 13.

HOSPITAL WORKERS

Camillus de Lellis (1550-1614): Born at Bocchianico, Italy; former soldier addicted to gambling; lost all of his earnings and lived in poverty at Naples; studied to become a Franciscan Capuchin but was denied entrance into the Order because of a diseased leg he acquired from his days of fighting the Turks; eventually permitted to become a priest by his confessor, St. Philip Neri; died in Rome on July 14; canonized by Pope Benedict XIV in 1746.

Camillus devoted himself to caring for the sick after he was turned down by the Franciscan Capuchins. When he was finally allowed to be ordained at a later time, he formed his own congregation known as the Ministers of the Sick (the Camillians). He became director of the St. Giacomo Hospital in Rome. Camillus founded a hospital at Naples and received official approval of his order from Pope Gregory XIV in 1591. Later, Camillus sent his servants to help wounded soldiers in Hungary and Croatia. He was declared patron of the sick with St. John of God by Pope Leo XIII. Pope Pius XI also declared him patron of nurses. Feast day July 14.

John of God (1495-1550): John was a Portuguese soldier who converted to the faith after a long battle with the Turks. He later opened up a religious-article and book shop in Granada (1538). He eventually founded a house to serve the sick and the poor. His newly founded house expanded into the Order of Brothers Hospitalers, which in turn became known as the Brothers of St. John of God. Feast day March 8. (See *Booksellers.*)

Jude Thaddeus (first century): One of the Twelve Apostles chosen by Christ (Lk 6:16). He is also known as Judas or Lebbeus. Jude is considered to be the brother of James the Less. He is the one who asked the Lord why He did not manifest Himself to the rest of the world (see Jn 14:22-23). It is not clear why Jude is the patron of hospital workers. Feast day October 28. (See *Desperate Situations* under "Special Needs.")

HOSPITALERS

Julian the Hospitaler (date unknown): Legendary figure who reportedly married a wealthy widow as a gift from the king; when his wife put his parents up for a night while he was gone, Julian returned home and, thinking there was a man in bed with his wife, killed them both; remorseful, he engaged in great acts of penance; later built an inn for travelers and a hospital for the poor; a leper visited him, and he gave him his own bed; legend says that the leper was an angel sent to test his faith.

Julian left his home after his crime (see above) because of great restlessness and guilt. He was determined to do penance for the rest of his life. Once on a journey he came to a wide river where people would cross. In a dream, he heard a voice ask him to cross the river and help the people to the other side. When he went to them, he found one nearly dead from the cold. He started a fire, bedded him down, and nursed him back to health. Suddenly this sickly man became bright like the sun and ascended into heaven. Julian understood this miracle as a sign that God accepted his penance. He is the patron of hotelkeepers, travelers, and boatmen. His feast is celebrated on February 12.

HOUSEWIVES

Anne (first century B.C.): According to the apocryphal *Protevangelium of James*, Anne was the wife of Joachim and mother of the Blessed Virgin Mary. She is an ideal role model for all mothers and housekeepers, having raised the Mother of God and providing a loving atmosphere in which to nourish the faith. Anne married at the age of twenty and gave birth to Mary at the age of forty (supposedly because the prayers of the barren couple were answered by an angelic messenger from God). Legend claims that Anne died just after the birth of Christ. Feast day, July 26. (See *Cabinetmakers*.)

HUNTERS

Eustachius (d. c. 118): Legend surrounds this saint (he may not even have existed); a Roman under Emperor Trajan; originally named Placida until a conversion experience led to the formal change of his name (Eustachius or Eustace); married to Theopistis but separated after birth of sons, Agapitus and Theopistus; lost his fortune; later reunited with his family; entered the army and won many battles; refused to honor pagan gods and was roasted to death; one of the Fourteen Holy Helpers.

According to legend, Eustachius had a conversion experience while hunting at Guadagnolo, Italy. He saw a stag coming toward him with a figure of Christ on the cross between his antlers. A voice was heard from this vision which called him by name. Feast day, September 20.

Hubert (d. 727): Married servant of Pepin of Heristal; converted after wife's death; became priest under St. Lambert; succeeded Lambert as Bishop of Maastricht (705); later moved his see to Liège; known for miracles; died on May 30 at Tervueren near Brussels.

Hubert's patronage of hunters is based upon a legend that he was converted while hunting. Feast celebrated on November 3.

INFANTRYMEN

Maurice (d. c. 287): Martyred under Emperor Maximian for refusing to worship the pagan gods.

Maurice was a Christian soldier of the Theban Legion under Emperor Maximian Herculius. He and his fellow infantrymen refused to pray to the Roman gods at the request of Maximian in order to help assure victory over the Bagaudae. Maurice was martyred along with his 6,000-man army. Feast day, September 22. (See *Dyers*.)

INNKEEPERS

Amand (584-679): Amand was a monk at Bourges, France. He later engaged in missionary work in Flanders, Carinthia, and Germany. Amand founded several monasteries throughout Belgium, and his hospitality toward all visitors and his own flair for organization were well-known. He became abbot of an abbey in Elnon, where he spent the remainder of his life. Feast day, February 26. (See *Wine Merchants*.)

Martha (first century): Sister of Mary and Lazarus in Bethany. Martha served Jesus and her other guests during his visit to her home (Lk 10:38-42). She provided for guests while her sister Mary spent her time silently contemplating the teachings of the Lord. Feast day July 29. (See *Cooks*.)

JEWELERS

Dunstan (910-88): Dunstan was made Archbishop of Canterbury in 959. Prior to that, he had served as abbot of the Glastonbury Abbey. Dunstan's talents were widely known in his day: metalwork, goldsmithing, locksmithing, jewelry making, and illuminating manuscripts. Feast day, May 19. (See *Armorers*.)

Eligius (c. 590-660): Born at Chaptel, Gaul; became a metalsmith; good to the poor; built many churches; built the monastery at Solignac in 632; founded a convent in Paris; became Bishop of Noyon and Tournai in 640; died at Noyon on December 1.

Eligius came from a family of artisans. His father taught him the trades of engraving and smithing. He eventually served an apprenticeship for goldsmithing under Abbo, who was in charge of a mint at Limoges. Eligius left for France to pursue his trade thereafter. King Clotaire II commissioned him to make a chair of state, adorned with gold and precious stone. He ended up making two thrones and so impressed the king that he hired him to be master of his mint. Eligius's name was printed on several gold coins at Paris and Marseilles during the reigns of Dagobert I and Clovis II. Feast day, December 1.

JOURNALISTS

Francis de Sales (1567-1622): Born at Thorens in Savoy on August 21; studied at Jesuit college of Clermont in Paris (1580-88); studied law and theology at University of Padua; received doctorate at age twenty-four; ordained in 1593; spent five years as missionary in the Chablais; converted thousands to Catholicism; became bishop of Geneva in 1602; famous preacher, teacher, and intellect; founded many schools and taught catechetics; spiritual director of St. Frances de Chantal; founded the Order of the Visitation (the Visitandines) with Frances in 1610; beatified the year of his death — 1622 — by Pope Gregory XV, the first formal beatification and one of the fastest ever; canonized by Pope Alexander VII in 1665.

Francis de Sales was declared a Doctor of the Church by Pope Leo XIII (1877) because of the many spiritual classics he wrote, including *Introduction to the Devout Life* (1609) and *Treatise on the Love of God* (1616). These works stressed that sanctity and perfection are possible for every Christian, showing ways to achieve these goals. He is the patron of authors and the Catholic press. Feast day, January 24.

JURISTS

John of Capistrano (1386-1456): Born at Capistrano, Italy; married for a brief time; received a dispensation to enter a Religious order during his marriage; joined the Friars Minor in 1416; ordained in 1420; famous preacher; became a papal diplomat under Pope Nicholas V; died at Villach, Austria, on October 23, possibly from the plague; canonized by Pope Alexander VIII in 1690.

John had studied law at Perugia and worked as governor of the same city in 1412. Also declared patron of military chaplains on February 10, 1984. Feast day, October 23.

KINGS

Casimir of Poland (1458-84): Born the third of thirteen children to King Casimir IV of Poland and Elizabeth of Austria, daughter of Emperor Albert II of Germany; known for his early devotion to the saints and the Church as a child; refused marriage for the sake of serving God and country; miracles reported at his tomb; canonized by Pope Adrian VI in 1522.

Casimir was viceroy for his father's throne during the king's absence from 1479-83. Although never technically a king himself, Casimir came from a royal family and served his country well. Feast day, March 4. (See *Bachelors.*)

Dagobert II (d. 679): Son of King St. Sigebert III; friend of St. Wilfrid of York; died while hunting on December 23 in a forest of Lorraine.

Dagobert succeeded his saintly father as King of Austrasia in 656. Still a child, Dagobert was exiled by his guardian Grimoald, son of Pepin of Landen, who gave the crown to his own son, Childebert. Feast day, December 23. (See *Hunters*.)

Edgar (944-75): Born to a royal family in England; married Ethelfleda the Duck (so named because of her homeliness); had one child, the future St. Edward, with her; married Elfrida after the death of Ethelfleda; had two more children; once involved with the rape of Wulfrida, a woman who lived in Wilton Abbey; later repented his sinful act, delaying his coronation for seven years at the command of St. Dunstan; as a result of the rape, Wulfrida gave birth to the future St. Edith of Wilton.

Edgar replaced his brother Eadwig as king in 959. He recalled St. Dunstan from exile and ruled with such peace and good will that he earned the name "the Peaceable." During his reign, Edgar helped to influence the religious revival of his day. Religious communities were encouraged to practice their faith more diligently. Ecclesiastical reforms were instituted under this Christian king. Edgar's son, the future St. Edward, followed his father as King of England. Edgar ruled as king for two years. He is buried at the Glastonbury Abbey. Many miracles have been reported at his tomb. Feast day not yet determined. (See *Widowers*.)

Edmund (d. 870): King of East Anglia; captured by barbarian Northmen in 866; tortured and decapitated for his faith.

Edmund was only fifteen years old when he was crowned king of East Anglia in 855. He was a fair and just ruler, practicing his faith in a heroic manner. During his torture at the hands of his enemies, Edmund reportedly called upon the name of Jesus to comfort and console him. Feast day not established. (See *Victims of Torture* under "Special Needs.")

Edward the Confessor (1003-66): Born at Islip, England; son of King Ethelred III; King of England (1042-66); built St. Peter's Abbey at Westminster; known for piety and compassion for the poor; died in London on January 5; body found to be incorrupt; canonized in 1161 by Pope Alexander III; feast day, October 13.

After Edward became King of England in 1042, his chief minister (Earl Godwin) had a daughter named Edith whom Edward married in order to pacify him. Edward was partly Norman, and many of his advisers were as well; however, Godwin was not. This "political marriage" pleased the chief minister because it would increase his influence and balance the power of the Norman influence in the government. Most felt that Edward married in order to keep peace with the Earl rather than out of love for Edith. It was well-known that the marriage did not produce children, and some even said that there was no physical contact. Many who knew Edward felt that he agreed with Edith to dedicate his life to God and live a life of chastity and obedience; others felt that he just didn't love her. Tensions increased when Godwin's sons became earls in Edward's court. One of them — Swein — caused a scandal by seducing an abbess. Another son challenged the leadership of Edward and caused severe strains among the in-laws. Eventually, the Godwins were told to leave the country. Edward even sent his wife away to avoid further tensions and embarrassment to his throne. Godwin and sons returned later and challenged Edward for the throne. Eventually a settlement was reached, and Godwin's family received various honorary titles and parcels of land. Feast day on October 13.

Edwin (585-633): Son of King Aella of Deira in South Northumbria; King Ethelfrith of Bernicia in North Northumbria stole his kingship away; Edwin spent the next thirty years in Mercia and reclaimed the throne through the efforts of King Baedwald of East Anglia, who killed King Ethelfrith at the Battle of Idle River in 617; Edwin married but became a widow in 625; he then married Ethelburga, the sister of King Eadbald of Kent; Edwin finally gained control and power over all of England; he was defeated and killed at the Battle of Heathfield on October 12.

As King of England, Edwin established law and order. He intended to build a church at York but died at the hands of King Penda of Mercia in the Battle of Heathfield before it happened. Edwin was considered a martyr by Pope Gregory XIII. His father (King Aella of Deira) died when Edwin was only three years old. Thereafter for a number of years, Edwin was forced to live in one home after another before he regained his rightful throne. Feast day, October 12.

Louis IX (1215-70): Louis IX, King of France, married Margaret, daughter of Raymond Berenger, Count of Provence, at the age of nineteen. They would eventually have eleven children (five sons, six daughters). Louis' favorite son, young Louis, died at the age of sixteen. It was a tragic loss for the king, one from which he would never quite recover. After Louis became king, he defeated King Henry III of England and put an end to the revolts in southern France. Louis made a pilgrimage to the Holy Land between 1250-54 after his crusade in 1248. He founded many Religious houses and educational centers. Louis was responsible for changes in the tax system, simplifying the administration of the government and founding the first French naval fleet. During his reign, France prospered as a nation. He was known for his justice, charity, and personal piety. Later in his reign, Louis suffered the loss of another son, Jean-Tristan, to an illness. Feast day, August 25. (See *Crusaders*.)

Olaf II (d. 1030): Established Christianity throughout Norway; led his country from 1015-30 as king; killed trying to reclaim his throne at the Battle of Sticklestad

Olaf Skottkonung, son of Eric the Conqueror, is often confused with Olaf II Haraldsson ("the Fat"), patron of Norway, because he defeated King Olaf I Tryggvesson of Norway at the Battle of Svolder in 1000 and annexed part of his country. Feast day, July 29. (See *Norway* under "Countries and Nations.")

Solomon (d. 874): Nephew of King Nominoius, hero of Brittany; Erispoius (King Nominoius' son) was next in line for the throne when the King died, but Solomon killed his cousin out of envy and took the throne himself; saved Brittany from the Franks and the Northmen; later converted and did much good (such as preserving the remains of St. Maxentius in Brittany and protecting them from the Northmen); assassinated by rivals in 874.

When he became king, Solomon repented the murder of his cousin Erispoius and performed great penances. After his conversion, he contributed to the building and upkeep of many Religious houses. Feast day unknown.

Stephen of Hungary (975-1038): Born at Esztergom in Hungary; baptized in 985 at the age of ten; married Gisela, the half-sister of Duke Henry III of Bavaria (who became Emperor Henry II in 1002); ruled the Magyars beginning in 997; in 1001, became first King of Hungary (the crown came from Pope Sylvester II); Stephen elected Hungary's first archbishop and established many sees in his country; united the Magyars; died in Szekesfehervar, Hungary, on August 15; canonized by Pope Gregory VII in 1083.

Stephen built many churches during his reign as Hungary's first king. He also completed the building of St. Martin's Monastery, which had been started by his father. Stephen is also considered the patron of bricklayers. Feast day, August 16.

KNIGHTS

Gengulphus (d. 760): Also known as Gengulf or Gengoul, Gengulphus was a Burgundian knight. He was known for his virtuous life and even temper. Although married, he lived as a recluse after retirement.

This virtuous leader helped the needy and practiced great penance. He is especially admired in Holland, Belgium, and Savoy. Gengulphus was married to a woman who was unfaithful to him. Hurt and shamed by the actions of his beloved wife, he had her taken care of by his servants as he moved alone to his castle in Avallon. Later, Gengulphus was reported killed by his wife's lover. He was found murdered in his own bed. Feast day, May 11.

Julian the Hospitaler (date unknown): Legendary figure who reportedly married a wealthy widow as a gift from the king; when his wife put his parents up for a night while he was gone, Julian returned home, thought they were a man in bed with his wife, and killed them both; remorseful, he engaged in great acts of penance; later built an inn for travelers and a hospital for the poor; a leper visited him, and he gave him his own bed; legend says that the leper was an angel sent to test his faith. Julian left his home after killing his parents (see above) because of his great restlessness and guilt. He was determined to do penance for the rest of his life. Once on a journey he came to a wide river at a place for people to cross. In a dream, he heard a voice ask him to cross the river and help the people to the other side. When he went to them, he found one nearly dead from the cold. He started a fire, bedded him down, and nursed him back to health. Suddenly this sickly man became bright like the sun and ascended into heaven. Julian understood this miracle as a sign that God accepted his penance.

Julian was born of a noble family. He spent much of his early youth in joyful activities such as hunting. It is unclear why Julian is patron of knights. Perhaps the legendary account of his heroic journey symbolizes the true courage and leadership qualities found in the knights of old. Julian is also the patron of hotelkeepers, travelers, and boatmen. His feast is celebrated on February 12.

LABORERS

Isidore the Farmer (1070-1130): Isidore was from a poor family of Madrid, Spain. He worked as a farmhand for John de Vergas as a young child. He was to remain there under John's service all of his life. Isidore was a model worker and fine Christian. He started every day out by going to Mass, then worked the fields all day as he continually prayed. It is reported that Isidore frequently communicated with his guardian angel and various saints. Many miracles are associated with his work and intercession for others. Feast day May 15. (See *Farmers.*)

John (Don) Bosco (1815-1888): Born of a poor family at Becchi, Piedmont, Italy; ordained in Turin; co-founded the Daughters of Mary Help of Christians (for girls); built many churches; died in Turin on January 31; canonized by Pope Pius XI in 1934.

John Bosco worked for abused and orphaned boys in Becchi, Piedmont, Italy. He founded the Salesians in 1859 (for the education of boys). In 1863, there were 39 Salesians. When he died, there were 768.

Today, there are thousands across the world. Salesian accomplishments include an enormous output of work and effort over the years: schools from primary grades through colleges and seminaries, adult schools, technical schools, agricultural schools, hospitals, foreign missions, and pastoral work. In addition, they are known for their printing and bookbinding shops. Feast day, January 31.

LAWYERS

Genesius (third century): It is unclear why Genesius is patron of lawyers. Perhaps the association is made because he was brought before the court of the Roman persecutors for professing his Christian faith. Genesius was later tortured and beheaded. (See *Actors.*)

Ivo of Kermartin (1253-1303): Son of the lord of the manor of Kermartin, Brittany; studied theology, philosophy, and law; ordained in 1284; resigned in 287 to become a parish priest at Tredrez and Lovannec; built a hospital and cared for the poor; known for his preaching.

Ivo studied canon law at Paris and civil law at Orleans. When he returned to Brittany, he became judge of the Rennes diocesan court. In his own diocese of Treguier, he became known as "the poor man's advocate" for his defense of the poor and his refusal to accept fees from his poor clients. Feast day, May 19.

Thomas More (1478-1535): Born on February 6 in Milk Street, Cheapside; English martyr; received a law degree from Oxford; married Jane Holt in 1505; declared undersheriff of London in 1510; married Alice Middleton (a widow) after the death of his first wife in 1511; statesman, chancellor under King Henry VIII; elected Lord Chancellor in 1529 after Cardinal Wolsey's reign; author of *Utopia* (1515-16) and various well-known poems, treatises, devotional books, and prayers; opposed Henry's deposing Catherine of Aragon and his subsequent marriage to Anne Boleyn; refused to renounce authority of papacy; accused of treason and imprisoned at the Tower of London for fifteen months; beheaded; canonized by Pope Pius XI in 1935.

Thomas More was known for his quick wit and brilliant mind. He was born the son of a lawyer and judge (John More). In 1501, Thomas was admitted to the bar after successfully studying law at Lincoln's Inn (Oxford University). Feast celebrated on June 22.

LECTORS

Pollio (d. 304): Leader of the Christians in the diocese of former Bishop Eusebius, who was martyred for his faith under the persecutions of Diocletian; Pollio himself died at the hands of Diocletian's henchmen in the town of Cybalae in Lower Pannonia (now Mikanovici, Yugoslavia, also the birthplace of the Roman Emperors Gratian, Valentinian, and Valens); burned at the stake for refusing to honor the pagan gods.

Pollio was known in his day as an extraordinary lector in his local church. Feast day, April 28.

Sabas (d. 372): One of fifty-one Gothic martyrs particularly venerated by the Greeks; early convert to Christianity; served as a cantor or lector in the church; martyred at Targoviste near the city of Bucharest, Romania.

Sabas was a famous lector to the priest Sansala. During his great speeches, Sabas condemned the practice in which the Gothic persecutors forced pagans and Christians alike to eat meat that had been previously consecrated to the gods. Because of his outspokenness, Sabas was forced out of the city. After returning at a later date, he again proclaimed his faith and condemned the practice. Sabas was martyred for his faith. Feast day, April 12.

LIBRARIANS

Jerome (342-420): Born at Strido near Aquileia, Dalmatia; studied at Rome under Donatus; became a master of Greek, Latin, and classical writers; baptized by Pope Liberius in Rome (360); settled in Antioch by 374; saw Christ in a vision, which encouraged him to solitude, prayer, and study at Chalcis in the Syrian desert, where he lived for four years; wrote biography of St. Paul of Thebes; returned to Antioch; later went to Constantinople to study Scripture under St. Gregory Nazianzen; became secretary of Pope Damasus in 382; in 386, he moved to Bethlehem with companions Paula and Eustochium to lead a life of prayer and solitude; founded a monastery for men there, and Paula founded several convents; under Damasus' suggestion, he translated the Bible from its Hebrew and Greek origins to Latin (the so-called *Vulgate*, 390-405, which became the official version of the Catholic Church, proclaimed so at the Council of Trent); died at Bethlehem after a long illness; author of many fine works, including over 120 letters which are still extant, as well as many Biblical commentaries; one of the Doctors of the Church.

Patron saint of librarians: Besides his work on the Latin Vulgate (390-405) and much correspondence, Jerome wrote such important works as *Adversum Helvidium* (382), *Altercatio luciferiani et orthodoxi* (a treatise written in the late 370s), *Adversus Jovianianum* (393), *Contra Vigilantium* (393), *Apologetici adversus Rufinum* (395), *Dialogi contra Pelagianos* (415), and *De viris illustribis* (date unknown). Feast day, September 30.

LIGHTHOUSE KEEPERS

Venerius (d. 409): Second Bishop of Milan (the first was St. Ambrose); friends with Sts. Paulinus of Nola, Delphinus of Bordeaux, and Chromatius of Aquileia; supported and defended Council of Carthage in 401; St. Charles Borromeo brought his relics to the Cathedral of Milan in 1579.

It is not clear why Venerius is the patron of lighthouse keepers. Perhaps it has to do with the fact that St. Charles Borromeo once elevated his relics and placed them for all to see in Milan's great cathedral. As a lighthouse guides the ships through the night, so an elevated saint is a sign and special comfort for all of the faithful. Feast day, May 4.

LINGUISTS

Gotteschalc (d. 1066): Abotrite prince; student at Abbey of St. Michael in Luneburg, Germany; renounced his faith and left the abbey in 1030 when his father Uto was killed at the hands of a Saxon; attacked various Saxon groups in revenge; captured and imprisoned by Duke Bernard of Saxony; later released; left for Denmark and joined the army of King Canute; married his daughter; participated in wars with Norway and England; returned to his own country in 1043 and became chief of the Abotrites; reconverted to the faith; brought priests into his country; founded many monasteries throughout the land; participated in missionary work; killed in the city of Lenzen on June 7, 1066, during a Christian persecution.

Gotteschalc helped his local priests to translate sermons and instructions into his Slavonic language soon after his religious conversion. Feast day, June 7.

LOCKSMITHS

Dunstan (910-88): Born of nobility at Baltonsborough near Glastonbury, England; educated by monks; served in the court of King Athelstan while still a youth; became a Benedictine monk in 934; ordained in 939 by his uncle, St. Alphege, Bishop of Winchester; made abbot of Glastonbury by King Edmund in 943; became famous for his monastic reforms and establishing centers of learning; adviser to King Edred after Edmund was murdered; became Bishop of Worcester in 957 and of London in 958; appointed Archbishop of Canterbury in 959 by King Edgar; remained Edgar's adviser for sixteen years; appointed legate by Pope John XII; restored ecclesiastical discipline and continued to reform the Church and state in England; died in Canterbury after a brief time of teaching school there; famous musician, hymnist, metalworker, and illuminator of manuscripts.

Dunstan is patron of armorers, goldsmiths, blacksmiths, locksmiths, and jewelers because of his fame and talent in these areas. There was also a popular legend that claims that he once grabbed the nose of the devil with his pair of blacksmith's tongs after a period of long temptation. Feast day, May 19.

MAGISTRATES

Nicholas of Flüe (1417-87): Born of a wealthy family near Sachseln, Obwalden Canton, Switzerland, on March 21; married Dorothy Wissling and had ten children; fought a war with Zurich (1439) and later served as captain in the Thurgau War (1453); became magistrate and councillor for Obwalden; in 1467, became a hermit with his wife's consent and settled at Ranft near Sachseln; he spent his last nineteen years there, existing on only the Holy Eucharist for his food; known as "Bruder Klaus," he was respected for his piety and wisdom and became Switzerland's most famous saint (although he never became her patron); died in his cell at Ranft; canonized by Pope Pius XII in 1947.

After returning from the Thurgau War (1453), Nicholas was appointed magistrate and councillor by his fellow countrymen of Obwalden. His role of judge and councillor was known to be respected, for he was a man of great fairness and justice to all. Nicholas was responsible for the Edict of Stans, which resulted in the inclusion of Fribourg and Soleure in the Swiss Confederation (1481) after independence had been won from Charles the Bold of Burgundy. Feast day, March 22.

MAIDS

Zita (1218-78): Born at Monte Sagrati, Italy; served in the house of a wool dealer in Lucca at the age of twelve; other servants jealous of her holiness and miracles, but later grew fond of her; helped the poor and imprisoned; canonized in 1696.

At the age of twelve, Zita began to work as a housekeeper for Pagano di Fatinelli at Lucca. She rose during each night for prayer and attended Mass every morning before beginning her duties. Zita frequently gave away food to the poor. She was the object of ridicule and scorn from her jealous co-workers, but bore these insults patiently. One time, a fellow worker tried to seduce her, but she scratched her way out of the attempted rape. When her boss later questioned the man about his injured face, Zita remained silent, secretly forgiving him in her heart. Zita took care of the children of the landowners and fellow servants. Many miracles of the multiplication of food were reported by witnesses, especially when the household was short or the poor begged for a meal. She ended up serving the same family for forty-eight years. Feast day, April 27.

MARBLE WORKERS

Clement I (d. c. 100): Roman martyr; baptized by St. Peter; succeeded Cletus as Pope (88-97); forced out of Rome by Emperor Trajan; missionary work abroad; wrote an influential letter to the Corinthians to help in their disputes.

Clement worked the quarry mines in the Crimea as a result of his banishment by Emperor Trajan. While working at manual labor, he preached among the people and renewed their faith. It is reported that a spring miraculously appeared near the mine when the people were short of water. Some seventy-five churches were founded by Clement during his exile from Rome. Because of his missionary work among the people, he was condemned to death and thrown in the sea with an anchor around his neck. His feast day is November 23.

MARINERS

Michael: One of the three archangels mentioned in the Bible (the others being Gabriel and Raphael); he is mentioned twice in the Old Testament (Dn 10:13ff.; 12:1), where he is depicted as the protector of the Chosen People; Michael appears twice in the New Testament: in Jude 9, where he argues with the devil over Moses' body; and in Rv 12:7-9, where he throws the devil and his demons out of heaven; the "captain of the heavenly host"; found in numerous apocryphal literature of the early Christian centuries; a special helper for those at the moment of death.

Michael's role as patron of mariners is unclear. Perhaps his role as the leading archangel and guide of the angelic forces prompts sailors to look to him for guidance and protection against the forces of nature as well. Michael is also invoked as protector against evil spirits. Feast celebrated on September 29 (Michaelmas Day), a day chosen in the sixth century to honor the founding of a basilica in his name on the Salerian Way in Rome. Since 1970, Raphael and Gabriel are joined together with Michael on September 29 in the feast of the archangels.

Nicholas of Tolentino (1245-1305): Born at Sant' Angelo, Ancona, Italy; joined Augustinians; ordained in 1270; famous for preaching and as a confessor; became a hermit; charitable toward the poor, the sick, the needy, children, and criminals; known for miracles and the healing of the sick; died at Tolentino on September 10; canonized by Pope Eugene IV in 1446.

According to Jordan of Saxony in his *Life of St. Nicholas* (1380), a man was once killed by a group of adversaries and thrown into a lake thereafter.

During his struggle to survive, he prayed to Nicholas for protection. But his assailants ignored his prayers and killed him anyway. One week later, Nicholas appeared, removed his body from the water, and brought him back to life. In a short time, he was to die, but only after having been given the chance to confess his sins and bear witness to the fact that Nicholas had answered his prayers. Feast day, September 10.

MEDICAL RECORD LIBRARIANS

Raymond of Peñafort (1175-1275): Born at Peñafort, Catalonia, Spain; taught philosophy in Barcelona at age twenty; studied law at Bologna; received doctorate in 1216; joined Dominicans in 1222; noted preacher; confessor of Pope Gregory IX; named Archbishop of Tarragona (1235); systematized and codified canon law, in effect until 1917; master general of Dominicans (1238); compiled *Summa de poenitentia* (1223-38); died at Barcelona on January 6; canonized by Pope Clement VIII in 1601.

It is unclear why Raymond is named the patron of medical record librarians. Perhaps it is due to his great organizational abilities. Pope Gregory IX assigned Raymond to gather all the existing decrees and legislation of all the popes and councils to update what was last done by Gratian in 1150. The collection took him three years to complete, and it appeared in five books known as "Decretals." This has been recognized as the best arrangement of canon law until a later Code of Canon Law was promulgated in 1917. Feast day, January 7. (Also see *Canonists*.)

MEDICAL SOCIAL WORKERS

John Regis (1597-1640): Born at Fontcouverte in the Diocese of Narbonne; educated at the Jesuit college of Beziers; entered the Jesuits in 1615; known for his piety and profound humility; studied theology at Toulouse in 1628; ordained in 1631; engaged in missionary work for the next ten years (Vivarias, Velay, Le Puy, etc.); famous preacher; devoted to helping the poor and imprisoned; influenced St. John Vianney (the Curé of Ars) to become a priest.

John Regis once fell and broke his leg on the way to helping a parishioner in need. It is claimed that he continued, reached his destination, and gave absolution to the one who sought him for confession. Later that same day, he had his leg examined by a doctor but found that his broken leg had completely healed. Feast day, June 16.

MEDICAL TECHNICIANS

Albert the Great (1206-80): Born the oldest son of the count of Bollstadt at a castle in Swabia, Germany; studied at the University of

Padua; became a Dominican in Padua despite his parents' opposition (1223); taught at Cologne in 1228; also taught at Hildesheim, Freiburg-im-Breisgau, Regensburg, and Strasbourg; famous for his teaching and intellect; earned his doctorate at the University of Paris (1245); taught St. Thomas Aquinas while serving at the university; became provincial of Dominicans in 1254; served as personal theologian to Pope Alexander IV while in Rome; became Bishop of Regensburg in 1260; resigned in 1262 and began to teach at Cologne; participated in the Council of Lyons; reorganized the education of young Dominicans; tried to get the Greek Church united with Rome; defended St. Thomas Aquinas's teaching; influenced the founding of the scholastic method; died after two years of illness in Cologne (November 15); canonized by Pope Pius XI in 1931; also declared Doctor of the Church by the same pope.

Albert was one the great theologians of the Catholic Church. His background included the natural sciences, for which he was also to become famous. He knew a great deal about biology, chemistry, botany, physiology, metaphysics, logic, mathematics, the Bible, and theology. Because of his great learning and influence in the medical-natural sciences, Albert is also known as the patron saint of the students of natural sciences. Feast day, November 15.

MERCHANTS

Francis of Assisi (1182-1226): Francis is invoked as a patron of merchants because of his family background. His father, Peter Bernadone, was a wealthy silk merchant from Assisi, Italy, during Francis' youth. Although Francis was originally given the baptismal name of John by his mother during Peter's absence from home, he returned and insisted that young John be renamed "Francis." It was after Francis' conversion that he denounced his worldly father in public, stripped himself of his clothes, and dedicated his life to God in a spirit of humility and poverty. This was a true and heroic test of his faith, for by renouncing his wealth and worldly ambitions Francis not only sacrificed everything he held dear for so long — he also left his immediate family for the more important kingdom of God. Feast day, October 4. (See *Ecologists*.)

Nicholas of Myra (d. c. 350): Born at Patara, Lycia, Asia Minor; legendary aspects of life; ordained Bishop of Myra; known for holiness and miracles; imprisoned for faith under Emperor Diocletian; participated at Council of Nicaea (325); opponent of Arianism; according to legend, gave money and gifts to the poor; saved three girls from prostitution by throwing bags of gold in their home, causing all three to eventually marry; this and other traditions (such as restoring three dead girls back to life) started the practice of giving children Christmas gifts in his name for good luck; Nicholas became Sint Klaes to the Dutch, then Santa Claus.

It is not clear why Nicholas is patron of merchants. Perhaps it is because of the fact that after his death his relics were brought by sea to Bari, Italy, in 1087, where they remain in the St. Nicholas Basilica. There is one claim that he miraculously interceded for a group of sailors who were threatened by a storm off the coast of Lycia. Nicholas is also the patron of Russia, Greece, Apulia, Sicily, Lorraine, coopers, and children. Feast day on December 6.

MESSENGERS

Gabriel: It was the archangel Gabriel who came to the Blessed Virgin Mary at her home in Nazareth to announce that she would become impregnated by the Holy Spirit (the Incarnation) and give birth to the Son of God and Savior of the world (the Nativity). These stories are related in the Gospel of Luke (1:26-35). Gabriel was also the angel who convinced Joseph that he should marry the Blessed Virgin because she was pregnant by the power of the Holy Spirit (Mt 1:18-21). Likewise, Gabriel warned Joseph in a dream about Herod's plans to massacre all the infants under age two in order to kill Jesus (Mt 2:13-15). He told Joseph to head for Egypt until the threat was over (Mt 2:13). Gabriel appeared before the high priest Zechariah and told him about Elizabeth's pregnancy with John the Baptist (Lk 1:5-23).

The very name Gabriel means "messenger." His feast is celebrated on September 29 along with the archangels Michael and Raphael.

METALWORKERS

Eligius (590-660): Son of Gallo-Roman parents; born at Chaptel, Gaul; in charge of the mint under King Clotaire I in Paris; known for his generosity to the poor; helped kidnaped slaves; built several churches; founded the monastery at Solignac in 632; founded a convent in Paris shortly after; became chief counselor to Dagobert I in 629; ordained in 640; made Bishop of Noyon and Tournai; converted many throughout Antwerp, Ghent, and Courtrai; served as adviser to Queen-regent St. Bathildis; died at Noyon.

Eligius' father was a metalsmith. He had his son apprentice under Abbo the goldsmith at a mint in Limoges. After he completed his training, Eligius went to work for Bobbo, the royal treasurer, and later became master of the mint for King Clotaire I in Paris. His skills in metalwork were known throughout the country. Feast day, December 1.

MIDWIVES

Margaret of Cortona (1247-97): Born at Laviano, Tuscany, Italy; when she was seven, her mother died; raised by a harsh stepmother; ran away from home and lived with a young nobleman from Montepulciano; the couple had one son; her lover was murdered nine years after Margaret decided to live with him; she converted and made a public confession of her sins; shamed by her past lifestyle, her father refused to let her back into his home; two ladies in Cortona allowed Margaret and her son to stay with them; she became a Franciscan tertiary; known for her fasts and penances; recipient of many mystical graces; cared for the poor and sick; visions of Christ; founded a hospital for the sick at Cortona; converted many; known for her miraculous powers; died at Cortona; canonized by Pope Benedict XIII in 1728.

Margaret earned a living as a midwife before she became fully involved in her ministry to the sick and the poor. Feast day, February 22.

MILITARY CHAPLAINS

John of Capistrano (1386-1456): Born at Capistrano, Italy; studied law at Perugia; governor of Perugia in 1412; married shortly thereafter; received a dispensation to enter a Religious order during his marriage; joined the Friars Minor in 1416; ordained in 1420; famous preacher; became a papal diplomat under Pope Nicholas V; died at Villach, Austria, on October 23, possibly from the plague; canonized in 1690; declared patron of military chaplains on February 10, 1984.

John led a military campaign against the left wing of the Christian army at the Battle of Belgrade in 1456. The failure of the Turks to capture this city prevented Europe from being taken over by the Turks. Feast day, October 23.

MISSIONS, BLACK

Benedict the Black (1526-89): Born a slave near Messina, Italy; illiterate and poor; after being freed by his master, became a solitary and settled with hermits at Montepellegrino; made superior of his community; became a Franciscan lay brother; cook at St. Mary's convent near Palermo; again appointed superior of his community; asked to be relieved of his position because of great humility; returned to cooking; known for his miracles, holiness, and as confessor; died at the convent; canonized in 1807 by Pope Pius VII.

Despite an early upbringing which found him surrounded by hecklers and prejudiced people who gave him a hard time because of his color,

Benedict remained a holy and pious boy. Benedict is patron of blacks in the United States. Feast day April 4.

Peter Claver (1580-1654): Peter was a Jesuit sent as a missionary to New Granada in 1610. He helped the plight of the poor slaves in Cartegena, Colombia, by offering them food, medical supplies, and housing. Peter Claver worked with the lepers in St. Lazarus Hospital and heard the confessions of the local prisoners. (See *Colombia* under "Countries and Nations.")

MISSIONS, FOREIGN

Francis Xavier (1506-1552): Born near Pamplona, Navarre, Spain on April 7; studied at the University of Paris; met Ignatius Loyola there; one of the first seven Jesuits who took vows at Montmartre in 1534; ordained at Venice in 1537 with Ignatius and four other Jesuits; went to Rome in 1538; canonized by Pope Gregory XV in 1622; proclaimed patron of foreign missions by Pope Pius X.

Francis was a missionary to the Far East (beginning in 1540). He came to be known as "the Apostle of the Indies" and "the Apostle of Japan." He died on the island of Shangchwan (China) on December 3. Feast day, December 3.

Thérèse of Lisieux (1873-97): At one point in her life, Thérèse desired to serve with the Carmelites at Hanoi in Indo-China (who wished to have her), but a disease she encountered which caused her to hemorrhage at the mouth prevented her from going. She resigned herself to her convent and considered her sufferings in accordance with God's will. It was this fate which later made Thérèse exclaim that she would practice the way of "spiritual childhood," the way of trust and absolute self-surrender. From June of 1987, she was confined to bed. Thérèse died of tuberculosis on September 30. Feast day, October 1. (See *Florists.*)

MISSIONS, PARISH

Leonard of Port Maurice (1676-1751): Born at Porto Maurizio, Italy; began studies at Jesuit Roman College at age thirteen; joined Franciscans of the Strict Observance at Ponticelli in 1697; ascetical writer; known for devotion to the Cross, the Blessed Sacrament, the Sacred Heart, and Mary; preached missions throughout Italy; died at St. Bonaventure's in Rome on November 26; canonized by Pope Pius IX in 1867.

Leonard preached missions throughout Italy during the course of his priesthood, especially in the region of Tuscany. He conducted missions in Rome for six years. In 1744, Pope Benedict XIV sent him to Corsica to preach. Feast day, November 26.

MOTHERS

Monica (332-87): Born at Tagaste, North Africa; married to Patricius, a pagan; they had three children, one being St. Augustine; widowed in 371; prayed for years for conversion of Augustine, who lived most of his youth in worldly pleasure; Monica died at Ostia, Italy.

Monica was the model of the patient mother. After years of praying for the conversion of her son St. Augustine, her wishes were finally granted. Augustine converted in 386 after hearing a sermon from St. Ambrose in Milan. He was baptized on Easter in 387. Monica is also regarded as the patron of married women. She married a pagan (Patricius), who did not convert until 370. He had previously been a difficult person and exhibited a terrible temper. This was all changed as a result of Monica's years spent in prayer for the conversion of her family. Her feast is celebrated on August 27.

MOTORCYCLISTS

Our Lady of Grace (see unit on "Our Lady").

MOTORISTS

Christopher (d. c. 251): legendary figure who allegedly made a living by bringing people across a river; one day he was taking a young man across who was so heavy that the boat nearly sank; then the young man revealed himself as Christ, who claimed to be carrying the weight of the sins of the world on his shoulders; Christopher means "Christ-bearer"; entered into the Roman calendar in 1550.

Christopher is the patron of travelers and motorists. The legend surrounding his life did not emerge until the middle ages. His feast day is traditionally celebrated on July 25.

Frances of Rome (1384-1440): Born at Trastevere near Rome; married at thirteen; model wife for forty years; served the poor throughout Rome; visions of St. Alexis; predicted the end of the Great Schism; known for her gift of healing and prophecy; helped many during the plague; cared for her sick husband till he died; later joined the Benedictines of Monte Oliveto (1436); died in Rome on March 9; canonized by Pope Paul V in 1608.

It is not clear why Frances is a patroness of motorists. Perhaps it is because she was guarded by an archangel for twenty-three years of her life. This archangel was visible only to her, but helped to keep Frances out of danger. Feast day, March 9.

MOUNTAINEERS

Bernard of Montjoux (996-1081): Born in Italy; became a priest; elected Vicar General of Aosta; built schools and churches in his diocese;

missions in the Alps; declared patron saint of both alpinists and mountaineers by Pope Pius XI in 1923.

Bernard became patron and protector of mountaineers because of his four decades spent in missionary work throughout the Alps. He also founded two hospices there for the benefit of lost travelers in the mountain passes of Great and Little Bernard (appropriately named after him). Feast day, May 28.

MUSICIANS

Cecilia (second or third century): Born in Rome of a patrician family; married against her will to Valerian; convinced him to let her keep her virginity and to live a Christian life; known for charitable works; died a virgin-martyr by a soldier who attempted to behead her; he only partially completed the job, leaving her to bleed and suffer for three days before she finally expired; date of death unknown.

Cecilia is considered patron of musicians. It is claimed that during her marriage ceremony she heard no music because of her ecstatic singing to God. Feast day, November 22.

Dunstan (910-88): Born of nobility at Baltonsborough near Glastonbury, England; educated by monks; served in the court of King Athelstan while still a youth; became a Benedictine monk in 934; ordained in 939 by his uncle, St. Alphege, Bishop of Winchester; made abbot of Glastonbury by King Edmund in 943; became famous for his monastic reforms and establishing centers of learning; adviser to King Edred after Edmund was murdered; became Bishop of Worcester in 957 and of London in 958; appointed Archbishop of Canterbury in 959 by King Edgar; remained Edgar's adviser for sixteen years; appointed legate by Pope John XII; restored ecclesiastical discipline and continued to reform the Church and state in England; died in Canterbury after a brief time of teaching school there; noted metalworker and illuminator of manuscripts.

Dunstan was a well-known musician of his day. He played the harp and composed several hymns, his most famous being *Kyrie Rex splendens*. Dunstan is also patron of armorers, goldsmiths, blacksmiths, locksmiths, and jewelers because of his fame and talent in these areas. There was also a popular legend which claims that he once grabbed the nose of the devil with his pair of blacksmith's pincers after a period of long temptation. Feast day, May 19.

Gregory the Great (540-604): Born in Rome, the son of a wealthy family; converted to Catholicism and changed his home into St. Andrew's Monastery during the reign of Valentius; later became a monk there; founded six monasteries in Sicily; ordained by Pope Pelagius II and made one of the seven papal deacons (578); papal nuncio to the Byzantine court from 579-85; returned to monastic life in 586 and became Abbot of St. Andrews; left to preach in England but was recalled to Rome by Pope Pelagius during the plague (589-90); Pelagius caught the plague and died; he was succeeded by Gregory on September 3, 590; as Pope, Gregory initiated ecclesiastical reform, removed immoral clerics from office, abolished clerical fees for burials and ordination, and was known for his charitable actions toward all; fed victims of a famine; protected Jews from ill treatment; negotiated a peace settlement with the Lombard king; sent St. Augustine of Canterbury to evangelize England; denounced the title of "Ecumenical Patriarch" claimed by John, the Patriarch of Constantinople; invented the papal title "Servant of the Servants of God"; known for his preaching; his famous writings include *Dialogues* and *Liber regulae pastoralis*, plus hundreds of sermons and letters; began the practice of saying thirty consecutive Masses for the dead; last of the Latin Doctors of the Church; known as "the Great"; founder of medieval papacy; died in Rome on March 12; canonized soon after his death.

Gregory is considered patron of musicians because of his enormous influence on the liturgical music of the Church. It was during his reign that the famous Gregorian Chant was perfected. He was also a compiler of the Antiphony on which the Roman *schola cantorum* was based, and wrote several hymns while in office. Feast day, September 3.

NOTARIES

Luke the Evangelist (first century): Luke is thought to be author of the Gospel which bears his name. This book was written sometime between A.D. 80-90. He is considered author of the Book of Acts, originally written as a second part to his Gospel. Luke as patron of notaries is a well-deserved role. Many consider his Gospel to be one of the most beautiful pieces of literature ever written. Feast day, October 18. (See *Butchers*.)

Mark the Evangelist (d. c. 74): Possibly the John surnamed Mark in Acts 12:12,25; a relative of St. Barnabas (Col 4); a Levite and Cypriot; journeyed with Paul and Barnabas to Cyprus (Acts 8:5); later returned to Jerusalem after Paul remained awhile at Perga in Pamphylia (Acts 13:13); after a disagreement with Paul, Mark joined Barnabas on a journey to Cyprus; reconciled with Paul later on; helped Paul in Rome when he was imprisoned (Col 4:10); revered as author of the first Gospel (c. A.D. 70); tradition says that after Jesus' resurrection, Mark lived in Alexandria and became its bishop; supposedly founded a church there; tortured and imprisoned for his faith; during his confinement, he was visited by an angel and the Lord Himself; today, his bones are preserved at the Basilica of St. Mark in Venice, Italy (brought there from Alexandria in the ninth century).

According to Clement of Alexandria, Irenaeus, and Papias, Mark was the personal friend and interpreter of St. Peter. Thus he is invoked as the patron of notaries. Feast day, April 25.

NURSES

Agatha (d. 250): Born to a wealthy family of Palermo, Italy; consecrated to a life of chastity; refused the advances of Roman consul Quintian; died a martyr's death by being thrown on hot coals; her intercessions helped to calm the eruptions of Mt. Etna.

During a prison stay for her refusal to renounce her faith and because of her rejection of the advances of Quintian, Agatha was tortured and beaten. Still, she remained calm through it all. At one point she was burned and had iron hooks penetrate her body. Then her breasts were cut off. The governor ordered that she not receive any food or medicine to aid her in health or to relieve the pain. St. Peter appeared to her in the dungeon, gave her comfort, and healed her. Agatha's feast is celebrated on February 5.

Camillus de Lellis (1550-1614): Born at Bocchianico, Italy; fought against the invading Turks; a heavy gambler, became broke and destitute at Naples; desired to become a Franciscan Capuchin, but was denied because of a diseased leg which occurred during his fighting the Turks; died in Rome on July 14; canonized by Pope Benedict XIV in 1746.

Camillus cared for the sick and was director of St. Giacomo Hospital in Rome. He was eventually given permission for ordination by his confessor (St. Philip Neri). He founded the Camillians (Ministers of the Sick). He was declared patron of the sick (along with St. John of God) by Pope Leo XIII. Camillus was declared patron of nurses and nursing groups by Pope Pius XI.

John of God (1495-1550): John of God is named patron of nurses because of his identity with helping and caring for the sick. He started a house which served the sick, and this began his Order of Brothers Hospitalers (the Brothers of St. John of God). Feast day, March 8. (See *Booksellers.*)

Raphael: One of seven archangels who stand before the throne of the Lord (Tb 12:12,15); sent by God to help Tobiah and Sarah; accompanied Tobiah into Media disguised as a man named Azariah; besides Raphael, Michael and Gabriel are the only archangels mentioned by name in the Bible.

Raphael's name means "God heals." This identity came about because of the Bible story that claims he "healed" the earth when it was defiled by the sins of the fallen angels in the apocryphal Book of Enoch (10:7).

Raphael is also identified as the angel who moved the waters of the healing sheep pool (Jn 5:1-4). He is also the patron of the blind. Feast celebrated on September 29 by Christians and Jews alike.

NURSING SERVICES

Catherine of Siena (1347-80): Catherine served the sick at hospitals and devoted herself to caring for patients with particularly dreadful diseases such as leprosy and cancer. In her own life, Catherine would suffer a paralytic stroke which caused her death eight days later. Feast day, April 29. (See *Italy* under "Countries and Nations.")

Elizabeth of Hungary (1207-31): When her husband died, Elizabeth devoted herself to caring for the sick when she became a Franciscan tertiary in 1228. She spent time at Marbourg at a hospice serving the sick, the poor, and the orphaned. Feast day, November 17. (See *Bakers*.)

ORATORS

John Chrysostom (347-407): Born at Antioch, Syria; studied rhetoric and theology; baptized by Bishop Meletius (369); became a hermit under St. Basil and Theodore of Mopsuestia (374); left his reclusive life when he became ill; ordained a deacon in 381; chosen Patriarch of Constantinople in 398 (against his wishes); helped the poor and reformed the Church; he was condemned on twenty-nine counts by Theophilus and thirty-six bishops because of jealousy; eventually banished to Cucusus in Armenia by Emperor Arcadius (404); wrote 238 letters during his exile; later exiled to Pityus on the Black Sea and died on the way at Comana, Pontus, from exhaustion; wrote *The Priesthood*; declared a Doctor of the Church at the Council of Chalcedon in 451.

John Chrysostom was famous for his preaching; in fact, his popularity was such that he soon became known as the "Golden Mouth." After 390, he gave eloquent discourses on the books of the New Testament. His output was enormous: for example, there were 88 homilies on John, 90 on Matthew, and 32 on Romans. He also established a reputation as an apologist and promoter of the faith. Named patron of preachers by Pope Pius X. Feast day, September 13.

ORGAN BUILDERS

Cecilia (second or third century): Born in Rome of a patrician family; married against her will to Valerian; convinced him to let her keep her virginity and to live a Christian life; known for charitable works; died a virgin-martyr by a soldier who attempted to behead her; he only partially completed the job, leaving her to bleed and suffer for three days before she finally expired; date of death unknown.

Cecilia is considered patron of musicians. It is claimed that during her marriage ceremony she heard no music because of her ecstatic singing to God. Feast day, November 22.

PAINTERS

Luke the Evangelist (first century): A legend claims that Luke painted several portraits of the Virgin Mary after visiting her several times in Jerusalem. Feast day, October 18. (See *Butchers*.)

PARATROOPERS

Michael the Archangel: It is unclear why Michael is patron of paratroopers. Perhaps the tradition arose because of the story of how Michael threw the devil and his cohorts out of heaven and down to earth during the cosmic battle between good and evil (see Rv 12). Feast day, September 29. (See *Grocers*.)

PAWNBROKERS

Nicholas of Myra (d. c. 350): Nicholas's role as patron of pawnbrokers is unclear. Perhaps it is because he is associated with providing money (bags of gold) to three children who were poor in order that they could afford a dowry for marriage. (See *Russia* under "Countries and Nations.")

PHARMACISTS

Cosmas and Damian (d. 303): Patron of barbers and physicians. Both Cosmas and Damian studied medicine and became famous for their skills. They offered their services free of charge. Many healings from their intercessions have been claimed throughout the centuries. Feast on September 26. (See *Barbers*.)

PHARMACISTS (HOSPITALS)

Gemma Galgani (1878-1903): Born at Camigliano, Tuscany, Italy; extraordinary mystical experiences: visions of Christ and Mary; daily appearance of guardian angel; diabolical assaults; experienced the sacred stigmata (1899-1901); remained a lay person; died from a long illness in Lucca at age twenty-five; beatified by Pope Pius XI in 1933; canonized by Pope Pius XII in 1940.

Gemma Galgani suffered from tuberculosis of the spine for many years. This caused her to have a curvature of the spine. No medicine would help her situation. A miraculous cure came through the intercession of St. Gabriel of the Sorrows. Still, because of her continued sickly state, Gemma was denied entrance into the Passionist Order of nuns. She resigned herself to God's will and offered up her suffering for the benefit of all. She is a good example of how the Lord can serve as healer or comforter in the light of suffering. Her feast is celebrated on April 11.

PHILOSOPHERS

Justin Martyr (100-165): Born at Flavia Neapolis to Greco-Roman parents; studied philosophy, rhetoric, history, poetry, and Christian literature; converted at the age of thirty; famous writer and preacher; first of the Christian apologists; reconciled faith and reason; scourged and beheaded for refusing to sacrifice to the Roman gods.

Justin Martyr traveled around his country teaching others philosophical truths and engaging in debates. He eventually founded a school of philosophy in Rome. His most famous works are *Apologies* (defending Christianity against enemies) and *Dialogue with Trypho* (defending Christianity over Judaism in a discourse to Trypho, an educated Jew). Feast day, June 1.

PHYSICIANS

Cosmas and Damian (d. c. 303): Arabian twin brothers, physicians; studied medicine in Syria; charitable to the poor; defied death by water, fire, and crucifixion before they were finally beheaded with their three brothers during Diocletian's persecution.

Patrons of barbers and physicians. Both Cosmas and Damian studied medicine and became famous for their skills. They offered their services free of charge. Many healings from their intercessions have been claimed throughout the centuries. Feast on September 26.

Luke the Evangelist (1st century): According to Paul's letter to the Colossians, Luke was a physician by trade (Col. 4:14). He is also revered as author of the Gospel which bears his name and the Book of Acts. Feast day, October 18. (See *Butchers*.)

Pantaleon (d. 305): Many legends surround Pantaleon; son of a pagan named Eustorgius of Nicomedia; raised a Christian by his mother Eubula; martyred under the persecutions of Diocletian; after six other attempts to kill him had failed (drowning, fire, wild beasts, etc.), he was finally beheaded.

Pantaleon became the personal doctor of Emperor Maximian. He came to enjoy the life of royalty so much that he gave up his faith. After Hermolaos helped Pantaleon to reconvert, he sold his possessions, gave the money to the poor, and donated his medical services free of charge to those in need. Feast day, July 27.

Raphael: One of seven archangels who stand before the throne of the Lord (Tb 12:12,15); sent by God to help Tobiah and Sarah; accompanied Tobiah into Media disguised as a man named Azariah; besides Raphael, Michael and Gabriel are the only archangels mentioned by name in the Bible.

Raphael's name means "God heals." This identity came about because of the Bible story that claims he "healed" the earth when it was defiled by the sins of the fallen angels in the apocryphal Book of Enoch (10:7). Raphael is also identified as the angel who moved the waters of the healing sheep pool (Jn 5:1-4). He is also the patron of the blind. Feast celebrated on September 29 by Christians and Jews alike.

PILGRIMS

James the Greater (d. c. 44): Galilean, son of Zebedee, brother of John (called "Son of Thunder" with him); a fisherman, called with Peter and John to follow Jesus and witness with them to miracles, the Transfiguration and Agony in the Garden; first of the Apostles to die, by the sword in the reign of Herod Agrippa.

St. James is patron of pilgrims because of a legend that he journeyed to Spain, and relics said to be kept at his shrine at Compostela. (See also *Rheumatism* under "Special Needs and Conditions.")

POETS

Cecilia (date unknown): Cecilia reportedly experienced a miraculous blessing at her wedding. During the ceremony, she did not hear the music playing; rather, all she could do was sing to the heavenly sound of angels she heard in her heart. Feast day, November 22. (See *Musicians*.)

POLICEMEN

Michael the Archangel: Michael is probably invoked as patron of policemen because of his past role as protector against all evil forces. (See *Grocers*.)

PORTERS

Christopher (d. c. 251): Legendary figure who allegedly made a living by bringing people across a river; one day he was taking a young man across who was so heavy that the boat nearly sank; then the young man revealed himself as Christ, who said He was carrying the weight of the sins of the world on His shoulders; Christopher means "Christ-bearer"; entered into the Roman calendar in 1550.

Christopher is patron of porters, who are "doorkeepers" and ones who "carry burdens." Presumably, the burden of carrying Christ across the river holds a special identity with this legendary figure. Feast celebrated July 25.

POSTAL EMPLOYEES

Gabriel: It was the archangel Gabriel who came to the Blessed Virgin Mary at her home in Nazareth to announce that she would become impregnated by the Holy Spirit (the Incarnation) and give birth to the Son of God and Savior of the world (the Nativity). These stories are related in the Gospel of Luke (1:26-35). Gabriel was also the angel who convinced Joseph that he should marry the Blessed Virgin because she was pregnant by the power of the Holy Spirit (Mt 1:18-21). Likewise, Gabriel warned Joseph in a dream about Herod's plans to massacre all the infants under age 2 in order to kill Jesus (Mt 2:13-15). He told Joseph to head for Egypt until the threat was over (Mt 2:13). Gabriel appeared before the high priest Zechariah and told him about Elizabeth's pregnancy with John the Baptist (Lk 1:5-23).

The very name Gabriel means "messenger." Because postal workers carry special-delivery mail to the public and serve as channels of our communication, their identity with Gabriel is obvious. His feast day is celebrated on September 29, along with the archangels Michael and Raphael.

PRIESTS

John Vianney (Curé of Ars) (1786-1859): Born at Dardilly, France, on May 8; drafted into army in 1809 but later deserted; entered seminary at Lyons in 1813; ordained in 1815; appointed to Ars in 1818; opened a school for girls in 1824; noted confessor; long battles with the Evil One; died at Ars on August 4; built a famous shrine dedicated to St. Philomena; canonized by Pope Pius XI in 1925.

John Baptist Vianney (the "Curé of Ars") was an extraordinary priest. He often spent 16-18 hours a day in the confessional. John was also known for his gift of reading minds and souls, and he was continually sought for his spiritual wisdom and direction. He was declared patron of parish priests by Pope Pius XI in 1929.

PRINCES

Boris and Gleb (d. 1015): Sons of Vladimir of Kiev; each had ten stepbrothers and two stepsisters from Vladimir's first marriage;

great-grandmother was St. Olga (the first Russian canonized saint); when Vladimir died, each of his twelve sons was to receive an inheritance of his property and territory; a brother named Svyatopolk tried to defraud Boris and Gleb of their rightful inheritance; both were stabbed to death by Svyatopolk's companions; canonized by Pope Benedict XIII in 1724.

Boris and Gleb remained firm in their Christian faith, even when their lives were threatened. As legitimate princes, Boris and Gleb were known for their piety and kindness. They died peacefully, fully submitting to death and recognizing it as the will of God. Feast day, July 24.

Casimir of Poland (1458-84): Born the third of thirteen children to King Casimir IV of Poland and Elizabeth of Austria, daughter of Emperor Albert II of Germany; known for his early devotions to the saints and the Church as a child; refused marriage for the sake of serving God and country; miracles reported at his tomb; canonized by Pope Adrian VI in 1522.

Casimir was viceroy for his father's throne during the king's absence 1479-83. Although never technically a king himself, Casimir did serve as a prince in his country. He was known for his devotion to the Blessed Virgin and the Eucharist. Feast day, March 4. (See *Bachelors*.)

Gotteschalc: (d. 1066): Abotrite prince; student at Abbey of St. Michael in Luneburg, Germany; renounced his faith and left the abbey in 1030 when his father Uto was killed at the hands of a Saxon; attacked various Saxon groups in revenge; captured and imprisoned by Duke Bernard of Saxony; later released; left for Denmark and joined the army of King Canute; married his daughter; participated in wars with Norway and England; returned to his own country in 1043 and became chief of the Abotrites; reconverted to the faith; helped his local priests to translate sermons and instructions into his Slavonic language soon after his religious conversion; killed in the city of Lenzen on June 7, 1066, during a Christian persecution.

After his conversion, Prince Gotteschalc brought priests into his own country and founded many monasteries throughout the land. He also participated in several missionary works. Feast day, June 7.

PRINCESSES

Adelaide (931-99): Daughter of Rudolf II of Upper Burgundy; married the son of Hugh of Provence (Lothair); he eventually became King of Italy; the couple had one child named Emma, who ended up marrying Lothair II of France; Lothair died in 950; Adelaide refused to marry Berengarius's son and was imprisoned in a castle on Lake Garda; released by Otto the Great of Germany after he came into Italy and conquered Berengarius's army;

Otto married Adelaide on Christmas in Pavia (951), thus combining his German Empire with Italy; they had five children; Otto was crowned emperor at Rome in 962; in 973, Otto died and was succeeded by his eldest son, Otto II; Adelaide founded monasteries for monks and nuns; she died at her monastery at Seltz on the Rhine near Strasbourg; canonized by Pope Urban II in 1097.

Adelaide was known for her kind treatment of the poor during her time as princess and later during her reign as empress. She brought about a reconciliation between the wife of her son Otto II (Theophania), her servants, and herself. Adelaide helped to convert many pagans in her country and forgave her enemies. Her feast day is December 16.

Dymphna (d. c. 650): According to popular legend, Dymphna was the daughter of a pagan Celtic chieftain. She left home after her father tried to seduce her. Dymphna built an oratory near Amsterdam and lived there as a hermit. Seeking revenge, her father eventually found her and had her beheaded for not giving in to his carnal desires. Feast day, May 15. (See *Victims of Rape* under "Special Needs.")

PRINTERS

Augustine of Hippo (354-430): Patron of printers because of his enormous literary output and his influence on Catholic readers throughout the centuries. Augustine is one of the greatest and most influential Christian writers and theologians of all time, penning such classics as *Confessions* (his autobiography, 397-401), *On the Trinity* (a fifteen-book work written 400-16), *City of God* (413-26), and *Retractations* (426); it is reported that he wrote an incredible thousand books and 118 treatises in his lifetime! Feast day, August 28. (See *Theologians.*)

John of God (1495-1550): When John returned to Gibraltar, he opened a store and sold religious books and articles (1538). John of God was known for helping the sick and the poor. He started a house for this purpose, which was the beginnings of the founding of the Order of Brothers Hospitalers, or the Brothers of St. John of God. Feast day, March 8. (See *Booksellers.*)

PUBLIC RELATIONS

Bernardine of Siena (1380-1444): Born in Massa Marittima, Italy, the son of the local governor; orphaned at age seven and raised by his aunt; began schooling in Siena at age twelve; enrolled at age seventeen in a confraternity of Our Lady, where he helped the poor and sick; worked at a hospital in Siena during the plague (1400); later joined the Franciscans; professed and ordained in 1403; engaged in some preaching, but lived a life of retirement and prayer; became known as a great apostle and reformer; in 1417 he preached in Milan, beginning his fame as a public speaker; eventually preached all over Italy and encouraged devotion to the Holy Name; elected Vicar General of the Friars of the Strict Observance (1430) after turning down the offer to become Bishop of Siena (Pope Martin V, 1427); died at Aquila during a mission in 1444; many miracles reported at his tomb; canonized by Pope Nicholas V in 1450, only six years after his death.

Bernardine is the patron of advertisers, communications personnel, and public relations because of his evangelization and conversions of thousands to his beloved Franciscan Order. Bernardine founded many convents and reformed the rules of the Observance. Through preaching and teaching, his influence was felt throughout his country. Feast day, May 20.

PUBLIC RELATIONS (HOSPITALS)

Paul the Apostle (d. c. 67): St. Paul was known for his three great missionary journeys throughout Europe and Asia Minor: Cyprus, Pamphylia, Iconium, Lystra, and Derbe (first journey); Phrygia, Galatia, Philippi, Thessalonica, and Berea (second journey); and Macedonia and Greece (third journey). Throughout his travels he preached the Gospel, taught others about Christ and morality, and converted thousands to the faith. Indeed, Paul is the "Great Apostle," the most successful public relations man the Church has ever known. (See *Malta*.)

QUEENS

Clotilde (474-575): Clotilde (or Clotilda) was the daughter of King Chilperic of Burgundy. In 492, she married King Clovis of the Franks and converted him to Christianity on Christmas Day in 496. After the death of her husband, Clotilde spent the remainder of her life serving the sick and the poor in Tours. Feast day, June 3. (See *Death of Children* and *Parents of Large Families* under "Special Needs and Conditions.")

Elizabeth of Portugal (1271-1336): Elizabeth was the daughter of King Peter III of Aragon. She married King Denis of Portugal when she was only twelve years old. Elizabeth was known for her charitable actions toward the sick and the poor, and she founded several convents, hospitals, and shelters for wayward girls. When Denis died in 1325, Elizabeth desired to become a nun. She later changed her mind and became a Franciscan tertiary. Feast day, July 4. (See *Victims of Jealousy* and *Victims of Unfaithfulness* under "Special Needs.")

Hedwig, Queen of Poland (1374-99): Youngest daughter of King Louis I of Hungary; became Queen of Poland; under political pressure and against her will, Hedwig obediently married Jagiello, Prince of Lithuania; once engaged to William, Duke of Austria, the real love of her life; pressured to forfeit the marriage for political reasons; Hedwig offered her marriage to Jagiello as a sacrifice to God, uniting her cross to that of the Savior; husband eventually converted and baptized because of Hedwig's influence; died after a difficult childbirth at the young age of twenty-eight; miracles reported at her tomb.

After King Louis I of Hungary died in 1382, Hedwig succeeded her father, becoming Queen of Poland because Louis was nephew and successor to King Casimir III of Poland. During her reign Hedwig was known for her charitable acts and helped pass laws to benefit the poor. Honored in Poland on February 28.

Margaret of Scotland (1045-93): In 1070, Margaret married King Malcolm III of Scotland at Dunfermline Castle. She was known for her piety and kindness toward everyone. Margaret was particularly helpful toward the sick and the poor. She fought against Church abuses of her day, such as simony and usury. She also regulated the Lenten fast and Easter Communion. Feast day, November 16. (See *Death of Children* and *Parents of Large Families* under "Special Needs and Conditions.")

Matilda (895-968): Matilda (Maud, Mechtildis) was the daughter of Count Dietrich of Westphalia and Reinhild of Denmark. She married Henry the Fowler, son of Duke Otto of Saxony, in 909. Henry was to become the King of Germany in 909. Together the couple had five children: Otto (who later became Emperor of the Holy Roman Empire), Henry the Quarrelsome (who would become Duke of Bavaria), St. Bruno (later the Archbishop of Cologne), Gerberga (who married King Louis IV of France), and Hedwig (future mother to Hugh Capet). Henry and Matilda brought up their children in a Christian environment. She was to suffer greatly, however, when her child Henry rebelled against his brother Otto. He eventually died during one of their quarrels.

Matilda was a dedicated Christian during the term of her queenship. She was responsible for building three convents and a monastery. In her later years, Matilda retired to the convent she had built at Nordhausen. Feast day, March 14.

RADIO WORKERS

Gabriel: It is unclear why Gabriel is the patron of radio workers. Perhaps his association with delivering important messages and therefore being an important channel of communication serves this purpose. Feast day, September 29. (See *Messengers*.)

RADIOLOGISTS

Michael the Archangel: One of the three archangels mentioned in the Bible (the others being Gabriel and Raphael); he is mentioned twice in the Old Testament (Dn 10:13ff; 12:1), where he is depicted as the protector of the Chosen People; Michael appears twice in the New Testament: in Jude 9, where he argues with the devil over Moses' body; and in Rv 12:7-9, where he throws the devil and his demons out of heaven; the "captain of the heavenly host"; found in much apocryphal literature of the early Christian centuries; a special helper at the moment of death.

Michael's role as patron of radiologists is unclear. He is also invoked as protector against evil forces. Feast day celebrated on September 29 (Michaelmas Day), a day chosen in the sixth century to honor the founding of a basilica in his name on the Salerian Way in Rome. Since 1970, Raphael and Gabriel are joined together with Michael on September 29 as the feast of the archangels.

SACRISTANS

Guy of Anderlecht (d. 1012): Born near Brussels, Belgium, to a poor laboring family; poverty prevented him from getting a decent education; known for his deep faith and piety; served in the Church but left after a business opportunity promised him fortune; repented and returned to the faith after his ship wrecked on a journey and destroyed his merchandise; made many pilgrimages thereafter (such as Rome and Jerusalem); returned to Belgium; died of an illness in Anderlecht; many miracles reported at his tomb.

Guy was given the opportunity to serve as a sacristan in the Church of Our Lady at Laeken near Brussels. He was known for his piety and was beloved by everyone who came to know him. Because he was poor, a wealthy ship merchant offered Guy a chance to go into business with him. He accepted and left the Church with worldly ambitions. A shipwreck later on resulted in Guy's second conversion. Thereafter, he was a faithful servant of the Church. Feast day, September 12.

SADDLERS

Crispin and Crispinian (d. 287): Legendary figures of Christian history; Roman brothers; preached the Gospel in Gaul; settled at Soissons; converted many; tortured for their faith; attempted killings by Rictiovarus failed (such as boiling and drowning); because of his failure, Rictiovarus committed suicide; eventually beheaded under the Emperor Maximian.

Crispin and Crispinian worked as shoemakers during the night. During the day, they spent their free time helping to convert the people of Gaul.

They are also considered the patrons of shoemakers, leatherworkers, and cobblers. Feast day, October 25.

SAILORS

Brendan (c. 484-577): Born near Tralee, Kerry, Ireland; raised by St. Ita; ordained in 512; founded many monasteries in Ireland, including Clonfert (559), where he became its abbot; missionary journeys to England and Scotland.

Brendan once made a seven-year journey by sea to search for a fabled paradise (the Land of Promise). He was also known as "Brendan the Navigator." He may have sailed to North America, but the legends are not supported by fact. Feast celebrated May 16.

Christopher (d. c. 251): The legendary account of Christopher helping Christ across the water accounts for this patronage. Feast day, July 25. (See *Motorists*.)

Cuthbert (d. 687): Background uncertain; many allege that he was a Scot, others that he was Irish or English; orphaned as a child; a young shepherd; fought the Mercians; became a monk at Melrose Abbey; left for Ripon Abbey with St. Eata in 661; returned to Melrose in 662; eventually became prior of the abbey; elected Bishop of Hexham in 685; later became Bishop of Lindisfarne; cared for the sick and poor; miraculous healings attributed to his intercession; known for lengthy time spent in prayer; had the gift of prophecy.

Cuthbert was quite the traveler. He engaged in missionary work which took him to Lindisfarne, Ireland, and to a nearby island (Farnes Islands) near Bamborough. He preached the Gospel from the coast of Berwick to the Solway Firth. He may have visited the Picts of Galway as well. If he did, Cuthbert sailed with two companions and landed at the estuary on the Nith one year on the day after Christmas. Because of the snowy weather, he and his companions could not penetrate inland and were in danger of starving. His faith firm and through intense prayer, Cuthbert found a slice of dolphin's flesh to feed them and soon the weather cleared for passage. Because of this supernatural intervention, a church was later built on the spot in the town of Kirkcudbright in honor of St. Cuthbert. Feast day, March 20.

Erasmus (d. c. 303): Legendary figure; also known as Elmo; Bishop of Formiae, Campagna, Italy; he once fled to Mount Lebanon during the persecutions of Emperor Diocletian; he lived a life of solitude there for some time, being fed by a raven; after the emperor discovered his whereabouts, he was tortured and thrown in prison; legend claims that an angel released him and he departed for Illyricum; eventually suffered a martyr's death; one of the Fourteen Holy Helpers.

Legend records that when a blue light appears at mastheads before and after a storm, the seamen took it as a sign of Erasmus's protection. This was known as "St. Elmo's Fire." The blue electrical discharges under certain atmospheric conditions have also been seen on the masks or riggings of ships. Erasmus is also invoked against stomach cramps and colic. This came about because at one time he had hot iron hooks stuck into his intestines by persecutors under Emperor Diocletian. These wounds he miraculously endured. Feast day, June 2.

Eulalia of Merida (d. 304): Born in Spain; rejected Emperor Diocletian's demand that she sacrifice to the gods at the age of twelve; Eulalia's mother took her into the country for protection; she again refused to honor the pagan gods before Dacian; tortured and killed at Merida, Spain, for remaining firm in her faith; a church was built over the site of her tomb; relics now located in the Cathedral of Oviedo.

It is unclear why Eulalia is patron of sailors. Perhaps she was invoked by sea travelers who received many blessings from her intercession. Also the patron saint of runaways and victims of torture. Feast day, December 10.

Nicholas of Myra (d. c. 350): Born at Patara, Lycia, Asia Minor; legendary aspects of life; ordained Bishop of Myra; known for holiness and miracles; imprisoned for faith under Emperor Diocletian; participated at Council of Nicaea (325); opponent of Arianism; according to legend, gave money and gifts to the poor; saved three girls from prostitution by throwing bags of gold in their home, causing all to eventually marry; this and other traditions started the practice of giving children Christmas gifts in his name for good luck; Nicholas became Sint Klaes in Holland, then Santa Claus; relics brought to Bari, Italy, in 1087, where they remain in the St. Nicholas Basilica.

It is not clear why Nicholas is patron of sailors. Perhaps it is because of the fact that after his death his relics were brought by sea to Bari, Italy. Nicholas Basilica. There is one claim that he miraculously interceded for a group of sailors who were threatened by a storm off the coast of Lycia. Nicholas is also the patron of Russia, Greece, Apulia, Sicily, Lorraine, coopers, and children. Feast day on December 6.

Peter Gonzales (d. 1246): Also known as St. Elmo or St. Telmo; born to a Castilian family of nobility; educated by his uncle, the Bishop of Astorga; named canon of the local cathedral; famous for his penances and mortifications; joined the Dominican Order; preached; made chaplain of the court of King St. Ferdinand III; converted and influenced the soldiers of his country; evangelized; died on Easter Sunday; canonized by Pope Benedict XIV in 1741.

Peter Gonzales evangelized throughout his country and all along the coast. He had a special fondness for sailors. He used to visit them aboard their ships, preaching the Gospel and praying for their needs. Feast day, April 14.

SCHOLARS

Bridget (450-525): Bridget founded a monastery at Kildare in 470. She became the abbess of the convent, first in Ireland. Bridget developed this convent into a major center for learning and spirituality. Later, she founded a school of art in Kildare as well, which became famous for its illuminated manuscripts (such as the *Book of Kildare*). Feast day, February 1. (See *Ireland* under "Countries and Nations.")

SCIENTISTS

Albert the Great (1206-80): Albert was one of the Church's greatest intellects. He studied at the University of Padua and later taught at Hildesheim, Freiburg-im-Breisgau, Regensburg, and Strasbourg. He then taught at the University of Paris, where he received his doctorate in 1245. He was among the first and greatest of the natural scientists, gaining a reputation for expertise in biology, chemistry, physics, astronomy, geography, metaphysics, and mathematics. He was also very learned in biblical studies and theology. (See *Medical Technicians*.)

SCULPTORS

Castorius (d. c. 306): one of the "Four Crowned Martyrs"; imprisoned for refusing to sacrifice to the Roman gods under the reign of Emperor Diocletian; executed because he was falsely accused of killing Lampadius, Diocletian's officer; died at Pannonia in Hungary; buried on the Via Lavicana.

Castorius was hired as a carver under the Emperor Diocletian. He worked at the imperial quarries at Sirmium (Mitrovica, Yugoslavia). Although his work was well-known and pleased the emperor, he was sentenced to death for refusing to honor the Roman gods. Feast day, November 8.

SEAMEN

Francis of Paola (1416-1507): Born at Paola, Italy; education with Franciscans at a friary in San Marco; became a hermit near Paola at fifteen; founded Mimim Friars with two companions in 1436; built a monastery;

lived a life of penance, sacrifice, and charity; known for miracles, prophecies, and reading hearts; many miracles attributed to his intercession; founded the Hermits of St. Francis of Assisi in 1492 (later changed the name to Minim Friars); died at his monastery in Plessis, France, on April 2; canonized by Pope Leo X in 1519.

It is unclear why Francis is considered the patron of seamen. Perhaps he used the waterways in his frequent travels throughout Italy, where he established many foundations and built several monasteries. Feast day, April 2.

SECRETARIES

Genesius (d. c. 300): Genesius was a comedian who performed satirical plays depicting religious scenes and the sacraments. One day he was converted during a play before Emperor Diocletian in Rome. He received a vision of an angel who showed him his sins in a heavenly book. These sins were wiped clean before his eyes — a sign that he had been forgiven of his past offenses with his newfound faith. Genesius was eventually tortured and martyred for his faith. It is unclear why he is patron of secretaries, unless it alludes to the story of the angel serving as a "secretary" to his list of sins. Feast day, August 25. (See *Actors*.)

SEMINARIANS

Charles Borromeo (1538-84): Charles Borromeo was very instrumental in the formation of the decrees of the Council of Trent. He helped to revise the disciplinary measures and training procedures of the clergy, celebration of the liturgy, administration of the sacraments, giving of catechism on Sundays, and other important aspects of Church practice and devotion. He arranged for retreats for his clergy and served as a spiritual director to many. In 1578, Charles instituted a society of secular priests called the Oblates of St. Ambrose (now the Oblates of St. Charles). He also established the Confraternity of Christian Doctrine, whose schools numbered some 740 with 3,000 catechists and 40,000 pupils. Charles is considered the founder of the "Sunday school." Feast day, November 4. (See *Catechists*.)

SERVANTS

Martha (first century): Martha was the woman who served the guests and provided the food during Jesus' visit to her home (Lk 10:38-42). She lived with her sister Mary and brother Lazarus in Bethany. Because Mary had spent her time contemplating our Lord's words while Martha remained busy serving her guests, Jesus told Martha that "Mary had chosen the better part." This contrast reveals that Mary is an example of the prayerful, contemplative Christian whereas Martha best exemplifies the active Christian. Both are considered good, but Mary's role is superior. Feast day, July 29. (See *Cooks*.)

Zita (1218-78): Zita served the household of a wool dealer near Lucca, Italy for forty-eight years. She is an exemplary model of houseworkers everywhere, doing her ordinary daily duties to the best of her ability in a spirit of submission to the divine will. Many miracles are attributed to her intercession. Feast day, April 27. (See *Maids*.)

SHEPHERDESSES

Germaine Cousin (1579-1601): Germaine Cousin was a lowly poor girl from Pibrac near Toulouse, France. Her father was a farm laborer, and her mother died while she was still an infant. Germaine tended the family sheep daily, while praying the Rosary and making her work a spiritual experience. She was mistreated by her stepmother, since her sickly condition left her with a deformed neck and unattractive appearance. She was a victim of child abuse, being left to sleep in a small place behind the family stairs. Germaine never lost sight of her faith. She was found one morning dead on her straw mat under the stairs. Feast day, June 15. (See *Victims of Child Abuse* under "Special Needs and Conditions.")

Regina (second century): Daughter of the pagan Clement and Alice in Burgundy; mother died at birth; raised by a Christian woman; refused to marry Olybrius; tortured and martyred for her faith.

Regina was sent away by her father after he discovered that she was being raised a Christian. She was brought up in the home of a Christian woman, whom she served as a shepherdess. Feast day, September 7.

Solangia (d. 880): Born at Villemont, France; parents were vinedressers; known for her pious devotions and charitable acts; decapitated after refusing to marry the son of a count.

Solangia tended her father's sheep each day. Bernard de la Gothie, the son of the Count of Poitiers, sought her hand in marriage. Solangia refused his offer, having made a vow of virginity at the age of seven. She preferred to help her family and practice her faith. Bernard sought revenge and kidnapped her. He eventually cut off her head with his sword. Feast day, May 10.

SHEPHERDS

Cuthman (d. 900): Cuthman grew up as a poor child in the southern part of England. He helped his family out by working as a shepherd in their field. During his work day, Cuthman would frequently spend his time in prayer.

Cuthman was eventually forced to sell his father's livestock because of his mother's ill health. He left his home to look for work to help support his mother's medical expenses. After finding a suitable spot to settle down, Cuthman and his mother built a small cottage and he again worked the land. Eventually, he built a church next to his lot. Many miracles are attributed to Cuthman's intercession. Feast day, February 8.

Drogo (d. 1186): Drogo served as a shepherd to a kind woman at Sebourg named Elizabeth de la Haire. His reputation for sanctity was known throughout the land. Many people claimed to see him working the fields and attending Mass at the same time (the gift of bilocation). Drogo made several pilgrimages during his life, including nine trips to Rome. He eventually lived a life of a recluse in a small cell attached to the local church. Feast day, April 16. (See Orphans and Unattractive People under "Special Needs and Conditions.")

SHOEMAKERS

Crispin and Crispinian (d. 287): Legendary figures who were martyred for their faith. Crispin and Crispinian reportedly worked as shoemakers during the night while preaching the Gospel during the day. Their efforts resulted in the conversion of many people. Feast day, October 25. (See *Saddlers*.)

SILVERSMITHS

Andronicus (239-304): Born at Claudiopolis, Isauria; became a Roman soldier; left after his conversion to Christianity; arrested during the persecutions of Emperors Diocletian and Maximian; tortured for defending his faith; thrown to the wild beasts in an arena near Anazarbus; the animals were unable to kill him, so the gladiators killed him by sword instead.

It is unclear why Andronicus is patron of silversmiths. Perhaps it is due to his earlier feats using a metal sword as a young and valiant soldier; it may also have to do with the fact that it took the swords of the gladiators to kill Andronicus after the wild beasts were unable to end his life. Feast day, October 11.

SINGERS

Cecilia (second or third century): Born in Rome of a patrician family; married against her will to Valerian; convinced him to let her keep her virginity and to live a Christian life; known for charitable works; died a virgin-martyr; a soldier who attempted to behead her only partially completed the job, leaving her to bleed and suffer for three days before she finally expired; date of death unknown.

Cecilia is considered patron of singers and musicians. It is claimed that during her marriage ceremony she heard no music because of her ecstatic singing to God. Feast day, November 22.

Gregory I the Great (540-604): Gregory is considered the patron of singers and musicians because of his enormous influence on the liturgical music of the Church. It was during his reign that the famous Gregorian Chant was perfected. He was also a compiler of the Antiphony on which the Roman *schola cantorum* was based, and wrote several hymns while in office. Feast day, September 3. (See *Musicians*.)

SKATERS

Lydwine of Schiedam (1380-1433): Born at Schiedam, Holland, one of nine children of a workingman; after an injury in her youth, she became bedridden and suffered the rest of her life from various illnesses and diseases; experienced many mystical gifts, including supernatural visions of heaven, hell, and purgatory, apparitions of Christ, and the stigmata; Thomas à Kempis wrote a famous biography of her; canonized by Pope Leo XIII in 1890.

Lydwine suffered a fall while ice skating in 1396. During that fall, a friend collided with her and caused her to break a rib on the right side. From this injury she never recovered. An abscess formed inside her body, which later burst and caused Lydwine extreme suffering. Eventually, she was to suffer a series of mysterious illnesses which in retrospect seem to be from the hands of God. Lydwine heroically accepted her plight as the will of God, and offered up her sufferings for the sins of humanity. Some of the illnesses which inflicted Lydwine are: headaches, vomiting, fever, thirst, bedsores, toothaches, spasms of the muscles, blindness, neuritis, and the stigmata. Feast day, April 14.

SKIERS

Bernard of Montjoux (996-1081): Born in Italy; became a priest; elected Vicar General of Aosta; built schools and churches in his diocese; missions in the Alps; declared patron saint of both alpinists and mountaineers by Pope Pius XI in 1923.

Bernard became patron and protector of skiers because of his four decades spent in missionary work throughout the Alps. He also founded two hospices there for the benefit of lost travelers in the mountain passes of Great and Little Bernard (appropriately named after him). Feast day, May 28.

SOCIAL WORKERS

Louise de Marillac (1591-1660): Born on August 12 at Ferrières-en-Brie near Meux, France; tried to become a Capuchin sister but was turned down because of ill health; married Antony Le Gras in 1613; after his death in 1625, devoted to a life of faith and good works; St. Vincent de Paul became her spiritual director; died in Paris on March 15; canonized by Pope Pius XI in 1934.

Louise helped St. Vincent de Paul with serving the poor, the sick, and neglected children through the Ladies of Charity. She eventually formed the Sisters of Charity of St. Vincent de Paul (formally approved in 1655). In time, Louise wrote a rule for the new Order. She went all over France to establish her Order, which was dedicated to serving hospitals, orphanages, and other institutions. By the time of her death, Louise had founded over forty houses of her Order in France. The Sisters of Charity were to establish their mission throughout the world. She was declared patroness of social workers by Pope John XXIII in 1960. Feast day, March 15.

SOLDIERS

Ignatius of Loyola (1491-1556): Born of a noble family at Guipuzcoa, Spain, the youngest of thirteen children; served in the military before his conversion; founded the Society of Jesus (Jesuits) in 1534 at Paris; wrote *The Book of Spiritual Exercises* between 1522-23; active missionary; founded schools, colleges, and seminaries; died in Rome on July 31; canonized by Pope Gregory XV in 1622.

Ignatius had entered the army seeking fame and power as a brave soldier. He was wounded in his right leg during the siege of Pamplona in 1521. While recovering from his wound, he was converted after reading a life of Christ and a book on the saints. Also declared patron of retreats and spiritual exercises by Pope Pius XI. Feast day, July 31.

Hadrian (d. c. 304): Also known as Adrian; a pagan officer at the court of Nicomedia; married Natalia; thrown in prison and tortured for proclaiming his faith in Jesus Christ; one of his hands was severed as part of his torture; Natalia fled to Argryopolis near Constantinople after her husband's death and when an imperial official of Nicomedia insisted upon marrying her.

While serving as a soldier, Hadrian was converted after witnessing twenty-three Christians being tortured for their faith. Feast day, September 8.

George (d. c. 303): George may have served as a soldier in the army under Emperor Constantine, though a great deal known about his life is legend. A mythical story claims that George had slain a dragon to free the inhabitants of Sylene, Libya, from its terror. (See *Boy Scouts* under "Countries and Nations.")

Joan of Arc (1412-1431): Born to a farm family on January 6 at Domremy, France, youngest of five children; experienced supernatural visions at age thirteen (such as St. Michael, St. Catherine, and St. Margaret); told in these voices to save France by aiding the Dauphin; canonized by Pope Benedict XIV in 1920.

Joan led the French army in 1429 against the English invaders besieging Orléans. They were captured by Burgundians the following year and turned over to an ecclesiastical court in charge of heresy. Joan was found guilty and was burned at the stake. Her innocence was eventually declared in 1456. Joan of Arc was declared patroness of France; she is also known as the Maid of Orléans; feast day on May 30.

Martin of Tours (316-97): Martin was forced against his will to enter the army. In 337, he tore his cloak in half and gave half of it to a poor beggar freezing in the cold. It was later revealed to Martin that this beggar was Christ Himself. Because of this incident, he converted to Christianity, left the army, and became a hermit. (See *Beggars*.)

Sebastian (d. c. 288): Sebastian was a soldier in army at Rome in 283. During his service he preached to many prisoners and fellow soldiers, converting hundreds during his lifetime. Sebastian was martyred for his faith. (See *Archers*.)

SPINNERS

Seraphina (d. 1253): Born in San Gimignano, Italy, to a poor family; known for her self-denial and acts of penance as a young girl; a mysterious illness left this beautiful girl unattractive; her eyes, feet, and hands became deformed, and eventually Seraphina was paralyzed; mother and father both died while she was young; devoted to St. Gregory the Great; died on the feast of St. Gregory, exactly as she had been warned by Gregory in a dream.

Seraphina was a very helpful child around the family home. She did many of the chores, and helped her mother spin and sew. Feast day, March 12.

STENOGRAPHERS

Cassian (d. 298): Little is known of this Christian martyr; a shorthand writer; sentenced to death along with St. Marcellus in 298.

Cassian was an official record keeper (court stenographer) at the trial of St. Marcellus the Centurion before Deputy Prefect Aurelius Agricolan at Tangiers. He denounced the unjust death penalty given to Marcellus. For this judgment, he was imprisoned and put to death. Feast day, December 3.

STONECUTTERS

Clement I (d. c. 99): Clement was exiled to Crimea by Emperor Trajan for his belief in Christ. There he worked the mines among the other Christian prisoners. His preaching among the miners was so successful that it led to the order of his martyrdom. (See *Marble Workers*.)

STONEMASONS

Stephen of Hungary (975-1038): Stephen built many churches during his reign as King of Hungary (1001-1038). (See *Bricklayers*.)

STUDENTS/SCHOOLS

Joseph Calasanz (1556-1648): Also known as Joseph Calasanctius; born in a castle near Peralta de la Sal, Aragon, Spain, on September 11; received doctorate in law at University of Lerida; ordained in 1583 (although his father had wanted him to become a soldier); became vicar general of Trempe; left for Rome in 1592; known for his ministry to plague victims (1595); died in Rome on August 25; canonized by Pope Clement XIII in 1767.

Joseph Calasanz founded a free school for the poor in 1597. He supervised other teachers and opened other schools. In 1621, he founded the Clerks Regular of Religious Schools and became its superior general. His Order is also known as the Piarists or the Scolopi. Feast day, August 25.

Thomas Aquinas (1225-74: Born near Roccasecca, Italy, the son of Count Landulf of Aquino (who in turn was a relative of the Emperor and King of France); sent to Benedictine Monte Cassino Monastery at age five for his education; attended University of Naples in 1239; became a Dominican in 1244 at Naples; his family was so opposed to his joining the order that they kidnapped him for fifteen months; however, he rejoined the Order in 1445; studied at the University of Paris between 1245-48; ordained at Cologne in 1250; became master of theology at University of Paris (1256); known as the "Dumb Ox"; one of the greatest and most influential theologians of all time; died at the age of 50; canonized by Pope in 1323; declared Doctor of the Church by Pope Pius V.

Pope Leo XIII declared Thomas Aquinas to be patron of all universities, colleges, and schools. He is also considered the patron saint of students. Thomas was given these honors because of his past teaching experience. Besides being master of theology at the University of Paris (1256), he also taught at Naples, Anagni, Orvieto, Rome, and Viterbo between 1259-68. Thomas Aquinas wrote such masterpieces as *Summa contra Gentiles* (1261-64); *Summa Theologica* (1265-73); dozens of treatises, hymns, letters, commentaries on the Bible, and dissertations on the Lord's Prayer, the Angelical Salutation, and the Apostles' Creed. Feast day, January 28.

SURGEONS

Cosmas and Damian (303): Cosmas and Damian had studied medicine in Syria and practiced their trade in Aegeae, Cicilia, for which they became widely known. These martyrs served the poor free of charge. (See *Barbers*.)

Luke the Evangelist (first century): Luke is patron of surgeons because he was a physician prior to his call as a missionary (Col 4:14). (See *Butchers*.)

SWORDSMITHS

Maurice (d. c. 287): Maurice was a noble warrior who served in the army of the Theban Legion under Emperor Maximian Herculius. He was later martyred for refusing to worship the Roman pagan gods. (See *Coppersmiths, Dyers*.)

TAILORS

Homobonus (d. 1197): Born in Cremona, Italy, son of a merchant businessman; gave much of his fortune away to good causes and the poor; married a faithful girl; very devoted to the Blessed Sacrament; died before the Blessed Sacrament on November 13, his arms outstretched as if on a cross; canonized by Pope Innocent III only two years after his death; his head remains in the Church of St. Giles.

Homobonus grew up in a family of merchants, his father being a successful tailor. He soon gained a reputation for honesty and integrity in the business. He considered his trade a gift from God and a responsible duty to all the faithful. He is patron of both sailors and clothworkers (tailors). Feast day, November 13.

TANNERS

Crispin and Crispinian (d. 287): Legendary figures of Christian history; Roman brothers; preached the Gospel in Gaul; settled at Soissons; converted many; tortured for their faith; attempted killings by Rictiovarus failed (such as boiling and drowning); because of his failure, Rictiovarus committed suicide; eventually beheaded under the Emperor Maximian.

Crispin and Crispinian worked as shoemakers during the night. During the day, they spent their free time helping to convert the people of Gaul. They are also considered the patrons of shoemakers, leatherworkers, and cobblers. Feast day, October 25.

TAX COLLECTORS

Matthew the Apostle (first century): A Levite, son of Alpheus, born in Galilee; later worked as a tax collector (Mt. 9:9-13; 10:3); because of his tribal background, was also known as Levi; called by Christ to be His follower at the Lake of Capernaum (Sea of Galilee) (Mk 2:14; Lk 5:27-32); became one of the Twelve Apostles; revered as author of the first Gospel (c.a. 80-85), which was probably written in Aramaic, though our edition is an expanded Greek version; evidence from the Gospel reveals that it was written by a Jewish Christian of Palestine (probably in Antioch, Syria) for a3 Jewish-Christian audience; this Gospel stresses the importance of Jewish law and prophecy; tradition claims that Matthew preached throughout Judea, then went to the East, and died a martyr's death in Ethiopia (some legends say he died in Persia); also a patron of bankers and bookkeepers.

Patron saint of accountants, bookkeepers, and tax collectors because of his writing skills and his role as Roman tax collector, which required an ability with numbers. Feast day, September 21.

TEACHERS

Gregory the Great (540-604): Gregory was known for his preaching, teaching, and writing. Many famous treatises are attributed to this saint, such as *Dialogues* (a collection of visions, prophecies, miracles, and lives of the saints) and *Liber regulae pastoralis* (concerning the responsibilities of bishops). Gregory is the last of the Latin Doctors of the Church. He is known as "the Great," and many consider him to be the founder of the medieval papacy. Feast day, September 3. (See *Musicians*, or *West Indies* under "Countries and Nations.")

John Baptist de la Salle (1651-1719): Born at Rheims, France, on April 30, the eldest of ten children in a noble family; studied in Paris; ordained in 1678; known for his work with the poor; died at St. Yon, Rouen, on April 7; canonized by Pope Leo XIII in 1900.

John Baptist de la Salle was very involved in education. He founded the Institute of the Brothers of the Christian Schools (approved in 1725) and established teacher colleges (Rheims in 1687, Paris in 1699, and Saint-Denis in 1709). He was one of the first to emphasize classroom teaching over individual instruction. He also begin teaching in the vernacular instead of in Latin. His schools were formed all over Italy. In 1705, he established a reform school for boys at Dijon. John was named patron of teachers by Pope Pius XII in 1950. His feast day is April 7.

TELECOMMUNICATIONS WORKERS

Gabriel: Gabriel is patron of many different occupations involving mass communications. This identification comes from the fact that he was chosen by God in a special way to deliver divine messages to particularly chosen people for the benefit of the world. Gabriel's role as communications intercessor can best be seen in the Gospel of Luke. Feast, September 29. (See *Messengers*.)

TELEVISION WORKERS

Gabriel: It is unclear why Gabriel is patron of television workers. Perhaps this association is made because of Gabriel's role as a great communicator and intercessor for the faithful, as portrayed in the Gospel of Luke. Our modern-day communications revolve around television, radio, and the printed word. Feast, September 29. (See *Messengers*.)

THEOLOGIANS

Alphonsus de Liguori (1696-1787): Born at Marianelli near Naples, Italy, on September 21; received doctorate in canon and civil law at the University of Naples at age sixteen; practiced law for eight years; became an Oratorian priest in 1726; involved in missionary work around Naples for two years; founded the Redemptorines in 1731 after being convinced of a vision of Sister Mary Celeste which called for a new Order; in 1732, founded the Congregation of the Most Holy Redeemer (the Redemptorists) in Scala, devoted to missionary work; elected Superior of the Redemptorists in 1743; rule approved for men by Pope Benedict XIV in 1749 and for women in 1750; experienced the dark night of the soul; retired in Nocera after a series of illnesses; died on August 1; canonized by Pope Gregory XVI in 1839.

Alphonsus was famous for his many spiritual writings, including *Moral Theology* (1748) and *Glories of Mary* (1750). He was declared a Doctor of the Church by Pope Pius IX in 1871. Feast day, August 2. (See *Confessors*.)

Augustine of Hippo (354-430): Born the son of a Roman official, Patricius, and Monica at Tagaste in northern Africa; attended university at Carthage (370); gave up ambition to become a lawyer in order to succeed as a writer; later abandoned Christian faith; lived with a mistress for fifteen years; had a son named Adeodatus in 372; supported Manichaeism; taught in Tagaste and Carthage for ten years; studied in Rome in 383; became professor of rhetoric at Milan in 384; reconverted to Christianity through hearing the sermons of St. Ambrose in Milan; baptized in 387; his mother, Monica, died in 387 while he was traveling back to Africa; founded a monastery at Tagaste (388); ordained by popular acclaim in 391; made coadjutor to Bishop Valerius in Hippo (395); succeeded Valerius in 396; fought against such heresies as Manichaeism, Donatism, and Pelagianism; died at Hippo during Genseric's siege; known as the Doctor of Grace; patron saint of brewers and theologians.

Patron of theologians because of his enormous influence on Catholic thinking over the centuries. Augustine is one of the greatest and most influential Christian writers and theologians of all time, penning such classics as *Confessions* (his autobiography, 397-401), *On the Trinity* (a 15-book work written between 400-16), *City of God* (413-26), and *Retractations* (426); it is reported that he wrote an incredible 1,000 books and 118 treatises in his lifetime! Feast day, August 28.

TRAVELERS

Anthony of Padua (1195-1231): Anthony was known for his travels all over Italy, preaching the Gospel and converting hundreds to the faith. His fame as a preacher attracted large crowds throughout his country and brought him worldwide fame. (See *Portugal* under "Countries and Nations.")

WATCHMEN

Peter of Alcántara (1499-1562): Peter was in charge of the sacristy, the refectory, and later the gate of his convent at Manjaretes. He continued these duties during his novitiate in the Franciscan friars of the Observance. His penances were well known, and he spent part of many nights on his knees praying and the other part sleeping with his head against the wall. His prayerful "watchings" earned him the title of the patron saint of night watchmen. Feast day October 19. (See *Brazil* under "Countries and Nations.")

WEAVERS

Anastasius the Fuller (d. 304): Born to a wealthy family at Aquileia; suffered under the persecutions of Emperor Diocletian; painted a cross on his door in defiance of the Roman pagans; arrested and then thrown at sea with a weight around his neck; body found by Asclepia, who buried it in her garden; a cemetery and basilica were later built around his grave.

Anastasius took up the trade of weaver (fuller) in the town of Salona (Split) in Dalmatia, Yugoslavia. He dedicated himself to a humble laborer's job because he was influenced by St. Paul's words to the Thessalonians, "that you do your own business and work with your hands." Feast day, September 7.

Paul the Hermit (229-342): Born in Lower Thebaid, Egypt; orphaned at age 15; hid from the persecutions of Emperor Decius; his brother betrayed him and threatened to turn him in as a Christian in order to receive his estate; fled to the desert at age 22; known for his piety; miraculously fed each day by a raven; according to St. Jerome, lived to the age of 113.

While nearing his death, Paul asked St. Anthony to go and get him the cloak which he had received from Athanasius, Bishop of Alexandria. It was Paul's desire to be wrapped in this garment at the time of his death. The cloak had been made of palm-tree leaves patched together. When Anthony returned, Paul was already dead, just as he had predicted. Later, while walking down a road, Anthony saw Paul's soul ascend to heaven. Anthony kept the cloak that Paul had requested, wearing it himself for God's blessing on great festival days. Feast day, January 15.

WINE MERCHANTS

Amand (c. 584-679): Born at Nantes, France; became a monk in 604; made a missionary bishop in 629; did missionary work in Flanders, Carinthia, and Germany; established many monasteries throughout Belgium.

It is unclear why Amand is considered patron of wine merchants. Perhaps some of his monasteries eventually became known for producing fine wine. Feast day, February 6.

WOMEN'S ARMY CORPS

Geneviève (422-500): Born at Nanterre near Paris, France; dedicated her life to God at age seven; moved to Paris and became a nun at fifteen; many visions and prophecies; miracles reported at her tomb; died in Paris on January 3; life events not well-authenticated.

During the takeover of Paris by Childeric and the Franks, Geneviève brought in boatloads of food for the people. She also was successful in convincing Childeric to release many of the prisoners he had taken captive. An epidemic that came upon Paris in 1129 was reportedly stopped by her miraculous intercession. Feast day, January 3.

WORKINGMEN

Joseph (first century): Joseph was the husband of the Blessed Virgin Mary and the foster father of Jesus Christ. He is invoked as patron of workingmen because of his dedication to both his vocation as a carpenter and as the ideal family man. Feast day, March 19. (See *Carpenters.*)

WRITERS

Francis de Sales (1567-1622): Francis de Sales was declared a Doctor of the Church by Pope Leo XIII (1877) because of the many spiritual classics he wrote, including *Introduction to the Devout Life* (1609) and *Treatise on the Love of God* (1616). These works stressed that sanctity and perfection are possible for every Christian, showing the ways to achieve these goals. Feast day, January 24. (See *Authors*.)

YACHTSMEN

Adjutor (d. 1131): Norman knight; lord of Vernon-sur-Seine; first crusade in 1095; led a life of recluse his last years; died in Tiron on April 30.

Adjutor sailed the seas on the first crusade in 1095. He was captured by the Muslims, but later escaped and returned to France, where he became a monk at the abbey of Tiron. Feast day, April 30.

III. Special Needs and Conditions

ABANDONED

Flora (d. 851): Flora was raised a Christian by her mother, but her father remained a firm Muhammadan. She was eventually abandoned by her brother for not practicing the Islamic faith. Flora was scourged, imprisoned, but later escaped. She was eventually beheaded. Feast day, November 24. (See *Victim of Betrayal.*)

Germaine Cousin (1579-1601): Born in France at Pibrac; noted for extraordinary holiness; born with a deformed right hand, lived a sickly childhood, unloved by father and abused by his second wife; instructed children in the faith, attended daily Mass, and was devoted to the Rosary; buried in the Church of Pibrac; over 400 miracles attributed to her intercession; beatified on May 7, 1854 by Pope Pius IX; canonized by the same Pope on June 29, 1867.

Germaine was unloved and unwanted by her father (Laurent Cousin) and abused by his second wife. This was because she was born with a deformed right hand and was a source of shame and embarrassment to them. They even made her sleep in a stable outside the home or under the stairs. Out of fear of catching a disease from Germaine, her parents isolated her from her brothers and sisters. Germaine heroically bore these abuses through her love and good faith. She spent the remainder of her life serving as a shepherdess near her home. She was found dead on a straw mat under the family stairs at the age of 22. Feast day, June 15.

Pelagius (d. 925): Also known as Pelayo; lived during the reign of the Omayyad ruler Abd-ar-Rahman III; tortured and martyred for his faith; his remains were taken to three different places: Córdoba in Spain (925), León (967), and Oviedo (985), where they remain to this day.

When Pelagius was ten, he was handed over by his parents to be raised by his uncle Hermoygius, the Bishop of Tuy. Shortly thereafter, he and his guardian uncle were taken captive by the Moors in their battle with the Christians. They were sent to a prison in Córdoba. Bishop Hermoygius arranged for his own release by leaving behind young Pelagius with the promise to free some Moorish prisoners in Galicia. However, after the bishop was freed, Pelagius was abandoned by the bishop, who delayed the release of the Moorish captives. The exchange of prisoners never occurred for three years, and Pelagius heroically suffered his abandonment and persevered in his faith. Feast day, June 26.

ADOPTED CHILDREN

Clotilde (d. 545): Wife of King Clovis of the Franks. Clotilde was a devout Catholic who tried to convert her husband; he finally converted after defeating the Alemanni and was baptized on Christmas, 496. Clotilde and Clovis founded the church of the Apostles Peter and Paul in Paris (renamed St. Geneviève). Clovis was buried in Paris after his death in 511. Many family feuds over political power occupied Clotilde for years to come. She eventually married the Visigoth Amalaric, who treated her cruelly. Clotilde dedicated her later years to helping the sick and poor at Tours.

Clotilde had three sons with King Clovis: Clodomir, Childebert, and Clotaire, and a daughter named Clotilde. (Her first son had died in infancy shortly after his baptism). The children fought one another for control of land and power, which greatly grieved Clotilde for many years. She was to witness the death of her son Clodomir, who was killed by the brother of his cousin Sigismund after the latter had died from the hands of Clodomir. Clotilde later adopted Clodomir's three sons, but her natural son Clotaire killed two of these children (who were his elder nephews, age seven and ten) out of jealousy and rivalry. Feast day, June 3.

Thomas More (1478-1535): Thomas More was the son of attorney John More and Agnes Granger. His mother died while he was still a young child. Thomas, his brothers, and two sisters were placed in the care of a nurse named Mother Maud. Feast day, June 22. (See *Lawyers*.)

William of Rochester (d. 1201): Originally from Perth, Scotland; adopted a young boy named David; made a pilgrimage to Jerusalem; miracles reported from his intercession after death; canonized by Pope Alexander IV in 1256; a shrine dedicated to William at Rochester Cathedral.

William was killed by his adopted boy (David) while journeying to Canterbury. When a mentally deranged woman found his body and cared for it, she was miraculously cured of her mental problems. Feast day, May 23.

ALCOHOLISM

Monica (331-87): Monica was the mother of St. Augustine of Hippo. She helped to convert her pagan husband Patricius, who was known for his wild life, drinking habits, and violent temper. Monica also prayed for Augustine's conversion, which finally occurred in 386. Because of his previous reputation for the wild and carefree life, Augustine may once have been a victim like his father of wine, women, and song. Feast day, August 27. (See *Difficult Marriages* and *Mothers*.)

BACHELORS

Benedict Joseph Labre (1748-1783): From a very early age in childhood, Benedict Joseph Labre was dedicated to serving God. At the age of eighteen, he tried to enter two different religious orders (the Carthusians and the Cistercians), but was refused because of his tender age. Rejected by the religious, Joseph dedicated himself to a single life of prayer, sacrifice, and penance. Feast day, April 16. (See *Rejected by Religious Order*.)

Benezet (d. 1184): Known as "Little Benezet the Bridge Builder"; heard a heavenly voice three times during a solar eclipse in his native Savoy, asking him to build a bridge over the river in Avignon; through miracles he gained the approval of the Bishop of Avignon to begin the building in 1177; his body was eventually buried upon the bridge, and later a chapel was built over his body, found to be incorruptible; remains transferred to a church of the Celestine monks; the Order of Bridge Brothers was founded in 1189 in honor of Benezet.

From a very early age, Benezet sacrificed marriage for a life dedicated to God. He is also considered the patron of Avignon. His feast day is April 14.

Boniface of Tarsus (d. c. 306): In his youth, Boniface had a reputation as one who loved wine and women. However, after becoming acquainted with a good Christian girl named Aglae, he converted. Although he was fond of Aglae and all that she had done for him, he remained a confirmed bachelor all his life, dedicated to the service of God. Feast day, May 14. (See *Converts*.)

Caesarius (d. 369): From a family of saints; St. Gorgonia was his sister, and St. Gregory (Doctor of the Church) was his brother; distinguished physician at Constantinople; served at the court of Julian the Apostate; resisted Emperor Julian's pressure to deny his faith; later moved to Bithynia where he served Emperor Valens; donated all his possessions upon death to the poor; died after a long illness.

Caesarius had been a lifelong single man. During his time as a well-known and respected physician in Byzantium, a noble marriage and various honors (such as a place in the Senate) were offered him, but he declined. Feast day, February 25.

Casimir (1458-84): From early youth, Casimir lived a life of holiness and sanctity. He refused his father's efforts to have him marry, preferring a life dedicated to prayer and study. Feast day, March 4. (See *Lithuania* under "Countries and Nations.")

Cuthman (d. c. 900): Born to a pious family in southern England; a child of unusual prayer and sanctity; when father died he devoted many years to taking care of his mother, building her a home at Steyning in Sussex; built a church near his property in Sussex; many miracles attributed to him during life and after death.

Cuthman stayed at home and took care of his invalid mother after the death of his father. He spent all of his time working to support her, thus sacrificing a life of his own. Feast day, February 8.

Epipodius (d. 178): Tortured and martyred for the faith under the Roman persecutor Marcus Aurelius. Along with his friend St. Alexander, Epipodius dedicated his life to God and the service of others. He remained a bachelor all of his life. Feast day, April 22. (See *Victims of Betrayal*.)

Gerald of Aurillac (d. 909); Gerald was the Count of Aurillac in France. He suffered from various illnesses during youth and became totally blind in his later years. During his early reign, he gave away all of his possessions to the poor and lived a life of heroic sanctity. Enjoying a life completely dedicated to the service of God and humanity, Gerald remained a bachelor all his life. Feast day, October 13. (See *Counts* under "Occupations.")

Guy of Anderlecht (d. 1012): Born into poverty near Brussels; known as the Poor Man of Anderlecht; embraced poverty as God's will for him; later, was influenced to invest in worldly goods; after a ship carrying his goods was wrecked, he saw this as a sign from God that he must return to embrace poverty; in a penitential act, he walked to Rome, then later went to Jerusalem to visit the shrines; overexhausted from his journeys, he died on returning to Brussels; many miracles reported after his death.

Guy remained a bachelor all his life, even though his faith and piety made him known across Europe. Although he worked as sacristan for a priest near Brussels, Guy would eventually find a home as a guide to pilgrimages in the Holy Land. Feast day, September 12.

John Rigby (1570-1600): A Lancashire gentleman from a Protestant family; converted to Catholicism and imprisoned for his faith; helped to convert many during this time, including his own father; refused to go to a Protestant church or acknowledge the queen's supremacy; imprisoned at Newgate; executed at the command of Justice Gaudy at St. Thomas' Watering; tortured before death and disembowelled for refusing to attend Protestant services; died at the age of about thirty; one of the Forty Martyrs of England and Wales; canonized by Pope Paul VI in 1970.

Before John Rigby was sentenced to be hanged for refusing to renounce his faith, he was asked his marital status. Rigby proudly replied that he was "both a bachelor and a maid" (having once been a household servant of Sir Edmund Heddleston, an avid Protestant). After this comment, he was led to his death. John spent his entire life doing good deeds for everyone. Feast day, June 21.

Joseph Moscati (1880-1927): A brilliant physician and professor who dedicated his life early on to his faith and the field of medicine. Rather than marry, Joseph took a private vow of celibacy in 1913. He was famous for his cures and explained that much of his success relied upon both his prayers and medical skills working together. He was the only layman beatified by Pope Paul VI in 1975 and the only layman canonized by Pope John Paul II in 1988. Feast day, April 12. (See *Rejected by Religious Order*.)

Marino (fourth century): Also known as Marinus; born in the Republic of San Marino south of Rimini, Italy; stonemason by trade; worked in the quarries at Monte Titano; converted many to the faith through his preaching; became a deacon while continuing his trade; known as a model Christian; possibly founded a hermitage in a cave on Monte Titano; relics located in the Basilica of St.Marinus.

Marino remained a confirmed bachelor all of his life. According to one story, he was accused by a Dalmatian woman of being her former husband who had deserted her. Marino denied the story, panicked, and sought refuge as a recluse for the remainder of his life. He devoted his time to constant prayers and acts of penance. Feast day, September 4. (See *Falsely Accused*.)

Pantaleon (d. 305): Pantaleon was Emperor Maximian's physician during the persecutions of Rome. He gave up his faith after enjoying the high life of the royal court, but later reconverted and gave medical services free of charge to the poor. He never married, but devoted himself to the service of God and neighbor. Feast day, July 27. (See *Physicians* and *Victims of Torture*.)

Roch (1295-1327): Roch was the son of the governor of Montpellier, France. When he was twenty, both his parents died. Roch then gave away all his possessions to identify with the poor, and he set out for Italy to help the sick who were stricken by the plague. Roch remained single all of his life, preferring to be at the total service of God and humanity. Feast day, August 16. (See *Falsely Accused*.)

Serenus (d. c. 307): Serenus was a Greek who sacrificed the worldly life and marriage in order to love and serve God. He moved to Yugoslavia and bought a home with a garden. He spent his days doing humble chores, praying and meditating in the midst of his work.

Serenus was falsely accused of insulting a noblewoman who wandered into his garden without permission. The woman's story reached the ears of the local governor, who eventually had him killed for being a Christian. Feast day, February 23. (See *Falsely Accused*.)

Theobaldus (1017-66): Theobaldus was born at Provins in Brie, the son of Count Arnoul. At a very early age, he dedicated himself to the service of God and neighbor. He was particularly fond of reading the lives of the saints, and was determined to imitate their example in piety, self-denial, and perfection. Theobaldus lived a life of poverty and made several pilgrimages to Compostela and Rome. He was canonized less than seven years after his death by Pope Alexander II. Feast day, June 30. (See *Church Cleaners* under "Occupations and Vocations.")

BLINDNESS

Odilia (d. c. 720): Odilia (also known as Ottilia and Adilia) was born blind at Obernheim in the Vosges Mountains. She was given away by her parents, ashamed of her condition, to be cared for by a peasant woman. At the age of twelve, Odilia was placed in a convent at Baume, where she was baptized into the faith. It is reported that at the time of her baptism by Bishop St. Erhard of Regensburg, she was miraculously cured of her blindness when the bishop touched her eyes with chrism during the ceremony. Feast day, December 13. (See *Alsace* under "Countries and Nations.")

Raphael: One of seven archangels who stand before the throne of the Lord (Tb 12:12, 15). He was sent by God to help Tobiah and Sarah. At the time, Sarah's previous seven bridegrooms had been destroyed by demons on the night of their wedding. Raphael accompanied Tobiah to Media disguised as a man named Azariah. Raphael told him how to heal his father's blindness and safely enter marriage with Sarah. Besides Raphael, Michael and Gabriel are the only archangels mentioned by name in the Bible.

Raphael's name means "God heals." This identity came about because of the Biblical story which claims that he "healed" the earth when it was defiled by the sins of the fallen angels in the apocryphal Book of Enoch (10:7). Raphael is also identified as the angel who moved the waters of the healing sheep pool (Jn 5:1-4). The archangels' feast is celebrated on September 29 by Christian and Jew alike.

BODILY ILLS

Our Lady of Lourdes (see unit on "Our Lady").

CANCER PATIENTS

Peregrine Laziosi (1260-1345): Born at Forli, Italy, of a wealthy family; devoted to the Blessed Virgin; received an apparition of Mary, who advised him to go to Siena and join the Order of Servites; miraculously cured of cancer of the foot after a vision; canonized by Pope Benedict XIII in 1726,

After his superiors sent Peregrine to Forli to found a new house for his order, he developed a cancerous sore on his foot. Although the open wound repulsed those who came into contact with him, Peregrine continued with his ministry of preaching, celebrating Mass, and reconciling sinners to God. When the doctors suggested that he have his foot amputated, Peregrine prayed about the situation and was suddenly and miraculously cured of all signs of cancer. Feast day, May 1.

CHARITABLE SOCIETIES

Vincent de Paul (1581-1660): Born at Puoy, France, April 24; ordained in 1600; captured by pirates and sold into slavery in Algeria (1605); escaped in 1607; returned to France and became chaplain of Queen Margaret of Valois; became disciple of St. Francis de Sales; died in Paris; canonized by Pope Clement XII in 1737; declared patron of all charitable organizations by Pope Leo XIII in 1885.

Vincent de Paul founded the Congregation of the Missions (Vincentians, Lazarists) in 1625 and co-founded the Sisters of Charity in 1633. He was known for his work with the poor. His feast is celebrated on September 27.

CHILDLESS

Anne Line (d. 1601): Anne Line married Roger Line of Ringwood.They remained childless, however, when he died at a young age while in Flanders (1594). Feast day, February 27. (See *Converts*.)

Catherine of Genoa (1447-1510): Catherine married Julian Adorno at the age of sixteen. She suffered greatly because of his careless and spendthrift ways. They never did have any children. After Catherine converted Julian, they agreed to live celibate lives together and dedicated themselves to the sick and the poor. Feast day, September 15. (See *Difficult Marriages*.)

Gummarus (d. 774): Gummarus served in the court of Pepin the Short. He had married a noble woman named Guinmarie, whose temperament and overbearing ways caused him great suffering for the many years they were married. Luckily, they had no children together, for Gummarus ended up getting a permanent separation from her in his later years. Guinmarie was reportedly very proud, arrogant, ruthless, and oppressive to all who served her husband. Feast day, October 11. (See *Courtiers*.)

Henry II (d. 1024): Succeeded his father as Duke of Bavaria in 995.

Although Henry married Cunegunda, the couple remained childless and vowed their lives to sexual abstinence in favor of serving God and humanity. At one point before he rose to power, Henry contemplated becoming a priest. Feast day, July 13. (See *Dukes*.)

Julian the Hospitaler (date unknown): A legendary figure who reportedly married a wealthy widow as a gift from the king. The couple remained childless all their lives. When his wife put his parents up for a night while he was gone, Julian returned home, thought there was a man in bed with his wife, and killed them both. Remorseful, he engaged in great acts of penance. Later, Julian built an inn for travelers and a hospital for the poor. A leper once visited him, and he gave him his own bed. Legend says that the leper was an angel sent to test his faith. Julian left his home after killing his parents (see above) because of his great restlessness and guilt. He was determined to do penance for the rest of his life. Julian once left on a journey and came upon a wide river at a place where people would cross. In a dream, he heard a voice ask him to cross the river and help the people to the other side. When he went to them, he found one nearly dead from the cold. He started a fire, bedded him down, and nursed him back to health. Suddenly this sickly man became bright like the sun and ascended into heaven. Julian understood this miracle as a sign that God accepted his penance. Feast day, February 12. (See *Ferrymen* under "Occupations.")

CHILDREN

Nicholas of Myra (d. c. 350): Nicholas was once the Bishop of Myra in Asia Minor. He is best known for the legend which surrounds the story of Santa Claus. The name "Saint Nicholas" was changed to Sint Klaes by the Dutch and then into "Santa Claus." According to one legend, Nicholas once heard about a poor man who could not afford the dowries for his three daughters to be married. Nicholas threw a bag of gold into the open window of the man's house, and soon his eldest daughter was married. Later, he did the same for the other two girls; hence, the tradition started that Santa Claus gives gifts and blessings to all young people at Christmas time. Feast day, December 6. (See *Russia* under "Countries and Nations.")

CONVERTS

Afra (d. 304): Born in Augsburg, Bavaria, West Germany; once a well-known prostitute; after her conversion, Emperor Gaius demanded that she honor the pagan gods; she refused and was taken to an island in the river Lech to await death by fire; she finally suffocated from the smoke at the stake; Afra's mother and her three former servants (who were also prostitutes) all converted and were also martyred by being burned at the stake; her remains are located at the Church of Sts. Ulrich and Afra in Augsburg.

Afra converted from her former sinful life as a prostitute during the persecutions under Diocletian. When the Bishop of Gerona was forced from his office, Afra's mother, Hilaria, took him into her home and protected him from danger. Both Hilaria and Afra were converted through his guidance and influence. After repenting her former sins, Afra did great penance and dedicated herself to helping the poor. Feast day, August 5.

Alban (d. 304): A legendary figure who was probably a martyr from Great Britain. Alban lived in Hertfordshire, England, during his younger years. While there, he hid a priest from the persecutors under Emperor Diocletian. The priest so influenced Alban that he was converted to Christianity. Bravely, Alban exchanged clothes with the real priest, handed himself in, and refused to honor the Roman pagan gods. For this sacrificial act he was beheaded by the authorities. Many miracles were reported on the way to his execution. Feast day, June 22. (See *Victims of Torture*.)

Anne Line (1569-1601): A convert to Catholicism who married Roger Line of Ringwood; widowed in 1594; put in charge of house of refuge for clergy in London through the Jesuit Father John Gerard; died a martyr's death by hanging alongside the Jesuit Roger Filcock.

Anne was the daughter of William Heigham, a loyal Protestant from Dunmow in Essex. He disowned Anne and his son for converting to Catholicism. She was sentenced to death for hiding a priest.Her feast is celebrated on February 27.

Boniface of Tarsus (d. 306): Martyr and convert to the Catholic faith; beheaded for defending Christians who were being tortured while passing through Tarsus; Algae found his remains, which she had brought back to Rome; today his relics are found in the Church of St. Alexius and St. Boniface.

Boniface was a convert to the Catholic faith through the influence of a beautiful Roman lady named Aglae. They had been living together in Rome at the time. Boniface was hired by Algae to be her steward, for her wealth allowed her to entertain and put on shows for the citizens of Rome. She encouraged him to search for the relics of saints in the East because she heard that they would bring great glory to those who found and venerated them. During his journey, Boniface was converted. Feast day, May 14.

Caedwalla (d. 689): After many years of killing his opponents for the crown of England, he converted to the faith after suffering a wound during his attack on the Isle of Wight. Later on, he was known for his generosity to the Church. Caedwalla was baptized in 689, the year of his death. Feast day, April 20. (See *Murderers*.)

Charles Lwanga and Companions (d. 1886): Charles Lwanga succeeded Joseph Mkasa, a Catholic, as the master of pages in the court of King Mwanga of Uganda. Mwanga was a fierce antiCatholic. After Charles publicly ridiculed him for murdering a Protestant minister and engaging in homosexual activities, Mwanga ordered the death of Charles Lwanga, who was burned in 1886. Feast day, June 3. (See *Victims of Torture*.)

Edwin (585-633): Son of King Aella of Deira in South Northumbria; King Ethelfrith of Bernicia in North Northumbria stole his kingship away; King Edwin's father died when he was only three years old; thereafter for a number of years, Edwin was forced to live in one home after another before he was raised and regained his rightful throne; Edwin spent the next thirty years in Mercia and reclaimed the throne through the efforts of King Baedwald of East Anglia, who killed King Ethelfrith at the Battle of Idle River in 617; Edwin married but became a widower in 625; he then married Ethelburga, the sister of King Eadbald of Kent; Edwin finally gained control and power over all of England; established law and order; intended to build a church at York but died at the hands of King Penda of Mercia in the Battle of Heathfield before it happened; considered a martyr by Pope Gregory XIII.

Edwin was converted after he married the Christian woman named Ethelburga, who was the sister of King Eadbald of Kent. His conversion took place about 627. Feast day, October 12.

Flora (d. 851): The daughter of a Muhammadan who converted to Christianity after meeting Mary, a sister of a deacon who had recently been martyred. Mary and Flora both dedicated their lives to serving Christians during the persecutions. As a result, both were eventually beheaded. Feast day, November 24. (See *Victims of Betrayal*.)

Genesius (third century): A legendary figure who reportedly was converted while performing in a Christian play before the Roman Emperor Diocletian. During that performance, Genesius played a young catechumen about to be baptized in a satirical act portraying this Christian sacrament. He later proclaimed his newfound faith before the emperor, who had him tortured and beheaded. Feast day, August 25. (See *Actors, Comedians* under "Occupations and Vocations.")

Helena (d. 330): Daughter of an innkeeper and mother of the future Roman Emperor, Constantine the Great. She was converted to Catholicism at age 63, according to Church historian Eusebius (260-340). She built many churches and aided the poor. Helena moved to Jerusalem shortly after Constantine became Emperor of both the East and West. She reportedly discovered the True Cross. Later, Helena built basilicas on the Mount of Olives and at Bethlehem. She traveled throughout Palestine, helping the soldiers and tending to the poor and imprisoned. Feast day, August 18. (See Empresses under "Occupations and Vocations.")

Hermengild (d. 585): Born to a heretical family, which included his Arian father, Leovigild, the King of the Visigoths; later married a Catholic named Indegundus and converted to the faith; he publicly renounced the heresy; waged war against all Arians, appealing for support from Romans; was betrayed, as the Romans kidnapped his wife and son; reconciled with father; later, stepmother made them enemies again, which resulted in his being thrown in prison at the tower of Seville for the act of treason; tortured and finally died unshaken in his faith.

Hermengild was converted from Arianism to the Christian faith after he married a devout Christian princess named Indegundus(576). Hermengild's stepmother Goswintha resented the marriage, for she was a staunch Arian. Family objections kept the young couple under constant pressure, but Hermengild remained firm in his newfound faith. Eventually his father King Leovigild had Hermengild axed to death. He died a heroic martyr and helped to promote the movement against the Arian heresy of his day. Feast day, April 13.

Joseph of Palestine (d. 356): Assistant to Rabbi Hillel, after his conversion, he built churches in Tiberias, Nazareth, Capernaum, Bethsan, and Diocaesarea through the support of Constantine the Great; fought Arianism and the Jews; during the reign of Constantius, he harbored persecuted priests at Scythopolis in a Christian house he founded there; died in Palestine at the age of seventy.

Joseph was secretly baptized into the Catholic faith at his deathbed. Before, Christ spoke with him and encouraged him to convert. Feast day, July 22.

Lucian and Marcian (d. 250): Former devil worshipers and practitioners of black magic. When their powers failed to curse a young Christian woman (she gave them a Sign of the Cross and the evil spirits fled), Marcian and Lucian were converted. Before their lives had ended, these two went around denouncing demonic worship and black magic throughout the city of Nicomedia. Feast day, October 26. (See *Possessed.*)

Ludmila (860-921): Ludmila converted to Christianity after her husband (Borivoj, Duke of Bohemia) was baptized in 871 by St. Methodius, the "Apostle of the Slavs." The couple's newfound faith was opposed by both sides of the family, but they remained firmly committed to Christ and His Gospel message. Feast day, September 16. (See *Bohemia; Duchesses.*)

Margaret Clitherow (d. 1586): Margaret was brought up a Protestant by the wealthy wax chandler Thomas Middleton and his wife. Margaret married the butcher John Clitherow in 1571. Soon after the marriage, she converted to Catholicism. Persecutions against Catholics were frequent during this time in Protestant-dominated England, and Margaret suffered for her newfound faith. She was imprisoned once for two years, but upon her release she started a Catholic school for young children. Eventually, Margaret was executed at York. Feast day, March 25. (See *Businesswomen.*)

Natalia (d. 857): Wife of the Muhammadan Aurelius, who practiced his newfound Christian faith in secrecy while openly conforming to the Islamic faith; Sabigotho was a former Moor who took the name Natalia upon her Christian baptism; Natalia was martyred along with several other companions (including St. Aurelius) for helping to convert many Muhammadans from their faith to Christianity.

Natalia eventually proclaimed her new faith openly by visiting the churches in Córdoba, her face open and unveiled. She was arrested along with her husband Aurelius for apostasy from Islam. Natalia was beheaded in front of Emirs Abdur Rahman II and Muhammad I. Feast day, July 27.

Olga (c. 879-969): Also known as Helga, born at Pskov, Russia; married Prince Igor of Kiev; husband murdered; Olga had his killers killed in return; spread the faith and promoted missionary work; died in Kiev on July 11.

Olga is the first Russian to have been baptized (Constantinople, 957). She is reportedly the first of the newborn Christian people of Russia. Before her conversion, Olga was known as a cruel, vindictive woman. After the assassination of her husband, Prince Igor of Kiev, she killed several hundred of his opponents and scalded with steam the few who were responsible for his death. Feast day, July 11.

Philemon (d. 305): Philemon was martyred along with St. Apollonius during the persecutions of Diocletian. He was a well-known dancer and piper. A miraculous conversion experience during a play at a pagan ceremony angered the local authorities, who had Philemon and Apollonius tortured and killed for refusing to honor the pagan gods. Feast day, November 22. (See *Dancers.*)

Theodota (d. 318): Theodota was a former harlot who converted to Christianity at a young age. She had lived during the persecutions of Agrippa. For refusing to worship and sacrifice to Roman gods, Theodota was scourged and stoned to death. Feast day unknown. (See *Victims of Torture.*)

Vladimir (975-1015): Born the illegitimate son of Grand Duke Sviastoslav and Malushka; his father gave him Novgorod to rule; left for Scandinavia after his half-brother Yarapolk killed his other half-brother (Oleg) and took over Novgorod; Vladimir sought revenge by recapturing Novgorod and killing Oleg (980); eventually became ruler of all of Russia and was known as Vladimir I of Kiev; cruel and ruthless ruler before his conversion; married six times; patron of all Russian Catholics.

Vladimir's conversion (989) was the beginning of the spread of Christianity in Russia. This came about after he was influenced by the faith of his future wife Anne (daughter of Emperor Basil II). His religious zeal caused him to repent his past ways, build schools and churches, and destroy pagan idols throughout his native Russia. Vladimir also imported Greek missionaries to Russia and helped St. Boniface in his mission to the Pechangs. At the end of his life, he gave away all of his wealth to the poor. Feast day, July 15.

CONVULSIVE CHILDREN

Scholastica (d. c. 543): Sister of St. Benedict; founder and abbess of convent at Plombariola near Monte Cassino; regarded as first nun of Benedictine Order; died at her convent.

It is unclear why Scholastica is patron of convulsive children. Perhaps the connection is due to the fact that she once interceded for her brother (St. Benedict) and the heavens "convulsed" with rain, thunder, and lightning. This miracle occurred because she wanted Benedict to spend the night in her convent for prayer and talk, sensing that she would not see him again in this earthly life. Benedict was not supposed to spend a single night away from his monastery, so he insisted upon leaving. The storm was so violent that Benedict was forced to remain at the convent until the next day. That night, the two siblings talked and prayed. Three days later, Scholastica died, just as she had foreseen. Feast, February 10.

DEAFNESS

Francis de Sales (1567-1622): Francis de Sales was a sickly and frail child, although he did eventually grow up to be an energetic and active man. In his later years, Francis became seriously ill with a paralytic seizure. Only gradually did he recover his speech and consciousness. It is not clear, but perhaps Francis also lost his hearing during this period of illness which took over his life. Feast day, January 29. (See *Authors* in "Occupations and Vocations.")

DEATH OF CHILDREN

Clotilde (d. 545): Wife of King Clovis of the Franks; married in 492; devout Catholic who tried to convert her husband; he finally converted after defeating the Alemanni; baptized at Christmas, 496; Clotilde and Clovis founded the church of the Apostles Peter and Paul in Paris (renamed St. Geneviève); buried Clovis in Paris after his death in 511; family feuds over political power occupied Clotilde for years to come; married the Visigoth Amalaric, who treated her cruelly; dedicated her later years to helping the sick and poor at Tours.

Clotilde had three sons with King Clovis: Clodomir, Childebert, and Clotaire, and a daughter named Clotilde. (Her first son had died in infancy shortly after his baptism). The children fought one another for control of land and power, which greatly grieved Clotilde for many years. She was to witness the death of her son Clodomir, who was killed by the brother of his cousin Sigismund after the latter had died from the hands of Clodomir. Clotilde later adopted Clodomir's three sons, but her natural son Clotaire killed two of these children (who were his elder nephews, age seven and ten) out of jealousy and rivalry. Feast day, June 3.

Dorothy of Montau (1347-94): Dorothy was married to the wealthy swordsman Albrecht of Danzig was she was seventeen. The couple had nine children. All but one of them died during childhood.The survivor — their youngest daughter — became a Benedictine nun. It was Dorothy's strong faith that pulled her through these agonizing years, for her husband became bitter and refused to offer her consolation. She was known for her piety, devotion to the Eucharist, and mystical experiences. Feast day, October 30. (See *Difficult Marriages* and *Parents of Large Families*.)

Elizabeth of Hungary (1207-31): Elizabeth married Herman I of Thurungia in 1221. They had three children: Herman, who died at age nineteen; Sophia, who lived to age sixty; and Gertrude, who became the Abbess of the Convent of Altenburg. Feast day, November 17. (See *Bakers*.)

Felicity and Her Seven Sons (d. second century): Roman Christian woman known for acts of charity, fasting, and great penance; whipped and beaten along with sons for converting many away from the false worship of Roman gods; her tomb was originally in the catacomb of Maximus on the Via Salaria; her remains (and those of her son Silenus) transferred in the eighth century to a crypt in the Church of Santa Susanna in Rome.

Each one of Felicity's sons was martyred for the faith, as was Felicitas, who was beheaded. Feast day, July 10.

Hedwig, Queen of Poland (d. 1243): Hedwig was the daughter of Count Berthold IV. She would later become Queen of Poland through her marriage to Henry I of Silesia, Poland. Hedwig and Henry were married in 1186, when she was only twelve years old and he was eighteen. The couple would have seven children, three of whom died during childbirth. Three more children died as adults. Feast day, October 16. (See *Silesia* in "Countries.")

Isidore the Farmer (d. 1130): Isidore was a very poor farmer from Spain. He married Maria Torribia and they had a son. The young baby died unexpectedly, however, causing the couple grief and anguish. After praying about their situation, Isidore came to the conclusion that the tragedy was the will of God. He and Maria dedicated the remainder of their lives to serving God and neighbor. They agreed to remain celibate for the rest of their lives. Many miracles are associated with the life of this poor and humble farmer. Feast day, May 15. (See *Farmers* in "Occupations.")

Julitta and Cyriacus (d. 304): Widow from Iconium; moved to Isauria with her son Cyriacus and two maids in order to practice her faith in a safer environment; however, Emperor Diocletian and Governor Alexander ended up killing her son as well as herself; venerated in both the East and the West.

During the persecutions under Emperor Diocletian, Julitta was put on trial for her profession of faith. She brought her child Cyriacus with her during the interrogations. After she was sentenced to death, Cyriacus was taken from his mother. The boy was then brought to Governor Alexander. After he kicked the governor and telling him that he too was a Christian, Alexander threw him on the ground and fractured his skull, killing Cyriacus immediately. Julitta was overcome with remorse as she witnessed the murder of her son. Angered at both the mother and the son, Alexander ordered Julitta to be beheaded and the body of Cyriacus to be disposed of outside the town. Heroically, Julitta prayed for her son, thanking God for his precious martyrdom. Feast celebrated on June 16.

Leopold (1073-1136): Leopold succeeded his father as Margrave of Austria at the age of twenty-three. He married Agnes, the daughter of Emperor Henry IV. The couple eventually had eighteen children, eleven of whom survived childhood. In addition to this, Agnes had been a widow and brought two other sons into the new marriage. Leopold was known for his piety and charity, and he founded several monasteries near Vienna and Mariazell. Feast day, November 15. See *Parents of Large Families*.)

Louis IX (1215-70): Louis IX, King of France, married Margaret, daughter of Raymond Berenger, Count of Provence, at the age of nineteen. They would eventually have eleven children (five sons, six daughters). Louis' favorite son, young Louis, died at the age of sixteen. It was a tragic loss for the king, one from which he would never quite recover. Later in his reign, Louis suffered the loss of another son, John-Tristan, to an illness. Feast day, August 25. (See *Crusaders*.)

Luchesius (d. 1260): Married to Buona dei Segni, who bore him several children. Luchesius sacrificed his faith for a life in pursuit of wealth and power. When his children died in his thirties, he converted to Christianity. From then on, Luchesius was dedicated to serving the sick, the poor, and prisoners. Feast day, April 28. (See *Lost Vocations*.)

Margaret of Scotland (1045-93): Queen Margaret of Scotland bore eight children with her husband, King Malcolm. Her son Edward was killed while trying to revenge his father's death to William Rufus of England (1093). She learned this terrible news from her son Edgar while bedridden. She threw up her hands to God, resigned to His will, and claimed that her sufferings would help to purify her soul. Feast day, November 16. (See *Widows*.)

Matilda (895-968): Matilda was the daughter of Count Dietrich of Westphalia and Reinhild of Denmark. She married Henry the Fowler, son of Duke Otto of Saxony, in 909. Henry was to become the King of Germany in 909. Together this couple had five children: Otto (who later became Emperor of the Holy Roman Empire), Henry the Quarrelsome (who would become Duke of Bavaria), St. Bruno (later the Archbishop of Cologne), Gerberga (who married King Louis IV of France), and Hedwig (future mother to Hugh Capet). Henry and Matilda brought up their children in a Christian environment. She was to suffer greatly, however, when her child Henry rebelled against his brother Otto. He eventually died during one of their quarrels. Feast day, March 14. (See *Falsely Accused*.)

Nonna (d. 374): Married Gregory the magistrate at Nazianzus in Cappadocia; converted him to Christianity from Judaism; he later became a Catholic priest and bishop (now known as St. Gregory Nazianzus the Elder); all three children became saints: St. Gregory Nazianzus, St. Caesarius of Nazianzus, and St. Gorgonia; known for her great fasts and penance, help for the sick and poor, and care for widows and orphans.

Nonna witnessed the death of two of her children, Gorgonia (who died in her arms) and her eldest son, Caesarius. Nonna was praised during the latter son's eulogy given by her other child, Gregory of Nazianzus. Feast day, August 5.

Perpetua (d. 203): Born in Carthage to a noble family; arrested during the persecutions of Emperor Severus; imprisoned in a private home; sentenced to death by the procurator Hilarion; when thrown to the wild beasts in the local amphitheater, Perpetua was miraculously protected from harm; eventually killed by the sword.

Perpetua was imprisoned while having a baby to take care of. Her tormentors brought the child to her prison cell, where she was allowed to suckle him. Although the baby was allowed to stay for a while in her care, it was later removed and sent to its grandfather. Her child was eventually killed along with Perpetua because she refused to renounce her faith. Feast day, March 7.

Stephen, King of Hungary (975-1038): Stephen married Gisela, sister of Henry, the Duke of Bavaria, when he was twenty years old. The couple had only one son, Emeric, who died in an accident while hunting bear. Feast day, August 16. (See *Bricklayers* under "Occupations.")

DESPERATE SITUATIONS

Jude Thaddeus (first century): Also known as Simon of Thaddeus; called "the brother of James" (another Apostle); Jude was the one who asked Jesus at the Last Supper why he would not manifest Himself to the whole world after His resurrection (Jn 14: 2223); little else known of his life; legend claims that he visited Beirut and Edessa; possibly martyred with St. Simon in Persia.

Jude is invoked for desperate situations because his New Testament letter stresses that the faithful should persevere in the environment of harsh, difficult circumstances, just as their forefathers had done before them. Feast day, October 28.

Rita of Cascia (1381-1457): Born at Roccaporena near Spoleto, Italy; married against her will at age twelve; bore two children and lived with a cruel husband for eighteen years; widowed when her husband was killed in a fight; after both her sons died, she tried to join the Augustinians in Cascia but was refused three times (because they only allowed virgins); she finally was accepted in 1413; famous for mystical experiences and great penances; received a permanent thorn wound on her forehead after hearing a sermon on the crown of thorns (a wound of the stigmata); died in Cascia; miracles reported at her tomb; canonized by Pope Leo XIII in 1900.

Rita is patroness of impossible and desperate situations. Perhaps this identity comes from the fact that she was married to a cruel husband for eighteen years, patiently enduring his ill treatment in a Christian-like manner. Rita's three rejections for admittance into the Augustinian Order may also contribute to her patronage, for her persistence finally paid off when she was accepted as a novice in 1413. Feast celebrated on May 22.

DIFFICULT MARRIAGES

Catherine of Genoa (1447-1510): Daughter of James Fieschi and Francesca di Negro; born at Genoa, Italy, the last of five children; desired a religious life, but after her father's death was married to Julian Adorno at age sixteen; became a Franciscan tertiary; worked at the Pammetone hospital with her husband; eventually moved into the hospital to devote more time to the sick; made directress in 1490; caught the plague of 1493, but survived; because of her illness, she was forced to resign as directress of the hospital in 1496; husband died in 1497; experienced many mystical gifts; Don Cattaneo Marabotto became her spiritual director in 1499; health continued to deteriorate in her last years; wrote the spiritual classics

Dialogue Between the Soul and the Body and *Treatise on Purgatory*; canonized by Pope Clement XII in 1737.

Catherine was married between 1463-97 to a cruel and annoying husband, Julian Adorno. He was a drifter, a spendthrift, and an unfaithful husband. Julian's carefree attitude about money caused the couple to live on the edge of poverty after ten years of marriage. Catherine bore these trials heroically, eventually causing her husband to convert by way of her pious example. Both of them eventually became Franciscan tertiaries and dedicated their lives to serving the sick. Feast day, September 15.

Dorothea of Montau (1347-94); Patroness of Prussia; married Albert Danzig the swordsmith at age seventeen; devoted to the Blessed Sacrament; had many visions and revelations during her life; had nine children, only the eldest surviving; Dorothea went alone on pilgrimage to Rome after her husband became ill; when she returned, Albert had already died; a widow at forty-three, she moved to Marienwerder, where she became a recluse in a church cell there; died one year later on May 25, with a reputation for holiness and extraordinary favors.

Dorothea suffered during her twenty-five years of marriage because of a quick-tempered and domineering husband. She patiently changed his position and encouraged him to make a pilgrimage to Aachen, Einsiedeln, and Cologne. Feast day on October 30.

Edward the Confessor (1003-66): Born at Islip, England; son of King Ethelred III; King of England (104266); built St. Peter's Abbey at Westminster; known for piety and compassion for the poor; died in London on January 5; body found to be incorrupt; canonized in 1161 by Pope Alexander III; feast day, October 13.

Edward's chief minister, Earl Godwin, had a daughter named Edith whom Edward married in order to pacify him. Edward was part Norman and many of his advisers were as well; however, Godwin was not.This "political marriage" pleased the chief minister because it would increase his influence and balance the power of the Norman influence in the government. Most felt that Edward married in order to keep peace with Godwin instead of doing so out of love for Edith. It was well-known that the marriage did not produce children, and some even said that there was no physical contact whatsoever. Many who knew Edward felt that he agreed with Edith to dedicate his life to God and live a life of chastity and obedience; others felt that he just didn't love her. Tensions increased when Godwin's sons became earls in Edward's court. One of them — Swein — caused a scandal by seducing an abbess. Another son challenged the leadership of Edward and caused severe strains among the in-laws. Eventually, the Godwins were told to leave the country. Edward even sent his wife away to avoid further tensions and embarrassment to his throne. Godwin and sons returned later and challenged Edward for the throne. Eventually a settlement was reached and Godwin's family received various honorary titles and parcels of land. Feast day on October 13.

Elizabeth, Queen of Portugal (1271-1336): Elizabeth was married at age twelve to King Denis of Portugal. She was known for her piety, gentleness, and charity toward the poor, and founded hospitals and shelters for wayward girls. Her husband was often involved in bitter disputes with their son Alfonso. Elizabeth eventually became known as "the Peacemaker," for she would faithfully interecede on behalf of both her husband and son in order to keep peace in the family. One time, after King Denis thought she was favoring Alfonso over him, he had her exiled. After Denis died in 1325, Elizabeth became a Franciscan tertiary and dedicated her life to serving others. Feast day, July 4. (See *Falsely Accused* and *Victims of Jealousy*.)

Fabiola (d. 399): Patrician lady of Rome; married, granted a civil divorce when husband proved unbearable; known for great acts of charity and donations to the Church; founded the first hospital in the Christian West; in 395, went to Bethlehem to visit St. Jerome, who became a good friend and supporter of her vocation; originally desired to live a solitary life in Bethlehem, but her vocation was never realized; instead, she returned to Rome; eventually founded a hospice for poor and sick pilgrims at Porto with St. Pammachius; her restless spirit took her on another journey, during which she died.

Fabiola received a divorce under Roman law after her husband had been unfaithful and cruel to her. Fabiola married again while her ex-husband was still living. Realizing that this was considered a sin, she did public penance at the Lateran basilica after her second husband had died. Fabiola was allowed to receive the Sacraments of the Church through the forgiveness of Pope St. Siricus. Feast day, December 27.

Gengulphus (d. 760): Gengulphus was a Burgundian knight in the Frankish kingdom. He married a woman of nobility who proved to be unfaithful and scandalous to him. Ashamed of her actions, Gengulphus put her under another's care and left for his castle in Burgundy, where he would practice a life of penance and charitable actions. Eventually he was murdered by his wife's lover while he lay sleeping in bed. Feast day, May 11. (See *Victims of Unfaithfulness*.)

Godelève (1049-70): Godelève married Bertolf of Gistel and soon became an enemy to his mother. It was rumored that the mother-in-law had someone else in mind to marry her son and decided to make life tough on poor young Godelève. She was so domineering that Bertolf respected her wishes by not going near the girl. After Godelièvе escaped from her home (her mother-in-law was her temporary custodian), she reported her physical and mental abuse to her father, Hemfried, the Lord of Wierre-Effroy. Outraged, he threatened to turn both Bertolf and his mother in to the state and the Church. Bertolf then faked a repentant attitude and took Godelièvе back. However, the abuse continued and she was eventually murdered by two of Bertolf's servants. Feast day, July 6. (See *Victims of Physical Abuse*.)

Gummarus (d. 774): Gummarus served in the court of Pepin the Short. He married Guinmarie, a woman from a noble family. Although he loved her dearly, Guinmarie proved to have a violent temper, was proud and vain, and impatient with everyone who crossed her path. Gummarus heroically suffered these trials for years. After he was sent away for eight years to help Pepin the Short fight several battles, when he returned he found that Guinmarie had abused and insulted the men of his household, oppressing them all the time he was gone. Finally, he was granted a separation from Guinmarie. He would live the remainder of his life alone as a hermit in Nivesdonck. Feast day, October 11. (See *Courtiers*.)

Hedwig (d. 1243): Daughter of Count Berthold IV and later Queen of Poland. Hedwig married Henry I of Silesia, Poland, when she was only twelve and he was eighteen. She was to suffer many tragedies during her marriage. Although the couple produced seven children, three of them died in childbirth and three others passed away as adults.

Furthermore, Henry was wounded in 1227 by the Duke of Pomerania. Later on, he was imprisoned by Conrad of Masovia. Eventually Hedwig bargained for his release, but had to make many concessions to do so. Feast day, October 16. (See *Silesia*.)

Helena (d. 330): Mother of Constantine and finder of the true Cross of Jesus Christ. When Helena was young, she married the Roman General Constantius Chlorus. They would have a child who would one day be known as "Constantine the Great." Because Helena was from a poor family (the daughter of an innkeeper), Constantius divorced her for a woman of higher nobility, Theodora, stepdaughter of the Emperor Maximian. Constantius lived fourteen more years until 306. At his death, Constantine became Caesar and eventually Roman Emperor. Feast day, August 18. (See *Empresses*.)

Louis IX (1215-70): Louis IX, King of France, married Margaret, daughter of Raymond Berenger, Count of Provence, at age nineteen. They would eventually have eleven children (five sons, six daughters). Louis' mother (Queen Blanche) was a very domineering and possessive woman, and she caused great stress upon her young son's marriage. Blanche did not like Margaret. She made every effort to break them apart. Blanche arranged for Louis to live in an apartment above her, while keeping Margaret in a separate apartment below her own quarters. Louis and Margaret managed to see each other anyway, however, through a stairway that connected the two quarters. It wasn't until Blanche's death in 1254 that the marriage was relieved of this terrible burden. Other problems plagued Louis and Margaret during their marriage. Louis' favorite son, young Louis, died at age sixteen. It was a tragic loss for the king, from which he would never quite recover. Later in his reign, Louis suffered the loss of another son, John-Tristan, to an illness. Throughout all of these trials and tribulations, King Louis IX remained a firm Catholic, participating in two crusades in order to free the lands from pagan domination. He was considered a saint during his lifetime and was canonized only twenty-seven years after his death. Feast day, August 25. (See *Crusaders*.)

Margaret the Barefooted (1325-95): Margaret was married to a gentleman from Cesolo, Italy. Although her marriage started out to be a happy one, he grew increasingly angry at her dedication to serving others and living the Christian faith. At one point, Margaret gave up wearing shoes in order to more closely identify with the poor people that she helped. Her husband was embarrassed by her pious actions and caused her great trials. Still, she bore her burden with heroic virtuosity and continued her Christian practice after her husband's death. Feast day, August 27. (See *Victims of Physical Abuse*, *Widows*, and *Young Brides*.)

Monica (331-387): Monica was the mother of St. Augustine of Hippo. She married a pagan from Tagaste named Patricius, who was known to have a violent temper. Although Patricius may never have physically hurt Monica, she patiently endured his jealous and irritable ways throughout their marriage. By 370, Monica was able to convert both Patricius and his mother after many years of prayers. Feast day, August 27. (See *Mothers*.)

Nicholas of Flüe (1417-87): Nicholas married Dorothea Wissling, and the couple had ten children. In 1467 (at the age of fifty), he decided to become a hermit at Ranft near Sachseln, Switzerland. There he would live in a small cell for the remaining nineteen years of his life. His wife and children, though faced with the extreme hardship of living a separated family life, agreed to the arrangement. Nicholas remained married, although the burden of being separated must have required a trust and patient disposition that could only come from an extraordinary faith. Feast day, March 22. (See *Councilmen* under "Occupations.")

Olaf II (995-1030): Olaf married a Swedish princess named Astrid. Although he remained faithful to Astrid for the remainder of their marriage, Olaf secretly loved her sister, another princess named Ingejerd. Olaf had originally asked Ingejerd's parents for permission to marry, but they refused him. Instead, they approved her marriage to the Russian Prince Jaroslav.

Olaf and Ingejerd continued to love each other, even though he settled for marrying her sister instead. Perhaps it was Olaf's way of keeping a bit of Ingejerd in his life. Feast day, July 29. (See *Carvers; Norway*.)

Pharaïldis (d. 740): Born in Gand; popular saint throughout Flanders; consecrated her virginity to God while still a youth; little else known about her life; many miracles claimed through her intercession; a legend claims that one time a beggar was praying before her tomb when joining him was a woman who had a loaf of bread with her; seeing the beggar, she hid the loaf; later, the bread had turned to stone; another legend claims that a miraculous spring came forth from the ground at Bruay near Valenciennes to help the thirsty harvesters of the area; the water is also suppose to relieve children's disorders.

Pharaïldis was forced to marry a wealthy man, despite her vow of virginity to God as a child. She refused to live with her new husband and promised to protect her pledge to God. As a result, her husband abused her for her actions. Eventually, the man died and left Pharaïldis a widow, her virginity still intact. Feast day not established.

Philip Howard (d. 1595): Philip Howard was the son and heir of the fourth Duke of Norfolk, Thomas Howard. He married Anne, daughter of Thomas, Lord Dacre of Gillesland, at the age of twelve. Anne returned to her Catholic faith after being a Protestant for years. When Philip began to serve in the court of Queen Elizabeth, he decided to please the royalty and neglected the concerns of his wife in the process. He also had their first child baptized a Protestant and named her Elizabeth in order to please the Queen. In time, Philip and Anne separated. Later on, they patched up their differences and both reconciled with the Church in 1584. From then on, Philip was a changed man, pious and devoted to his faith. Feast day, October 19. (See *Falsely Accused*.)

Thomas More (1478-1535): Thomas More married Jane Holt in 1505. They had four children: Margaret, Elizabeth, Cecily, and John. By the time the eldest child was five, Jane Holt died. Thomas then married Alice Middleton, who was seven years older than his thirty-four years. The marriage was a trying one for Thomas. She had been described by those who knew her as "blunt, rude, and narrowminded." Despite her stubbornness and selfish pride, Alice was considered a good stepmother to the children. Thomas and Alice brought up their family to be good, solid Christians. Feast day, June 22. (See *Lawyers*.)

DIVORCED

Fabiola (d. 399): Fabiola was married to a Roman patrician who was cruel and unfaithful to her. It was rumored that he beat her on occasion, so violent and unpredictable was his behavior. Fabiola was granted a divorce and later remarried. She repented marrying again while the first husband was still living (a sin according to Christian law). She made public penance of her sin at the Lateran basilica. Feast day, December 27. (See *Difficult Marriages*.)

Guntramnus (d. 592): King of Burgundy and one of four sons to King Clotaire I. He had married Mercatrude, but they later divorced. He even arranged for the murder of Queen Austrechild's physicians because they were unable to cure Mercatrude of her illness. He later converted to the faith and lavished great gifts upon the Church. He also founded many churches and monasteries and organized several synods. Feast day, March 28. (See *Murderers*.)

Helena (d. 330): Mother of Constantine and finder of the true Cross of Jesus Christ. When Helena was young, she married the Roman General Constantius Chlorus. They would have a child who would one day be known as "Constantine the Great." Because Helena was from a poor family (the daughter of an innkeeper), Constantius divorced her for a woman of higher nobility, Theodora, stepdaughter of the Emperor Maximian. Constantius lived fourteen more years until 306. At his death, Constantine became Caesar and eventually Roman Emperor. Feast day, August 18. (See *Empresses*.)

DYING

Joseph (first century): It is unclear why St. Joseph, the foster-father of Jesus, is patron of the dying. Perhaps it has to do with the fact that a tradition claims that Joseph was dead before the crucifixion and resurrection of Christ. The apocryphal *Protoevangelium of James* claims that he was an old man by the time he married the young Blessed Virgin. Despite his advancing years, Joseph performed his greatest task near the end of his life — that of raising Jesus Christ. He is the model of fathers and of family life. Feast day, March 19. (See *Carpenters* and *Korea*.)

EMIGRANTS

Frances Xavier Cabrini (1850-1917): In 1899, Frances was invited to visit New York by Archbishop Corrigan. Here she was called to work with the poor Italian immigrants of the city. Membership in her Missionary Sisters of the Sacred Heart would spread throughout America, as she traveled extensively and founded schools, hospitals, convents, and orphanages. In time, these institutions would open in South America, Central America, Italy, and England. Feast day, November 13. (See *Hospital Administrators*.)

EPILEPSY

Vitus (d. c. 300): Son of a senator from Sicily; legend surrounding life; converted at age twelve; known for miracles; tortured for not honoring Roman gods; died in Lucania, Italy.

Vitus is known as protector of epileptics and those suffering from St. Vitus Dance (chorea). It is not clear why he is designated patron of epileptics. Perhaps it is due to the fact that he miraculously freed the Emperor Diocletian's son of an evil spirit, only to be blamed by the Roman pagans of practicing sorcery. In those days, many reported demonic possessions were really seizures occurring from epileptic victims. Vitus is also protector against storms. He has been declared patron of dancers, actors, and comedians. Feast date, June 15.

Willibrord (658-739): Although its origin is unclear, a feast known as *Springende Heiligen* (Dancing Saints) occurs every year at Echternach on Whit-Tuesday. Willibrord is buried there in the abbey church. The feast has taken place every year since 1553 (except 1786-1802). It consists of a procession from a bridge over the Sure to St. Willibrord's shrine. Four or five people go arm-in-arm, hopping and dancing, taking three steps forward and two steps back. The local people dance to tunes played by a live band. Following the celebration is benediction with the Blessed Sacrament. This has become a penitential procession for all who suffer from epilepsy and similar maladies. Feast day, November 7. (See *Holland* under "Countries and Nations.")

EXPECTANT MOTHERS

Gerard Majella (1725-55): Born at Muro, Italy; turned down by Capuchins because of his youth; opened a tailor shop at Muro; became a Redemptorist lay brother (1748); professed by St.Alphonsus Liguori in 1752; extraordinary gifts: prophecy, bilocation, ecstasies, visions, and infused knowledge; spiritual director of several nuns; died at Caposele; canonized by Pope St.Pius X in 1904.

As a male, Gerard Majella holds the unusual distinction of being patron of expectant mothers. After his father's death, his own mother claimed that he was the ideal child, holy and pious from an early age on. She claimed that he prayed constantly, was devoted to the Blessed Eucharist, and that "he was born for Heaven." Later, Gerard returned home to live with his mother and sisters, where he helped provide for their care. His feast day is October 16.

Raymond Nonnatus (1204-40: Raymond Nonnatus is considered patron of expectant mothers and midwives because of the nature of his own birth. Although his mother died in labor, Raymond miraculously survived

the ordeal. His life is filled with legend, and even his last name —
Nonnatus — was supposedly given to him from the term *non natus*, which
means "not born." Raymond was reportedly born by caesarian operation.
Feast day, August 31. (See *Falsely Accused*.)

EYE DISEASES

Lucy (d. 304): Born of nobility at Syracuse, Sicily; refused marriage
during Diocletian's reign; martyred for being Christian; at first they tried to
burn her to death, but the fire did not harm her; later, she was stabbed in the
throat; patron of Syracuse.

Lucy is invoked by those suffering from eye diseases. This is based on
legend that she offered her eyes to a suitor she disliked who admired them,
tore them out for him, but they were miraculously restored. Another
possible reason is that the name "Lucy" means "light," and the eyes are the
recipients of light to each soul. Feast date, December 13.

FALSELY ACCUSED

Blandina (d. 177): A slave and victim of persecution under Emperor
Marcus Aurelius; tortured for her faith; body burned and ashes thrown in
the Tiber River.

Blandina was falsely accused of feeding on human flesh and
committing such atrocities as incest and unmentionable sexual perversions.
This occurred with many Christians at the time, for the persecutors under
Marcus Aurelius would do anything to have the believers condemned and
killed. Feast day, June 2.

Dominic Savio (1842-57): Dominic achieved great sanctity at a very
early age. One time, when the family moved to Mondonio, two boys filled
the school stove with snow and garbage during the cold winter months.
When the teacher came back into the room, they falsely accused Dominic
of doing the dirty deed. Although disciplined in front of the entire class,
Dominic refused to tell on the two mischievous boys. When the truth was
later revealed, Dominic was asked why he didn't confess to his innocence.
He remarked that he was imitating our Lord, who remained silent during
His persecutions and crucifixion. Feast day, March 9. (See *Choirboys*.)

Elizabeth of Hungary (1207-31): Elizabeth was once accused of
mismanaging the estate of her husband, the Landgrave Ludwig, after his
death, which occurred while he was on crusade with Emperor Frederick II.
The accusations began because of Elizabeth's great charity towards the
poor. She was known to give much of her wealth and property to those who
had nothing. Her brother-in-law forced her out of office and she went to

Marburg, where she entered the Franciscan Order as a tertiary in 1228. Feast day, November 17. (See *Bakers*.)

Elizabeth, Queen of Portugal (1271-1336): Elizabeth was exiled from her court by a jealous husband, King Denis of Portugal. She had often served as a peacemaker between Denis and their son Alfonso, who led several rebellions against his father. When Denis thought that Elizabeth was favoring Alfonso over him, he had her removed from power and sent away. After Denis' death, she became a Franciscan tertiary. Feast day, July 4. (See *Difficult Marriages, Jealousy, Queens, Tertiaries*, and *Victims of Jealousy*.)

Helen of Sköfde (d. c. 1160): Also known as Elin; born to a noble family; married; after her husband's death, dedicated her life to works of charity; known for her kindness to the poor and needy; built the Church at Sköfde with her own money; murdered; body brought to Sköfde; miracles reported at the tomb; canonized by Pope Alexander III in 1164.

When Helen's daughter's husband died, she was blamed for his death. Actually, his own servants had killed him because of his cruelty toward everyone who worked for him. After his death, Helen left on pilgrimage. During her absence, the servants falsely accused Helen of murdering her daughter's husband. To add substance to their story, they claimed that Helen left on pilgrimage to avoid suspicion. Believing their story, the parents of the murder victim attacked and killed Helen. Feast day, July 31.

Margaret of Cortona (1247-97): A famous Franciscan tertiary mystic, Margaret was once accused of having intimate relations with the friars she associated with. Jealous of her good works and piety, gossips spread the false story that she was having relations with her two spiritual directors, Frs. John de Castiglione and Giunta Bevegnati. She bore this heavy cross for a long time. It wasn't until Father Bevegnati moved away that the local people came to know the truth about this innocent holy soul. Feast day, February 22. (See *Tertiaries*.)

Marina (date unknown): Marina was the daughter of Eugenius, Bithynian who became a monk and brought Marina into the monastery disguised as a boy. She had to dress and act like a boy under her father's orders, until his death when she was seventeen. Marina was accused of making the daughter of the local innkeeper pregnant. She continued to hide her true identity and was banned from the monastery. She then took up a life of begging and approached her former monastery. Still remaining silent, she offered to take the son of the innkeeper's daughter into her custody and was readmitted to the monastery with the boy five years later. It was only upon her death that the religious community found out that "he" was a girl. Feast day, February 12.

Matilda (895-968): Daughter of Count Dietrich of Westphalia and

Reinhild of Denmark; raised by her grandmother (abbess of Eufurt convent); married Henry the Fowler, son of Duke Otto of Saxony (909); widowed in 936; known for her great charities; built three convents and a monastery; spent her later years at a convent at Nordhausen, a place she had built; died at the monastery Quedlinburg and buried there with her husband Henry.

Matilda was betrayed by her own son Otto after her husband, King Henry, had died. She favored her younger son Henry as successor to the throne, but Otto wanted the throne instead (indeed, King Henry had suggested that Otto replace him when he died). Despite his efforts, Otto failed to become king and took revenge on his mother. He falsely claimed that Matilda was squandering the money of the empire on herself and on extravagant charities. Otto demanded a public account. He even hired spies to trap her. In the end, Matilda found out that Henry and Otto were conspiring to eliminate her queenship. She bore these trials heroically. Later on, a reconciliation took place, and Matilda returned to the court. Feast day, March 14.

Philip Howard (1557-95): Son of fourth Duke of Norfolk, Thomas Howard; baptized a Catholic but raised a Protestant; married at age twelve to Ann Dacres; neglected his wife; reconverted to Catholicism (1584); imprisoned for treason and supporting his Catholic faith; died in prison on October 19; canonized by Pope Paul VI in 1970; one of the Forty Martyrs of England and Wales. Feast day, October 19. (See *Difficult Marriages, Separated Spouses, Victims of Betrayal*.)

Raymond Nonnatus (c. 1204-40): Born at Portella, Catalonia, Spain; born by caesarian operation; mother died in childbirth; became a Mercedarian; appointed cardinal by Pope Gregory IX; devoted his life to ransoming captives from the Moors; died at Cardona; canonized in 1657; patron saint of midwives; feast on August 31. (See *Expectant Mothers*.)

Roch (1295-78): Born at Montpellier, France; birth mark in the shape of a cross on his chest; orphaned at age twenty; went on pilgrimage to Rome; cared for plague victims there; contracted plague but recovered; known for miracles of healing; imprisoned five years for mistakenly being identified as a spy by his own uncle, the governor; died in prison; invoked against pestilence; known as Rocco in Italy; feast date, August 17. (See *Bachelors* and *Invalids*.)

Serenus (d. c. 307): Born in Greece; known as "The Gardener"; sacrificed all his possessions and worldly plans for a life of celibacy, prayer, and penance; left for Mitrovica, Yugoslavia, and bought a garden there; lived off his land and practiced a life of prayer and solitude;

beheaded for his faith after being falsely accused of mistreating a woman whose husband was a guard for the court of Emperor Maximian.

Serenus once found a woman wandering through his private garden in Yugoslavia. When he questioned her about her presence there, she grew angry and defensive. The woman wrote to her husband and falsely accused Serenus of insulting and harassing her. Her husband happened to be a guard in the court of the Christian-persecutor, Emperor Maximian. This charge was readily believed by the court, and they found other excuses to condemn poor Serenus as well. He was beheaded in the year 307. Feast day, February 23.

FATHERS OF LARGE FAMILIES (three or more children)
(See *Parents of Large Families*.)

FIRE PROTECTION
Catherine of Siena (134780): It is unclear why Catherine is the patron of fire protection. Perhaps it is due to the fact that in one of her many visions of Christ, she exclaimed, "Then I saw the God-and-man, as one sees the brightness of the sun, receiving that soul in the fire of His divine love." Catherine of Siena received the stigmata in Pisa in 1375. Feast day, April 29. (See Italy under "Countries and Nations.")

GUARDIANS
Guntramnus (d. 592): Son of King Clothaire I, Guntramnus would later serve as King of Burgundy. Guntramnus served as peacemaker between his brother's quarreling families, each one trying to take over the other's power and territorial rights. After the death of his two brothers, Chilperic and Sigebert, Guntramnus adopted and raised their children. Feast day, March 28. (See *Murderers*.)

Joseph of Palestine (d. 356): A Jewish convert who "guarded" or housed many priests who were subject to persecution under Emperor Constantius. His house was located in Sythopolis. Among the better-known saints that Joseph hid in his home were Eusebius of Vercelli (355) and Epiphanius. Feast day, July 22. (See *Converts*.)

Mamas (d. 275): Mamas was tortured and martyred for his faith under the persecutions of Emperor Aurelian. Although Aurelian had commanded his guards to burn Mamas with torches for refusing to honor the pagan gods, he was miraculously spared and the guards themselves were burned. Later, when the persecutors attempted to drown Mamas at sea, an angel protected him from the guards and they fled in fright. Eventually, Mamas died by the sword. Feast day, August 17. (See *Orphans* and *Victims of Torture*.)

HANDICAPPED

Alphais (d. 1211): A poor peasant girl born at Cudot in the Diocese of Orléans, France; helped support the family while still a child because her father was unable to make ends meet; many supernatural graces associated with her life; had the gift of inedia (living entirely on the Eucharist); great periods of fasting and penance; known for her holiness; gave advice to Queen Adela, wife of King Louis VII of France, who visited her three times; canonized by Pope Pius IX in 1874.

While still a young child, Alphais came down with leprosy. Because of this illness, she later lost her arms and legs and was forced to remain bedridden. Because of her holiness and extraordinary faith, the local archbishop had a church built next to her home so that she could assist at the services through a special window made for this purpose. It is claimed that Alphais was cured of her leprosy through the intercession of the Blessed Virgin. Feast day, November 3.

Gerald of Aurillac (d. 909): Gerald was the Count of Aurillac in France. He was known for his piety and fairness to all. In his elder years, he became blind. Feast day, October 13. (See *Counts*.)

Henry II (d. 1024): Henry succeeded his father as Duke of Bavaria in 995. Later, Pope Benedict VIII crowned him Holy Roman Emperor (1014). After a lifelong service to his country and God, Henry became lame in his latter years. Even so, he continued to serve as Duke of Bavaria until his death in 1024. Feast day, July 13. (See *Dukes*).

Seraphina (d. c. 1253): Born at San Gimignano, Italy, to a poor family; victim of numerous unexplainable illnesses as a youth, one of which left her paralyzed; offered up her sufferings in union with Christ; visions of her favorite saint, Gertrude the Great; after her death, heavenly scents emitted from her grave, including the appearance of white violets on her coffin; miracles reported. Feast day, March 12. (See *Spinners* under "Occupations.")

Servulus (d. c. 590): A beggar with palsy from youth; memorized many of the books of the Bible by heart; continually sang hymns of praise and thanksgiving, despite his constant pain; heard heavenly music and voices at the hour of his death; body buried in St. Clement's church.

Servulus was born with palsy and had to live as a beggar to sustain himself. He spent many hours in front of the church of St. Clement, begging for alms. He was unable to walk or move on his own accord, so much had the disease crippled his body. Instead, he relied on his mother and brother to carry him to the church each day and to move his limbs periodically. Feast day, December 23.

HAPPY MEETINGS

Raphael: One of seven archangels who stand before the throne of the Lord (Tb 12:12,15). He was sent by God to help Tobit, Tobiah and Sarah. At the time, Tobit was blind, and Tobiah's betrothed, Sarah, had had seven bridegrooms perish on the night of their weddings. Raphael accompanied Tobiah into Media disguised as a man named Azariah. Raphael helped him through his difficulties and taught him how to safely enter marriage with Sarah. Tobiah said that Raphael caused him to have his wife and that he gave joy to Sarah's parents for driving out the evil spirit in her. He also gave Raphael credit for his father's seeing the light of heaven and for receiving all good things through his intercession. Besides Raphael, Michael and Gabriel are the only archangels mentioned by name in the Bible.

Raphael's name means "God heals." This identity came about because of the Biblical story which claims that he "healed" the earth when it was defiled by the sins of the fallen angels in the apocryphal Book of Enoch (10:7). Raphael is also identified as the angel who moved the waters of the healing sheep pool (Jn 5:1-4). He is also the patron of the blind. The feast is celebrated on September 29 by Christian and Jew alike.

HEADACHE SUFFERERS

Teresa of Ávila (1515-82): Teresa was the victim of many illnesses and sufferings throughout her mystical life. When she reached the age of twenty-one, Teresa was afflicted with malignant malaria, but recovered through her hours spent in mental prayer. Around 1557, Teresa received a transverberation (mystical wound) of the heart. After her death, a cross-like image was imprinted in her heart. Teresa suffered from many other illnesses and was reported to have excruciating headaches during her life. She would die from a prolonged illness on October 4, 1582. Feast day, October 15. (See *Spain* under "Countries and Nations.")

HEART PATIENTS

John of God (1495-1550): John devoted himself to helping the sick and the poor after his release from a lunatic asylum in 1539. After living a carefree life as a soldier and feeling guilty about all the lives he had taken, John converted and sought to amend his ways. When he heard a sermon by St. John of Ávila (c. 1538), John had a mental breakdown because of his guilt and sadness. John of Ávila later helped him to recover. He founded the

Order of Brothers Hospitalers to serve the sick and poor. John was known for his long hours of helping the sick at the local hospital he helped to found. Feast day, March 8. (See *Booksellers* under "Occupations and Vocations.")

HOMELESS

Benedict Joseph Labre (1748-83): After being refused admittance to the Carthusian and Cistercian Orders, Benedict Joseph Labre left for Rome and took up residence there at the Coliseum. There he spent the rest of his life in prayer and begging for food. During the days he would often visit the many churches throughout the city. Feast day, April 16. (See *Rejected by Religious Order*.)

Edwin (585-633): Son of King Aella of Deira in South Northumbria; King Ethelfrith of Bernicia in North Northumbria stole his kingship away; Edwin spent the next thirty years in Mercia and reclaimed the throne through the efforts of King Baedwald of East Anglia, who killed King Ethelfrith at the Battle of Idle River in 617; Edwin married but became a widow in 625; he then married Ethelburga, the sister of King Eadbald of Kent; Edwin finally gained control and power over all of England; established law and order; intended to build a church at York but died at the hands of King Penda of Mercia in the Battle of Heathfield before it happened; considered a martyr by Pope Gregory XIII.

King Edwin's father (King Aella of Deira) died when he was only three years old. Thereafter for a number of years, Edwin was forced to live in one home after another before he was raised and regained his rightful throne. Feast day, October 12.

Elizabeth of Hungary (1207-31): Elizabeth was the daughter of Andrew II of Hungary and Gertrude of AndechsMeran. She was sent away to the Thuringian Castle of Wartburg near Eisenbeth at the age of four in order to prepare her for a future groom her parents had chosen. The prearranged marriage would be to Louis, the oldest son of Landgrave Herman of Thuringia. Louis was twenty-one when he married Elizabeth, and she was only fourteen. After Louis died, Elizabeth was accused of squandering her inherited estate. In reality, she was known for giving much of her wealth to the needy and poor. For her "crime," she was forced into exile by her brother-in-law. Thereafter, Elizabeth lived the life of a poor Franciscan tertiary. Feast day, November 19. (See *Bakers* under "Occupations.")

Lufthild (d. c. 850): Young Christian who was abused by a jealous stepmother for being so kind to the poor. According to legend, Lufthild (or Lufthildis) was forced to leave home and lived like a hermit, attending to a life of prayer and works for the poor. Feast day, January 23. (See *Victims of Child Abuse*.)

Margaret of Cortona (124797): This Franciscan tertiary mystic had been raised by a cruel stepmother after her real mother died when she was seven. The abuse became unbearable, and Margaret ran away from home. She ended up living with a nobleman for nine years before her conversion. Feast day, February 22. (See *Tertiaries*.)

INVALIDS

Roch (1295-1327): Roch attended to the plague victims in the city of Aquapendente, Italy. He continued his care for the sick in Cesena, Rome, Mantua, Modena, and Ravenna. When he reached Piacenza, Roch himself was stricken with the plague. After his recovery, many miracles were reported through his intercession. Feast day, August 16. (See *Falsely Accused*.)

JEALOUSY

Elizabeth, Queen of Portugal (see *Victims of Jealousy*).
Hedwig, Queen of Poland (see *Victims of Jealousy*).

KIDNAP VICTIMS

Arthelais (d. c. 560): Born in Constantinople; daughter of proconsul Lucius and his wife Anthusa; because of her beauty, the emperor demanded that she be his; frightened, the parents secretly sent her away to her uncle Narses Patricius in Benevento; known for her fasting and prayer; died of fever at sixteen.

Arthelais was kidnapped by robbers while on her way to stay with her uncle and was miraculously freed after three days of imprisonment. Arthelais offered gifts to Our Lady in thanksgiving for all the heavenly blessings she received. This occurred when she finally reached her uncle's home in Benevento, Italy. Feast day, March 3.

Dagobert II (d. 679): Son of King Sigebert, ruler of Austrasia for eighteen years; father died at age twenty-six when Dagobert was a child; his guardian was Grimoald, son of Pepin of Landen; Grimoald tried to steal the inherited throne away from Dagobert and give it to his own son, Childebert; exiled, Dagobert traveled throughout England; friend of St. Wilfrid of York; while in England, married a princess and had several children; forced to go to war with Theodericus III; died during a hunting accident in the forests of Woevre in Lorraine on December 23; buried at Stenay; remains transferred to the cathedral at Rouen.

Dagobert was kidnapped by his guardian and sent to Ireland under the custody of the Bishop of Poitiers. The kidnapping occurred because his guardian wanted his own son to inherit the throne after the death of King Sigebert in 656. Because of this incident, Dagobert's destiny would change, as God had better things in store for this holy young man from Austria. Feast day, December 23.

Simon of Trent (1472-75): According to a story in Trento, Italy, at age two he was kidnapped by a Jewish doctor named Tobias who crucified him out of hatred for Christ. The Jews of Trent were later falsely blamed for a conspiracy to murder young Christians. His body was later thrown in a canal. Many miracles were reported at his tomb at St. Peter's Church in Trent. Simon suffered agonizing pain as his torturers gagged, beat, whipped, and finally crucified him. He was pierced throughout his body with awls and bodkins. This occurred on Good Friday in 1475. His feast day is March 24. (See *Victims of Torture.*)

Wernher (d. 1275): Kidnapped by non-Christians when only a child; buried at Trier; miracles reported at tomb; feast especially popular in Germany.

Wernher was kidnapped after receiving Communion on Maundy Thursday (1275). His kidnappers hoped to make him spit up the host he swallowed by hanging him upside down. When this was not successful, they killed him. Wernher's blood was drained from his body and spilled into a pit at Bacherach. Later on, the killers were convicted and Wernher's bodily remains were found. Feast day unknown.

William of Norwich (1132-1144): Born in Norwich, England; became a tanner's apprentice; apparently murdered by ritual torture and crucifixion, blame placed on Jews; martyred like Christ, as his killers pierced him in the side, punctured his head with a crown of thorns, and ultimately crucified him in mocking disdain; miraculous intercessions after death; feast day celebrated on March 24. (See *Victims of Torture.*)

LEARNING

Ambrose (340-97): Ambrose was greatly known for his teachings and writings in theology and philosophy. Some of the better-known writings which contributed to his fame as a great defender of the faith were: *De Officiis ministrorum* (on the ethics of the clergy), *De Virginibus* (a discourse to St. Marcellina), and *De Fide* (an apologetic work condemning the Arians). Ambrose also wrote many hymns, poems, homilies, and Biblical commentaries. Feast day, December 7. (See *Chandlers.*)

LOST VOCATIONS

Gotteschalc (d. 1066): Abotrite prince; once attended the Abbey of St. Michael in Luneberg, Germany; after his father, Uto, was killed by a Saxon, he left the abbey and renounced his faith; thereafter he battled the Saxons, trying to regain his father's holdings; after victorious battles in Germany, Norway, and England, he returned home as a hero to the Abotrites; later returned to the faith and converted thousands; founded many monasteries; killed for defending the faith on June 7 in Lenzen.

Gotteschalc renounced his faith as a young man when his father was suddenly murdered. He was so bitter at the time that he even left the Abbey of St. Michael in Luneberg, Germany, where he was a student. It is not clear when Gotteschalc returned to the faith. After spending some twenty years attacking various territories, he reversed his actions and began a lifetime of converting lost souls. Feast day, June 7.

James Intercisus (d. 421): James served under King Ysdegerd I of Persia as a military officer. In order to excel as a soldier and to please the king (who was a persecutor of Christians), he renounced his faith. After the king's death, a letter from his Christian mother and wife left him so guilty that he later converted back to the faith. In time, James was tortured and martyred for his newfound belief. Feast day, November 27. (See *Victims of Torture*.)

Luchesius (d. 1260): Married lay saint; he and his wife Buona gave much to the poor, visiting the sick and imprisoned; St. Francis of Assisi preached in their town of Poggibonsi in 1221; the same year, Francis formed his Third Order for the laity; Luchesius and his wife may have been its first members; Luchesius experienced many ecstasies, levitations, and the gift of healing; the couple may have died on the same day, April 28. Cults approved for both Luchesius and Buona in 1273 and 1694 respectively.

Luchesius grew up indifferent to religion. During the early years of his marriage, he pursued wealth and political influence. He gained a reputation as a greedy merchant and extravagant speculator in his home at Poggibonsi. After the death of his children, Luchesius converted and eventually became a Secular Franciscan. Feast day, April 28.

MENTAL ILLNESS

Benedict Joseph Labre (1748-83): Benedict Joseph Labre was considered an eccentric in his day, for his penances and mortifications were extreme and severe. Indeed, his fragile condition and extreme practices led to his rejection by many religious orders. His body turned sickly and frail from the rigorous fasts he subjected himself to, and later on he lived as a poor beggar in the Coliseum at Rome. Feast day, April 16. (See *Rejected by Religious Order*.)

Drogo (1105-89): Drogo was crushed when he found out at the age of ten that his mother had died giving birth to him. She had sacrificed her own life to save his. Drogo imagined himself to be responsible for her death. This caused him great anguish and sadness throughout his life. He began to practice extreme penances in order to make up for his imagined sin. Eventually, Drogo made nine pilgrimages to Rome, but was afflicted with a repulsive hernia on his last trip. Ashamed, he hid himself in a cell attached to his local church and lived in seclusion. Feast day, April 16. (See *Shepherds, Orphans, Sickness,* and *Unattractive People.*)

Dymphna (d. c. 650): Legend surrounds this saint, daughter of a pagan Celtic chieftain, either Irish or a Briton; when her mother died, her father suffered from grief and nearly had a mental breakdown; he attempted to marry his own daughter Dymphna because she most resembled her mother; after her confessor told her of the sinful nature of this act, she ran away from home before it occurred; arrived in Antwerp and built an oratory there with her confessor, St. Gerebernus, and two friends; built another oratory at Gheel near Amsterdam; lived as a hermit at Gheel; tracked down by her father (who had mistreated her as a child); he had her companions killed and she was beheaded at age fifteen after refusing to return home; she was later buried in a tomb with epileptics, the insane, and the possessed; many miracles reported at the tomb.

Dymphna was the victim of sexual aggression by her cruel father. She eventually ran away from him when her mother died. Dymphna was regarded as a saint during her lifetime. Because of her father's madness which drove him to mistreat and kill his daughter, she is invoked by those suffering from mental illness and possession. Dymphna is also considered the patron of epileptics, runaways, and rape victims. Feast day, May 15.

MOTHERS

Monica (332-87): Born in North Africa at Tagaste near Carthage; lived a pious Christian life from a very early age; married Patricius, a pagan citizen of Tagaste; Patricius was a suspicious character, jealous, ill-tempered, and violent; Monica endured his criticisms of her Christian faith until he converted along with his mother in 370; widowed in 371; died at Ostia, Italy, while awaiting a ship to take her back home to Africa.

Monica was the mother of St. Augustine of Hippo (she had another son and a daughter as well). Augustine grew up a carefree soul attracted to the wild life. He was a follower of Manichean heresy before his conversion to Christianity in August of 386. It was because of Monica's Christian example and patient prayers for many years that helped lead to Augustine's conversion and change of heart. On Easter in 387, St. Ambrose (Bishop of Milan) baptized Augustine. Augustine became Bishop of Hippo in 396. He is one of the greatest theologians the Church has ever known, producing such spiritual classics as *Confessions*, the *City of God*, *De Trinitate*, *De doctrina christiana*, and *Enchiridion*. Feast day, August 27. (See *Difficult Marriages* and *Widows*.)

MURDERERS

Caedwalla (d. 689): Of English royalty (also called Cadwallader); exiled but returned to reclaim his royalty; claimed West Saxons his own; invaded Isle of Wight and Kent; later made King of Sussex; converted after being wounded; later founded a monastery; Caedwalla relinquished his throne, went to Rome, was baptized in 689, and received the baptismal name of Peter; died on April 20; his body is located in a crypt at St. Peter's Basilica.

Caedwalla killed King Aethelwalh of Sussex in 685 before his conversion to Catholicism. More killings came when he invaded Kent in 686 and made himself its king. The conversion came after he was wounded while planning to take over the Isle of Wight. Before he turned to Christianity, Caedwalla killed many of the residents on the Isle in order to have them replaced with citizens of his native Sussex. Later, he gave one fourth of the Isle of Wight to the Church for her use and entrusted it to St. Wilfrid. He was finally baptized in 689 in Rome before Pope Sergius. He died only ten days later at age thirty. Feast day, April 20.

Guntramnus (d. 592): Also known as Gontran; one of four sons of King Clotaire I; at age thirty-six, became King of Burgundy after his father's death; married to Mercatrude, but later divorced; held a council at Paris to decide how his brother's territory would be divided after his death; quarrels resulted in family war over the property; Guntramnus served as a peacemaker between his brothers; helped to fight invading Visigoths; adopted the children of his brothers when they died; known for his fairness and justice as king; supported the building of churches and monasteries; close friend of St. Gregory of Tours (d. 594); died at the age of sixty-eight after having served as king for thirty-one years; buried at the Abbey of Baume les Dames.

Before his conversion, Guntramnus ordered the execution of Queen Austrechild's physicians because they were unsuccessful at curing his wife, whom he later divorced. Feast day, March 28.

Julian the Hospitaler (date unknown): A legendary figure who reportedly married a wealthy widow as a gift from the king. The couple remained childless all their lives. When his wife put his parents up for a night while he was gone, Julian returned home, thought there was a man in bed with his wife, and killed them both. Remorseful, he engaged in great acts of penance. Later, Julian built an inn for travelers and a hospital for the poor. A leper once visited him, and he gave him his own bed. Legend says that the leper was an angel sent to test his faith. Julian left his home after killing his parents (see above) because of his great restlessness and guilt. He was determined to do penance for the rest of his life. He once left on a journey and came upon a wide river where people would cross. In a dream, he heard a voice ask him to cross the river and help the people to the other side. When he went to them, he found one nearly dead from the cold. He started a fire, bedded him down, and nursed him back to health. Suddenly this sickly man became bright like the sun and ascended into heaven. Julian understood this miracle as a sign that God accepted his penance. Feast day, February 12. (See *Ferrymen*.)

Solomon (d. 874): Nephew of King Nominoius, hero of Brittany; Erispoius (King Nominoius' son) was next in line for the throne when the king died, but Solomon killed his cousin out of envy and took the throne himself; saved Brittany from the Franks and Northmen; later converted and did much good (such as preserving the remains of St. Maxentius in Brittany and protecting them from the Northmen); assassinated by rivals in 874.

Solomon repented of the murder of his cousin Erispoius by performing great penances. After his conversion, he contributed to the building and upkeep of many religious houses. Feast day unknown.

Vladimir (975-1015): Vladimir I of Kiev became ruler of Russia. He captured and killed Yaropolk at Rodno in 980, claiming himself king over all his country. His reign was cruel and barbarous. Vladimir converted to Catholicism about 989. His conversion marks the beginnings of Christianity in Russia. In time, Vladimir would found many churches and monasteries there. He also brought Greek missionaries into the land. Feast day, July 15. (See *Converts*.)

ORPHANS

Aurelius (d. 852): Son of a wealthy Moor and Spanish woman; practiced his faith in secrecy after the Muhammadans came to power; later publicly expressed his belief after seeing a merchant named John scourged for professing his faith; married with two children; lived a life of piety and virtue; martyred for making a public confession of faith; beheaded on July 27, 852.

Both of Aurelius's parents died while he was only a youth. He was later placed in the care of his mother's sister, who raised him and educated him in the Catholic faith. Feast day, July 27.

Dagobert II (d. 679): Dagobert was the son of King Sigebert of Austrasia. When Sigebert died in 656, Dagobert was taken away by his guardian Grimoald, who tried to make his own son (Childebert) successor to Sigebert's throne. In order to arrange this, Grimoald had Dagobert purposely kidnapped and taken from the territory. Dido, Bishop of Poitiers, was given custody of Dagobert and brought him to Ireland. He was raised there and attended school at the court of the King. Feast day, December 23. (See *Kidnap Victims, Kings,* and *Parents of Large Families.*)

Drogo (1105-89): Orphaned at birth. His parents had been of Flemish nobility. After learning that his mother had died in labor while he had lived, Drogo became deeply depressed and felt guilty for her death. He spent a lifetime of practicing great acts of penance to atone for his imagined sin. Feast day, April 16. (See Shepherds, Mental Illness, Sickness, and Unattractive People.

Frances Xavier Cabrini (1850-1917): In 1868, when Frances was only eighteen years old, both her parents died. For a while she lived with her sister Rosa, but later moved to the House of Providence, an orphanage at Codogno. There she became administrator of duties. Eventually, Frances would move to an abandoned Franciscan friary and found her own order, the Missionary Sisters of the Sacred Heart (1880). In later years, Frances' fondness and experiences with orphanages led to her formation of many other schools, hospitals, convents, and orphanages throughout North and South America. Feast day, November 13. (See *Hospital Administrators.*)

Jerome Emiliani (1481-1537): Born at Venice, Italy; ordained in 1518; founded Somascan Fathers; died on February 8 at Somascha of an infectious disease; canonized by Pope Clement XIII in 1767.

Jerome founded the Somascan Fathers in 1532, a religious order dedicated to caring for orphans. He was declared patron saint of orphans and abandoned children by Pope Pius IX in 1928. Feast day, July 20.

Mamas (d. 275): Born to Rufina while she was in prison for defending her Christian faith. The persecutors under Governor Democritus took Mamas away from Rufina as part of her punishment. Along with Rufina, Mamas was martyred as a young boy for proclaiming his faith. Feast day, August 17. (See *Guardians* and *Victims of Torture.*)

Pulcheria (399-453): Daughter of Emperor Arcadius and Empress Euxodia. Her mother died when she was five years old and her father when she was nine. Pulcheria was placed in an orphanage. Her brother Theodosius II became Emperor at age seven, but because of his age the empire was really ruled through the guardianship of Anthimus. When Anthimus died,Theodosius was still only thirteen. Pulcheria took over as "Augusta" and served as her brother's partner in ruling the empire. Feast day, September 10. (See *Empresses.*)

PARENTS OF LARGE FAMILIES (three or more children)

Adalbald of Ostrevant (d. 650): Son of a noble family; worked in the court of Dagobert I and Clovis II; became Duke of Douai; married Lord Ernold's daughter, Rictrude; opposition from many in-laws and relatives, though they were happily married; had four children; Adalbald was recalled to Gascony and was killed by a jealous in-law on the way (650); after his death, Rictrude had Adalbald's body buried with honor; the body was preserved in the Monastery of St. Amand les Eaux in Elanone, France; his head was later transferred to Douai; Rictrude entered the monastery at Marchiennes after her children were raised; she became its abbess. Adalbald had four children: son Mauront and three girls (Eusebia, Clotsind, and Adalsind). They were known as a deeply religious family. Adalbald and Rictrude had raised them to be very good Catholics; in fact, all four children became saints, as well as Adalbald and Rictrude. In addition, Adalbald's grandmother (St. Gertrude of Halmage) was raised to the altar, as was Rictrude's sister (St. Bertha). All the children followed their mother by entering religious life. After the death of Rictrude, her daughter Clotsind took over as abbess of the monastery at Marchiennes. Feast day, February 2.

Adelaide (d. 999): She was to have six children of her own through two marriages: Emma with Lothaire, King of Italy; and Otto II, Henry, Bruno, and two daughters with Otto the Great of Germany. In addition, Adelaide adopted Otto's son Rudolph from his first marriage. Feast day, December 16.(See *Empresses*.)

Clotilde (d. 545): Wife of King Clovis of the Franks. Clotilde was a devout Catholic who tried to convert her husband; he finally converted after defeating the Alemanni and was baptised at Christmas 496. Clotilde and Clovis founded the church of the Apostles Peter and Paul in Paris (renamed St. Geneviève). Clovis was buried in Paris when he died in 511. Family feuds over political power occupied Clotilde for years to come. She eventually married the Visigoth Amalaric, who treated her cruelly. Clotilde dedicated her later years to helping the sick and poor at Tours.

Clotilde had three sons with King Clovis, Clodomir, Childebert, and Clotaire, and a daughter named Clotilde. (Her first son had died in infancy shortly after his baptism). The children fought one another for control of land and power, which greatly grieved Clotilde for many years. She was to witness the death of her son Clodomir, killed by the brother of his cousin Sigismund after the latter had died at the hands of Clodomir. Clotilde later adopted Clodomir's three sons, but her natural son Clotaire killed two of these children (his elder nephews, age seven and ten) out of jealousy and rivalry. Feast day, June 3. (See *Adopted Children, Death of Children, Queens, Widows*, and *Young Brides*.)

Dagobert II (d. 679): Dagobert married an English princess. The couple had several children, including two who were to become saints: Irmina and Adela. Feast day, December 23. (See *Kidnap Victims, Kings*, and *Orphans*.)

Dorothea of Montau (134-794): Dorothea married swordsmith Albert of Danzig when only seventeen years old. The couple had nine children, the youngest daughter becoming a Benedictine nun. The rest of Dorothea's children died in childhood. Feast day, October 30. (See *Death of Children, Difficult Marriages, Widows*, and *Young Brides*.)

Edwin (d. 633): Nothing is known of Edwin's first marriage from historical records. He married a second time to Ethelburga, sister of Eadbald, the Christian King of Trent. The couple had at least four sons and a daughter. Feast day, October 12.(See *Converts, Homeless*, and *Kings*.)

Ferdinand III (1199-1252): King Ferdinand of Castile married Beatrice, daughter of King Philip of Swabia. They were to have seven sons and three daughters before her death. Later, Ferdinand married Joan of Ponthieu, who bore him two more sons and a daughter. All in all, he raised thirteen children during his busy life as King of France. Feast day, May 30. (See *Engineers*.)

Ivetta (1158-1228): Born at Huy near Leyden in the Netherlands; forced to marry by her father; after five years of marriage, her husband died when she was only eighteen; known for her care of lepers (ten years); became a recluse and was favored with many mystical experiences; received the gift of reading hearts and knowledge of distant events; received Communion miraculously; helped to convert her father and one of her sons; died at age seventy in Huy.

Ivetta bore three children during a forced marriage. Feast day unknown.

Leonidas (d. 202): Christian philosopher of Egypt; married and had seven sons, one of whom was to become the famous scholar Origen, raised by Leonidas; when Christians were persecuted in Alexandria, Leonidas was imprisoned; he was martyred in 202 at the command of the Governor of Egypt.

Leonidas's eldest son was the great Christian scholar Origen. He nurtured Origen's faith by training him in Scripture and the Greek literature of his day. Leonidas was a man of great prayer and instilled this value in all his sons. He was eventually imprisoned and beheaded for his faith. His wife and children were left in extreme poverty, as the state confiscated all his wealth and property. Feast day, April 22.

Leopold (1073-1136): Born at Melk, Austria; influenced in youth by St. Altmann, Bishop of Passau; succeeded his father as Margrave of Austria at age twenty-three; married Agnes, daughter of Emperor Henry, at thirty-three; founded Klosterneuburg near Vienna for Augustinian canons; also founded Benedictine Monastery of Mariazell, Styria, Austria; spread the faith throughout his land; held back invading Magyars; served forty years as Margrave; died at age sixty-three; buried at the Augustinian abbey of Klosterneuburg.

Leopold's wife was a widow, bringing two sons into their marriage. This faithful couple had eighteen more children during their happy marriage. Eleven children survived childhood, including Otto, who would become the Cistercian Abbot of Marimond in Burgundy. Feast day, November 15.

Louis IX (1215-70): Louis, King of France, married Margaret, daughter of Raymond Berenger, Count of Provence, at age nineteen. They would eventually have eleven children (five sons, six daughters). Louis's favorite son, young Louis, died at age sixteen. It was a tragic loss for the king, one from which he would never quite recover. Later in his reign, Louis suffered the loss of another son, John Tristan, to an illness. Feast day, August 25.(See *Crusaders.*)

Margaret of Scotland (1045-93): Queen Margaret and King Malcolm were blessed with eight children. There were six sons (Edward, Edmund, Edgar, Ethelred, Alexander, and David) and two daughters (Matilda and Mary). Margaret raised all of her children to be good Christians, including them in her spiritual exercises and prayers. Feast day, November 16. (See *Widows.*)

Matilda (895-968): Daughter of Count Dietrich of Westphalia and Reinhild of Denmark; married Henry the Fowler, son of Duke Otto of Saxony, in 909. Henry was to become the King of Germany in 909. Together this couple had five children: Otto (who later became Emperor of the Holy Roman Empire), Henry the Quarrelsome (who would become Duke of Bavaria), St. Bruno (later Archbishop of Cologne), Gerberga (who married King Louis IV of France), and Hedwig (future mother to Hugh Capet). Henry and Matilda brought up their children in a Christian environment, living a happy twenty-three years of marriage together. Feast day, March 14. (See *Falsely Accused.*)

Nicholas of Flüe (1417-87): Nicholas married Dorothea Wissling and fathered ten children. He later left his family (with their permission) for the life of a hermit at Ranft near Sachseln, Switzerland. Feast day, March 22. (See *Councilmen.*)

Richard Gwyn (1537-84): Born at Llanidloes in Montgomeryshire, Wales; raised a Protestant; attended St. John's College in Cambridge; opened his own school in Overton at Flintshire, Wales; converted to Catholicism; to avoid suspicion over his newfound faith, he left with his family for Erbistock; arrested in 1579 at Wrexham, but later escaped; recaptured and sent to prison; kept in chains and tortured; indicted for treason in 1584 at Wrexham; hanged in the same year; wrote many Welsh poems in prison; the first Welsh martyr of Queen Elizabeth I's reign; canonized in 1970 by Pope Paul VI as one of the Forty Martyrs of England and Wales. Richard Gwyn married after he moved to Overton in Wales (1562). In time, he was to have six children. Feast day, October 25.

Thomas More (1478-1535): Thomas More married Jane Holt in 1505.They had four children: Margaret, Elizabeth, Cecily, and John. By the time the eldest child was five, Jane Holt died. Thomas then married Alice Middleton, seven years older than his thirty-four years of age. Despite her rudeness and pride, she was considered a good stepmother to the children. Thomas and Alice brought up their family to be good, solid Christians. Feast day June 22. (See *Lawyers*.)

Vladimir (956-1015): Vladimir was the Grand Duke of Kiev and all Russia. Before his conversion he had five other wives. With these women he had ten sons and two daughters. (Polygamy was a common practice in medieval Russia.) After his conversion, he married Anna, daughter of Emperor Boris II and put aside his former wives. Feast day, July 15. (See *Converts*.)

PLAGUE PATIENTS

Sebastian (see *Archers* under "Occupations").

POSSESSED

Lucian and Marcian (d. c. 250): Former devil worshipers; after conversion, they publicly renounced Satanism and black magic; imprisoned and tortured by the Proconsul Sabinus for preaching the faith; burned alive in Nicomedia about 250.

Lucian and Marcian were once worshipers of the devil and practitioners of black magic. They once tried to put a spell on a Christian girl, but a Sign of the Cross caused the evil spirits to leave. Because of their inability to perform demonic rituals with success, Lucian and Marcian were converted. They burned books on witchcraft throughout the city of Nicomedia. Feast day, October 26.

Margaret of Fontana (d. 1513): Born in Modena, Italy; known for piety at an early age; vowed her virginity to God; entered the Dominican Third Order; helped the sick and the poor; spent entire nights in prayer; miraculous healings reported through her intercession. Margaret of Fontana had many battles with evil spirits. Her ability to drive them away through the Sign of the Cross led many to invoke this blessing for protection from demonic possession. Her miraculous powers of healing have also led to her role as patron of women who suffer in childbirth. No feast day yet established.

POVERTY

Armogastes (d. 455): Served King Geneseric's son Theodoric; tortured for his faith after Geneseric renounced the faith and became an avid persecutor of Christians; had his legs broken; suspended on a cord with his head hanging down; banished to Byzacena to work as a miner; later transferred to Carthage and tended cattle.

Little is known of Armogastes. He considered it a glorious thing to be dishonored and humiliated for the sake of his faith in Christ. Once a prestigious servant in the court of Theodoric (son of King Geneseric of the Vandals), he was commissioned to work lowly jobs such as mining and cattle grazing. Feast day, March 29.

Cuthman (d. 900): Cuthman was from a poor family in southern England. After his father's death, he had to help support himself and his mother, who was unable to work because of ill health. They sold the family's livestock and moved to Steyning in Sussex, where they built a small cottage and worked the land.

Feast day, February 8. (See Bachelors and Shepherds).

Julia (sixth century): Martyr from Corsica who was sold as a slave to a pagan merchant of Syria named Eusebius (439). She resigned herself to a life of humble service, recognizing her lot as God's will. Feast day, May 22. (See *Victims of Torture*.)

Macrina the Elder (d. 340): Mother of St. Basil the Great. Before her husband's death, they often suffered hunger. The pious couple were forced to live in the wild forests for seven years because of the threat of persecution from Galerius and Maximinus. Feast day, January 14. (See Widows.)

Regina (date unknown): Also known as Reine; few records about this saint; daughter of Clement, a pagan of Alise in Burgundy; raised a Catholic woman after her mother died in childbirth; rejected by father because of his pagan disapproval of the Christian upbringing; sent away to be raised by a nurse; refused marriage to the prefect Olympus; imprisoned in a dungeon, tortured for denying Olympus; tortured; constant appearance of a dove over her head helped to convert many observers; beheaded for her faith.

Regina was so poor as an orphaned child that she was forced to work for her daily food as a shepherdess at the home of her caretaker, a local nurse. Feast day, September 7.

Saturus (d. c. 455): A devout Catholic; ordered by Huneric to renounce his faith through the pressures of Genseric, King of the Vandals; Saturus refused; died about the year 455.

Saturus was threatened with losing his estate, his slaves, wife, and children for not renouncing his faith. His wife pleaded with him to give up his Christian practice, but he remained unwavering to the end. As a result, he lost all that he cherished and died in poverty. Feast day, March 29.

PRISONERS

Adelaide (d. 999): Kept in solitary confinement by Berengarius after she refused to marry his son Adalbert, she was imprisoned at the Castle of Garda until a priest named Martin dug a secret passage under her wall and allowed Adelaide to escape. Feast day, December 16. (See *Empresses*.)

Charles of Blois (1320-64): Born the son of Guy de Chatillon, Count of Blois, and Margaret, sister of King Philip VI of France; married Joan of Brittany in 1337; became Duke of Brittany; captured Nantes and fought rival factions; helped the sick and poor; founded religious houses; made a pilgrimage barefoot to Rennes in Guingamp; a good Christian soldier who attended Mass daily; in 1346, his rival John de Montfort (supported by King Edward III of England) defeated Charles in battle at La Roche Derrien near Treguier; tried to regain his former position as duke but was killed and defeated at Auray on September 29, 1364, by the British under Sir John Chandos; miracles reported at his tomb; canonized by Pope Pius X in 1904.

Charles of Blois was taken prisoner and deported to England after his defeat at the hands of John de Montfort. He was put in a tower and ransomed for money, but remained imprisoned for nine years before he returned home to France. All this time, he remained a devout Catholic and was faithful to prayer. He once felt a call to become a Franciscan friar instead of a political or military leader, but his dreams were never fulfilled. Feast day, September 29.

Dismas (first century): "Good Thief" crucified with Christ on Calvary (Lk 23:39-43). The other thief was known as Gestas. According to a legend from an Arabic Gospel of the Infancy, Dismas and Gestas were thieves who held up the Holy Family on their way to Egypt. Dismas convinced Gestas not to molest them. The Infant Jesus predicted both thieves would be crucified with Him in Jerusalem and that Dismas would accompany Him to heaven. Feast day, March 25. (See *Funeral Directors*.)

Joseph Cafasso (1811-60): Italian priest, renowned confessor; promoted devotion to the Blessed Sacrament; canonized by Pope Clement XIII in 1767.

Joseph was known for his work with prisoners and convicts around Turin, Italy. He once accompanied over sixty men to the scaffold, all of whom died converted to the faith. He would fondly call them his "hanging saints." Feast day on June 23.

Louis IX (1214-70): King Louis was the son of King Louis VIII of France. During one crusade which started in 1248, Louis was taken prisoner by the Saracens at El Mansura (1250). He was set free after ransoming himself and fled to the Holy Land, where he stayed until 1254. During that year he returned to France. Louis died of typhoid fever on another crusade in 1270. Feast day, August 25. (See *Crusaders.*)

PROTECTOR OF CROPS

Ansovinus (d. 840): Born at Camerino in Umbria, Italy; became a priest and then a hermit at Castel Raimondo near Torcello; known for his miracles and sanctity; had the gift of healing; confessor to Emperor Louis the Pious; worked with the poor; while visiting Rome he came down with a fatal fever; returned home to Camerino to die.

Ansovinus reportedly performed a miracle to feed the poor. One day, when the granary was empty and many were left unfed, the granary miraculously refilled itself until all the hungry had their fill. Feast day, March 13.

REJECTED BY RELIGIOUS ORDER

Benedict Joseph Labre (1748-83): Born at Amettes, France on March 25; eldest of eighteen children; pious at an early age; known for his great sanctity and prayers before the Blessed Sacrament; visited many shrines in Italy, Switzerland, France, Germany, and Spain; lived his last years in Rome under extreme poverty and practicing great penances; responsible for a miraculous multiplication of food for the poor; died in Rome on April 16; canonized by Pope Leo XIII in 1883.

Benedict was once refused admittance to the Trappists, Carthusians, and Cistercians because of charges that he was too young or eccentric. He tried many different times, but never realized his vocation to join a strict contemplative order. Benedict Joseph Labre was a misunderstood saint of his day. After finally giving up, he moved to Rome, lived in the Coliseum, and was known as "the beggar of Rome." Feast day, April 16.

Henry II (d. 1024): Succeeded his father as Duke of Bavaria in 995. He was later crowned Emperor of the Holy Roman Empire by Pope Benedict VIII (1014). Henry had long desired to become a priest before his rise to power, but he fell in love and married Cunegunda instead. Later in life, after heroic service to God and his country, he approached the Abbot of St.-Vanne at Verdun for admittance to his monastery. Henry wanted to end his life as a monk. The abbot refused him, however, and encouraged him to continue administration of his empire. Feast day, July 13. (See Dukes.)

Joseph Moscati (1880-1927): Born in Benevento, Italy, on July 25, seventh of nine children; a brilliant child, eventually studied medicine at the University of Naples; received a degree in medicine and surgery at the age of 23; helped to stop a local epidemic; visited the sick, often serving those who were poor at no charge; refusing to marry, he made a private vow of celibacy in 1923; helped to convert many; believed in healing both body and soul together; miraculous knowledge of illnesses and how to treat them; daily communicant; extraordinary acts of prayer and penance; died peacefully at home at the age of forty-six; two miracles accepted through his intercession in 1973; beatified by Pope Paul VI on November 16, 1975; canonized by Pope John Paul II on October 25, 1987: the only layperson beatified during 1975 and the only layman canonized for the Holy Year of 1987-88; buried in the Church of the Gesu Nuovo in Naples.

After consecration to a life of celibacy in 1913, Joseph Moscati wanted to enter the religious order called the Society of Jesus. He was refused by the Jesuits, who felt that his true vocation was in the world practicing medicine. Feast day, April 12.

Rose of Viterbo (d. 1252): Born in Viterbo in the Romagna to a peasant family; unusual sanctity as a child; experienced a vision of the Blessed Virgin at age eight during a severe illness; Mary indicated that she would one day become a Franciscan tertiary (lay Franciscan); began preaching in the streets at age twelve; lived a pious life at home; correctly predicted the approaching death of Emperor Frederick II in Apulia (December 13, 1250); canonized by Pope Callistus III in 1457.

Rose tried to enter the convent of St. Mary of the Roses at Viterbo, but was refused by the abbess because she lacked the necessary dowry. "Very well," said Rose. "You will not have me now, but perhaps you will be more willing when I am dead." Rose returned home and practiced her solitary life until her death in 1252 at the age of seventeen. On September 4, 1258, her body was transferred to the church at the convent of St. Mary of the Roses, as she had predicted. Later, the church burnt down but her bodily remains were preserved and relocated. Feast day, September 4

RETREATS

Ignatius of Loyola (1491-1556): Ignatius was a former soldier who converted to Christianity after being wounded, hospitalized, and reading lives of Christ and the saints. His first major retreat was taken at Manresa between 1522-23. Here Ignatius experienced many visions and was inspired to write his classic work *Spiritual Exercises* (published in 1548). He went on to found the Society of Jesus (Jesuits) with Francis Xavier, Peter Favre, Diego Laynez, Alfonso Salmeron, Simon Rodriguez, and Nicholas Bobadilla at Paris in 1534. His rule gained official approval in 1537. Feast day, July 31. (See *Soldiers*.)

RHEUMATISM

James the Greater (d. c. 44): Son of Zebedee; brother to the Apostle John; called by Jesus to be an Apostle while fishing at the Sea of Galilee (Mt 4:21-22; Mk 1:19-20; Lk 5:10); present at Jesus' cure of Peter's mother-in-law (Mk 1:29-31); nicknamed "Boanerges" (Son of Thunder) by Jesus (Mk 3:17); present with Peter and John at the raising of the official's daughter (Mk 5:37; Lk 8:51); with Peter and John at the Transfiguration (Mt 17:1-8; Mk 9:2-8) and at the Agony in the Garden (Mt 26:37-46; Mk 14:33-42); first martyred Apostle at Jerusalem, where he was beheaded under the orders of Herod Agrippa I (Acts 12:1-2); legend claims that before he died he had preached in Spain; later, his remains were transferred to Santiago de Compostela in that country.

James is also the patron of Spain. His role as patron for rheumatism is unclear. Perhaps he is identified with healings or cures because of his presence with Jesus during the cure of St. Peter's mother-in-law (see Mk 1:29-31). Feast day, July 25.

RUNAWAYS

Alodia (d. 851): Sister to St. Nunilo; both died as martyrs; lived at Huesca, Spain; her father was Muhammadan and her mother was Christian; mother remarried another Muhammadan after the death of her first husband; gave up the chance to marry for a life of virginity and devotion to God; ran away from home after being so mistreated; persecuted under the pagan Abdur Rahman; beheaded for their faith.

Alodia ran away from home when she was treated cruelly by her new stepfather, the second Muhammadan her mother married after her father's death. Feast day, October 22.

Dymphna (d. c. 650): Ran away from home after her mother died because her father had tried to seduce her. The evil father eventually found Dymphna and ordered his companions to kill her when she refused to give in to his lustful desires. Feast day, May 15. (See *Victims of Rape*.)

Eulalia of Merida (d. 304): During the persecutions of Diocletian, Eulalia was hidden in the country by her protective mother. At the time, she was only twelve years old. Wanting to proclaim her faith in a public manner, she heroically ran away and headed for Merida. There she confronted the local judge, Dacian, who demanded that she deny her faith and worship the Roman gods. She was severely tortured for her brave actions and died from fire. Feast day, December 10. (See *Sailors*.)

SCHOOLS

Joseph Calasanz (1556-1648): Also known as Joseph Calasanctius; born in a castle near Peralta de la Sal, Aragon, Spain, on September 11; received doctorate in law at University of Lérida; ordained in 1583 (although his father had wanted him to become a soldier); became vicar general of Trempe; left for Rome in 1592; known for his ministry to plague victims (1595); died in Rome on August 25; canonized by Pope Clement XIII in 1767.

Joseph Calasanz founded a free school for the poor in 1597. He supervised other teachers and opened other schools. In 1621, he founded the Clerks Regular of Religious Schools and became its superior general. His order is also known as the Piarists or Scolopi. Feast day, August 25.

Thomas Aquinas (1225-74: Born near Roccasecca, Italy, son of Count Landulf of Aquino (a relative of the Emperor and King of France); sent to Benedictine Monte Cassino Monastery at age five for his education; attended University of Naples in 1239; became a Dominican in 1244 at Naples; his family was so opposed to his joining the order that they kidnapped him for 15 months; however, he rejoined the order in 1445; studied at the University of Paris between 1245-48; ordained at Cologne in 1250; became master of theology at University of Paris (1256); known as the "Dumb Ox"; one of the greatest and most influential theologians of all time; died at the age of fifty; canonized in 1323; declared Doctor of the Church by Pope Pius V.

Pope Leo XIII declared Thomas Aquinas to be patron of all universities, colleges, and schools. He is also considered the patron saint of students. Thomas was given these honors because of his teaching experience. Besides being master of theology at the University of Paris (1256), he also taught at Naples, Anagni, Orvieto, Rome, and Viterbo between 1259-68. Thomas Aquinas wrote such masterpieces as: *Summa Contra Gentiles* (1261-64); *Summa Theologica* (1265-73); dozens of treatises, hymns, letters, commentaries on the Bible, and dissertations on the Lord's Prayer, the Angelic Salutation, and the Apostles' Creed. Feast day, January 28.

SEARCHERS FOR LOST ITEMS

Anthony of Padua (1195-1231): Anthony is known for his many miraculous intercessions for various causes, needs, and conditions. Indeed, his intercessory powers are so extraordinary since the time of his death that he is known by the nickname "The Wonder Worker." One tradition claims that a novice once ran away and carried off a valuable psalter Anthony was using. He prayed for its recovery, and the novice was visited by a heavenly apparition who frightened him into returning it. Feast day, June 13. (See *Portugal* under "Countries and Nations.")

SECOND MARRIAGE

Adelaide (d. 999): Adelaide married Otto the Great of Germany (twenty years her senior) a year after her first husband (Lothaire, King of Italy) had died. She brought one daughter, Emma, to the new marriage and had five more children with Otto: Otto II, Henry, Bruno, and two daughters who would become nuns. Feast day, December 16. (See Empresses.)

Matilda (895-968): Matilda was the daughter of Count Dietrich of Westphalia and Reinhild of Denmark. She married Henry the Fowler, son of Duke Otto of Saxony, in 909. Although Matilda would only marry once, Henry in fact had been married before to a woman named Hathburg. He received an annulment from that union. Henry was to become the King of Germany in 909. Together the couple had five children: Otto (who later became Emperor of the Holy Roman Empire), Henry the Quarrelsome (who would become Duke of Bavaria), St. Bruno (later the Archbishop of Cologne), Gerberga (who married King Louis IV of France), and Hedwig (future mother to Hugh Capet). Henry and Matilda brought up their children in a Christian environment. She was to suffer greatly, however, when her child Henry rebelled against his brother Otto. He eventually died during one of their quarrels. Feast day, March 14. See *Falsely Accused*.)

SEPARATED SPOUSES

Edward the Confessor (1003-66): Born at Islip, England; son of King Ethelred III; King of England (104266); built St. Peter's Abbey at Westminster; known for piety and compassion for the poor; died in London on January 5; body found to be incorrupt; canonized in 1161 by Pope Alexander III; feast day, October 13. Edward's chief minister, Earl Godwin, had a daughter named Edith whom Edward married in order to pacify the earl. Edward was part Norman, and many of his advisers were as well; however, Godwin was not. This "political marriage" pleased the chief minister because it would increase his influence and balance the power of Norman influence in the government.

Most felt that Edward married in order to keep peace with Godwin instead of doing so out of love for Edith. It was well known that the marriage did not produce children, and some even said there was no physical contact whatsoever. Many who knew Edward felt that he agreed with Edith to dedicate his life to God and live a life of chastity and obedience; others felt that he just didn't love her. Tensions increased when Godwin's sons became earls in Edward's court. One of them, Swein, caused a scandal by seducing an abbess. Another son challenged the leadership of Edward and caused severe strains among the in-laws. Finally, the Godwins were told to leave the country. Edward even sent his wife away to avoid further tensions and embarrassment to his throne. Godwin and sons returned later and challenged Edward for the throne. Eventually a settlement was reached, and Godwin's family received various honorary titles and parcels of land. Feast day on October 13.

Gengulphus (d. 760): A knight from Burgundy who was known for his bravery and virtuous life. He married an unfaithful woman who chose to sleep with another man. Ashamed at her actions and unable to convert her ways, Gengulphus separated from his beloved wife. She was put in the care of another, and he retreated to a castle in Burgundy, living a life of penance and good works. Eventually his wife betrayed him. She had her lover kill Gengulphus while he lay sleeping. Feast day, May 11.(See *Victims of Unfaithfulness.*)

Gummarus (d. 774): Gummarus served in the court of Pepin the Short. He married Guinmarie, a woman from a noble family. Although he loved her dearly, Guinmarie proved to have a violent temper, was proud, vain, and impatient with everyone who crossed her path. Gummarus heroically suffered these trials for years. After, he was absent for eight years to help Pepin the Short fight several battles. When he returned, he found that Guinmarie had abused and insulted the men of his household, oppressing them all the time he was gone. Finally, he was granted a separation from Guinmarie. He would live the remainder of his life alone as a hermit in Nivesdonck. Feast day, October 11. (See *Courtiers.*)

Nicholas of Flüe (1417-87): Nicholas married a Christian girl named Dorothea Wissling. The couple had ten children. Their marriage was a happy and prosperous one. When Nicholas turned fifty, he felt the urge to abandon the world and live a life as a hermit. After seeking permission from his wife, he left for Ranft, Switzerland, where he took up residence in a small cell. Nicholas was to remain there for the last nineteen years of his life. Feast day, March 22. (See *Councilmen.*)

Philip Howard (d. 1595): Son and heir of the fourth Duke of Norfolk, Thomas Howard. He married Anne, daughter of Thomas, Lord Dacre of Gillesland, at the age of twelve. Anne returned to her Catholic faith after being a Protestant for years. When Philip began to serve in the court of Queen Elizabeth, he decided to please the royalty and neglected the concerns of his wife in the process. He also had their first child baptized a

Protestant and named her Elizabeth in order to please the Queen. In time, Philip and Anne separated, but later they patched up their differences and were reconciled with the Church in 1584. From then on, Philip was a changed man, pious and devoted to his faith. Feast day, October 19. (See *Falsely Accused*.)

SICKNESS

Camillus de Lellis (1550-1614): Camillus was denied profession in the Franciscan Capuchins because of infection in a leg wounded while fighting the Turks. To make up for this loss, Camillus dedicated his life to serving the sick, becoming director of St. Giacomo Hospital in Rome. Later, he was ordained and founded his own order with two companions, the Ministers of the Sick (Camillians). The order was formally approved by Pope Gregory XIV in 1591. Feast day, July 14. (See *Nurses*.)

Drogo (1105-89): Flemish patron of shepherds; great acts of penance and mortification as in youth; early fame for sanctity; claims of bilocation at different churches while he remained working the fields at Sebourg; made nine pilgrimages to Rome; lived a life of seclusion on barley bread and water for forty years (gift of inedia); tomb a popular sight for pilgrims.

Drogo developed a severe hernia during one of his many pilgrimages. He must have looked awful, for he hid himself at Sebourg to raise sheep, not wanting anyone to see him in his condition. Eventually, he became even more a recluse, hiding in a cell built against the local church. From this cell he heard Mass, ate, prayed, and practiced great penance. He was to remain there for the last forty years of his life. Drogo is invoked for those with hernia problems and is also considered the patron of shepherds. Feast day, April 16.

Germaine Cousin (1579-1601): Born with a deformed and crippled right hand. In addition, she was a sickly child, suffering from swollen glands of the neck and malnutrition due to the abusive nature of her parents. She eventually died alone, her frail, weak body no longer able to sustain her. Feast day, June 15. (See *Abandoned*.)

Gorgonia (d. 374): Daughter of St. Gregory Nazianzen the Elder and St. Nonna; sister of St. Gregory Nazianzen and St.Caesarius; eventually married and bore three children; twice miraculously cured of illness; devoted to the Eucharist and charitable to the poor; late baptism.

Gorgonia suffered a fall from her carriage, stamped on by mules pulling it. Her internal organs were crushed, as well as many of her bones. But she recovered miraculously through the strength of her faith. Another time Gorgonia was plagued with a strange illness that gave her headaches, fevers, paralysis of mind and body, and temporary comas. While she was still able, Gorgonia went to the parish church, wept at the feet of a statue of Christ on the altar, and again was miraculously cured. Feast day, December 9.

John of God (1495-1550): John devoted himself to helping the sick and poor after his release from a lunatic asylum in 1539. After living a carefree life as a soldier, feeling guilty about all the lives he had taken, John converted and sought to amend his ways. When he heard a sermon by St. John of Ávila (c.1538), John had a mental breakdown because of his guilt and sadness. John of Ávila later helped him to recover. He founded the Order of Brothers Hospitalers to serve the sick and poor. Feast day, March 8. (See *Booksellers*.)

Louis IX (1214-70): Son of King Louis VIII of France. During one crusade which started in 1248, Louis was taken prisoner by the Saracens at El Mansura (1250). He was set free after ransoming himself and fled to the Holy Land, where he stayed until he returned to France in 1254. Louis died of typhoid fever during another crusade on August 25 in Tunisia. Feast day, August 25. (See *Crusaders*.)

Lydwine of Schiedam (1380-1433): Born at Schiedam, Holland, one of nine children of a workingman; after an injury in her youth, she became bedridden and suffered the rest of her life from various illnesses and diseases; experienced mystical gifts, including supernatural visions of heaven, hell, purgatory, apparitions of Christ, and the stigmata; Thomas à Kempis wrote a biography of her; canonized by Pope Leo XIII in 1890.

Lydwine suffered a fall while ice skating in 1396, when a friend collided with her and caused her to break a rib on the right side. From this injury she never recovered. An abscess formed inside her body which later burst and caused Lydwine extreme suffering. Eventually, she was to suffer a series of mysterious illnesses which in retrospect seem to be from the hands of God. Lydwine heroically accepted her plight as the will of God and offered up her sufferings for the sins of humanity. Some of the illnesses which afflicted Lydwine were headaches, vomiting, fever, thirst, bed sores, toothaches, spasms of the muscles, blindness, neuritis, and the stigmata. Feast day, April 14.

Michael the Archangel: It is not clear why Michael is patron of those who suffer from sickness. It is well known that his intercession has helped to cure many a soul throughout Christian history. Perhaps it is due to the fact that Michael represents goodness and wholeness while his counterpart the devil is a symbol of evil, wickedness, and death. His victory over the fallen angels (see Rv 12:7-12) confirms the fact that he is a particularly powerful advocate against all that is negative toward the wholeness and health of the human condition. Feast day, September 29. (See *Grocers, Mariners,* and *Paratroopers.*)

Syncletica (d. 400): Born at Alexandria, Egypt, to wealthy Macedonian parents; refused many offers of marriage because of her faith and loyalty to Christ her Spouse; overcame frequent temptations through rigorous fasts and acts of penance; left sole heiress to parents' estate when siblings died before her; gave away all her wealth to the poor; renounced the world and lived as a recluse; died at age eighty-four.

At age eighty, Syncletica began to suffer from burning fevers and a lung infection. She also had a gangrenous infection in her jaws and mouth which caused her to lose her speech. Even though cancer would take her life, she remained incredibly calm and patient through all her sufferings, joyful and confident in the Lord. Feast day, January 5.

SINGLE LAYWOMEN

Agatha (d. 251): Despite her natural beauty, Agatha rejected all offers of marriage, including that of Quintianus, Roman governor of her district. She had taken a vow of virginity at an early age and remained a virgin throughout her life. Feast day, February 5. (See *Nurses.*)

Alodia (d. 851): Sacrificed offers of marriage in favor of a life consecrated to God; she vowed her virginity to Christ and led a life of prayer, penance, and contemplation. Feast day, October 22. (See *Runaways.*)

Bibiana (date unknown): Also called Viviana; little known of her life; reportedly a native of Rome, daughter of Flavian and his wife Dafrosa, both ardent Christians; Flavian was burned in the face with a hot iron because of his faith; his wife was eventually beheaded; Bibiana and her sister Demetria were denied all their possessions at the hands of their persecutors; they fasted, prayed, and remained steadfast in their faith; Bibiana was tortured for remaining loyal to Christ; she was tied to a pillar and whipped with scourges loaded with lead; after she died from this beating, her body was left exposed for two days so that dogs might come and eat the remains; however, they refused to touch her.

Bibiana was placed in the care of a cruel woman named Rufina by order of the Governor Apronianus. He tried to use Rufina to encourage Bibiana to sacrifice her virginity for the governor, but her efforts were not successful. Angered by Bibiana's pious ways, Apronianus ordered her to be scourged and killed. Feast day, December 2.

Emiliana (d. c. 550): Aunt of St. Gregory the Great; received a vision of her widowed great grandfather (Pope St. Felix II), who showed her a place in heaven reserved for her; her knees and elbows were hardened from the hours spent in prayer; died on January 5, a few days after her sister Tharsilla.

Emiliana sacrificed married life for a life of penance and prayer. She and her sister Tharsilla became recluses at the home of their brother (St. Gregory the Great's father) in Rome. Feast day, December 24.

Flora (d. 851): Raised a Christian, Flora sacrificed marital life for service to God and humanity. She and her friend Mary (sister of a local deacon) dedicated their virginity to God and died as martyrs in 851. Feast day, November 24. (See *Victims of Betrayal*.)

Gudule (d. 712): Daughter of St. Amalberga; sister of St. Reinelda and St. Emembertus; cousin and godchild of St. Gertrude, who educated her and helped her spiritual development; attended Mass daily; once the lantern she used to find her way to church went out; miraculously, it lighted again after a few prayers; thus, her traditional picture shows her with a lantern or candle in her hand; died on January 8; remains interred at Morzelles during the reign of Charlemagne, then transferred to the Church of St. Michael in Brussels (about 988); in 1579, the church was vandalized and Gudule's remains were scattered. Their whereabouts are unknown to this day.

Gudule consecrated her virginity to God after her cousin Gertrude's death in 664. She is known for her steady practice of prayer, fasting, and almsgiving. Gudule is also considered patroness of Brussels. Feast day, January 8.

Julitta (d. 304): Julitta and her three-year-son Cyriacus were martyred for their faith under the persecutions of Emperor Diocletian. After she was widowed, Julitta and her son left Iconium for Isauria, but they were persecuted there by Governor Alexander. (See *Death of Children, Victims of Torture*, and *Widows*.)

Margaret of Cortona (1247-97): Mistress of a young man from Montepulciano after running away from home, Margaret bore a son and lived with her lover for nine years until he was murdered. Upon his death, Margaret converted and made public penance after confessing her past sin in the church at Cortona. Later, two ladies of Cortona took her and her child into their home. Eventually, she became a Franciscan tertiary (layperson) and devoted her life to prayer, penance, and acts of mercy. Feast day, February 22. (See *Tertiaries*.)

Nunilo (d. 851): Born at Huesca during the reign of Spain's notorious persecutor, the Moor Abdur Rahman II; sister to the martyr Alodia; father a Muhammadan and mother a Christian; after her father died, Nunilo's mother married another Muslim; both sisters sacrificed offers of marriage and vowed their virginity to God; arrested with Alodia for practicing the Christian faith; beheaded at the order of Abdur Rahman II.

Nunilo and her sister Alodia were treated cruelly by their stepfather after their mother remarried. Since he was a Muhammadan and they were raised Christian, Nunilo and Alodia suffered greatly for their faith throughout their youth. The two girls ran away from their stepfather and took up residence in the home of a Christian aunt. There they were free to practice their faith and spend their time in acts of mercy and prayer. Feast day, October 22.

Praxedes (second century): Roman who harbored and protected many Christians in her home during the persecutions of Emperor Antoninus; known for her kindness and charity toward the poor; unclear if she died a martyr; body originally buried in the Cemetery of Priscilla on the Salarian Way; later transferred to the Church of Santa Prassede (St. Charles Borromeo celebrated Mass there every morning during his stay in Rome).

Praxedes was a Roman maiden and sister of St. Pudentiana. She refused to marry in order to dedicate her life to the poor, persecuted, and suffering. Feast day, July 21.

Syncletica (d. 400): Born in Alexandria, Egypt, the daughter of a wealthy family, she achieved holiness and sanctity at a very young age, sacrificing a nobleman's proposal of marriage in favor of a life completely dedicated to God. Feast day, January 5. (See *Sickness*.)

Tharsilla (d. 550): Sometimes called Tarsilla; aunt of St. Gregory the Great, sister of Emiliana; known for great time spent in prayer and acts of penance; died a few days before Emiliana and appeared to her later.

Tharsilla and her sister Emiliana sacrificed married life for prayer and contemplation in Rome at the home of their brother (St. Gregory's father). Feast day, December 24.

Zita (1218-78): Zita served the Fatinelli family as a maid for forty-eight years. As a young girl, she devoted herself to God and the service of neighbor. She was known for her help to the sick, poor, and imprisoned. In younger days, Zita was pursued by a male fellow servant. She scratched the man's face when he made advances toward her. When her boss asked why he had been scratched, she denied he had done anything wrong in order to protect him from punishment. Feast day, April 27. (See *Maids*.)

STEPPARENTS

Adelaide (d. 999): Adelaide was widowed and then married Otto the Great of Germany, twenty years her senior. He brought a former child to the marriage, Rudolph. Besides a child of her own from her first marriage to Lothaire (Emma), Adelaide was to have five more children with Otto. Feast day, December 16. (See *Empresses*.)

Leopold (1073-1136): Succeeding his father as Margrave of Austria at age twenty-three, he married Agnes, the daughter of Emperor Henry IV. The couple eventually had eighteen children. In addition to this, Agnes had been a widow and brought two other sons into the new marriage. All in all, Leopold raised twenty children in the course of his life. He was known for his piety and charity, and he founded several monasteries near Vienna and Mariazell. Feast day, November 15. (See *Parents of Large Families*.)

Thomas More (1478-1535): Married Jane Holt in 1505. They had four children: Margaret, Elizabeth, Cecily, and John. By the time the eldest child was five, Jane Holt died. Thomas then married Alice Middleton, who was seven years older than his thirty-four years of age. Despite her rudeness and pride, she was considered a good stepmother to the children. Thomas and Alice brought up their family to be good, solid Christians. Feast day June 22. (See *Lawyers*.)

TERTIARIES

Delphina (d. 1360): Daughter and heiress to the Lord of Puy Michel; orphaned as an infant; raised by her aunt (an abbess); married St. Elzear of Sabran at age sixteen; a devout couple who sacrificed sexual union for the glory and honor of God; they moved to Naples in 1317, and Delphina served Queen Sanchia, wife of King Robert; Elzear died of illness on a trip to Paris; Delphina lived another thirty-seven years; when Queen Sanchia died, Delphina moved to Provence and lived a life of seclusion; gave away all she owned to the poor; with heroic patience, bore an illness that finally claimed her life; buried next to her husband at Apt; died on November 26.

It is reported that Delphina and her husband became Secular (lay) Franciscans and are honored by them to this day. She even convinced Queen Sanchia of Naples to become a Franciscan tertiary. Feast day, September 27.

Elizabeth of Hungary (1207-31): After Elizabeth's husband King Ludwig died of the plague while on a crusade, she became a Franciscan tertiary in 1228. Thereafter, Elizabeth devoted her life to serving the sick, poor, and orphaned. Feast day, November 17. (See *Bakers*.)

Elizabeth, Queen of Portugal (1271-1336): Daughter of Peter III, King of Aragon; known also as Isabella in Portugal, she was a niece of St. Elizabeth of Hungary; married at twelve to Denis, King of Portugal; had two children, son Alfonso and daughter Constance; lived a devout life of daily Mass, sacrifice, Matins, Lauds, and Prime; charitable to the poor; founded a hospital at Coimbra; died at Estromoz, Portugal on July 4; reported miracles through her intercession; canonized by Pope Urban VIII in 1626.

When her husband died in 1325, Elizabeth became a Secular Franciscan after being denied entry to the religious life. She moved into a house near the convent of the Sisters of St. Clare, which she founded in Coimbra. Elizabeth is buried in a church at the Poor Clare monastery in Coimbra. Feast day, July 4.

Elzear (d. 1323): Born at Ansouis in Provence; nephew of William of Sabran, Abbot of St. Victor's at Marseilles; educated in that monastery; married Delphina at age sixteen; lived a life of Christian virtue; recited the Divine Office daily; became Count of Ariano after his father's death; known for his fairness and justice toward the people; godfather to William of Grimoard (later to become Pope Urban V); came to Naples in 1317; helped tutor the son of King Robert (Charles); sent to Paris by King Robert to ask for the hand of Mary of Valois for Charles; returning, he became ill and died in the arms of a Franciscan friar, September 27, 1323; canonized by his nephew Pope Urban V in 1369.

Elzear joined the Franciscans as a tertiary (lay person) along with his wife Delphina. He and Delphina convinced Queen Sanchia of Naples to become a Franciscan Poor Clare after the death of her husband, King Robert. Feast day, September 27.

Ferdinand III (1199-1252): Became King of Castile at age eighteen. He married Beatrice in 1219. After the death of Beatrice, he married Joan of Ponthieu. Before his own death, Ferdinand, a strong Catholic who rebuilt cathedrals and local churches, became a lay Franciscan and was buried in the habit of the Friars Minor in the cathedral at Seville. Feast day, May 30. (See *Engineers*.)

Louis IX (1215-70): As King of France, was a strong Christian and able ruler. He participated in two separate crusades, dying of typhoid at Tunis during the second one. Louis recited the Divine Office daily. He established many religious houses, including the abbey in Royaumont. Louis received last sacraments on the day he died, August 25. (See *Crusaders*.)

Margaret of Cortona (1247-97): Born at Laviano, Tuscany, Italy, to a farm family; raised by a cruel stepmother after her own mother had died; she ran away and lived with a nobleman from Montepulciano, bearing a son; her lover was murdered nine years later; thereafter she converted, doing penance at the church in Cortona; known for miracles and visions of Christ; died in Cortona; canonized by Pope Benedict XIII in 1728.

Margaret repented her past life of living in sin and bearing a child out of wedlock. After her lover's death and her consequent conversion, she joined the Franciscans as a tertiary (order for the laity). Her spiritual directors were well-known masters, Frs. John de Castiglione and Giunta

Bevegnati. As a Franciscan, Margaret experienced the dark night of the soul. Her vocation as a Franciscan eventually came to be in serving the sick and poor. Feast day, February 22.

Rose of Viterbo (1235-52): Rose dedicated her life to God at a young age. On a vigil of the feast of St. John the Baptist she had a vision of Our Lady. The Blessed Virgin told her that she should join the Franciscans as a tertiary (lay member). As soon as Rose did, she recovered from a chronic illness she had acquired at age eight. Feast day, September 4. (See *Rejected by Religious Order.*)

THROAT DISEASES

Blase (d. c. 316): Born of wealthy parents; became bishop at young age; numerous legends surround his life; martyred under Governor Agricolaus of Cappadocia during Licinius's persecutions; blessing of throats on his feast comes from the tradition that he once saved the life of a boy who had swallowed a fish bone. Feast day, February 3.

TRAVELERS

Anthony of Padua (1195-1231): Anthony preached to the Moors in Morocco after 1221. He later preached successfully all over Italy, converting thousands as he went. Feast day, June 13. (See Portugal under "Countries and Nations.")

Christopher (d. c. 251): according to the legendary account, Christopher was an ugly giant who made his living carrying people across a river. He felt that no one was stronger than he. One day a young child he carried seemed so heavy that he feared they both would sink and drown. The child revealed Himself to be Christ, whose heaviness reflected the weight of the sins of the world He had to carry upon His shoulders. Feast day, July 25. (See *Motorists.*)

Nicholas of Myra (d. c. 350): Nicholas ("Santa Claus") is patron of travelers because of the legend claiming that he once interceded for a group of sailors who were threatened by a severe storm off the coast of Lycia. Feast day, December 6. (See *Russia* under "Countries and Nations.")

Raphael: One of seven archangels who stand before the throne of the Lord (Tb 12:12,15). He was sent by God to help Tobiah and Sarah. At the time, Tobit was blind and Sara's seven previous bridegrooms had expired on the night of their wedding. Knowing Tobiah's future, Raphael accompanied him into Media disguised as a man named Azariah. Raphael helped him through his difficulties and taught him how to safely enter marriage with Sarah. Besides Raphael, Michael and Gabriel are the only archangels mentioned by name in the Bible.

Raphael's name means "God heals." This identity came about because of the story that claims he "healed" the earth when it was defiled by the sins of the fallen angels in the apocryphal Book of Enoch (10:7). Raphael is also identified as the angel who moved the waters of the healing sheep pool (Jn 5:14). He is also the patron of the blind. The angels' feast day is celebrated on September 29 by Christian and Jew alike.

UNATTRACTIVE PEOPLE

Drogo (1105-1189): Drogo was victim of a terrible hernia which everyone could see. This occurred while he was tending sheep on a farm at Sebourg. He was so repulsive to others that he tried to hide himself from the community. Eventually he lived a reclusive life in a small cell attached to the local church. Through a small window in the cell which opened at the side wall of the church, he was able to attend Mass and receive Communion without causing attention. Drogo remained confined to this cell for the last forty years of his life. He was known for his prayers and piety, spending hours each day practicing acts of penance and mortification. Feast day, April 16. (See *Shepherds.*)

Germaine Cousin (1579-1601): Germaine was born with a deformed right hand and remained a sickly child. Eventually an illness led to scrofula (swollen neck glands that were very unbecoming in appearance). Because of these misfortunes, her parents abused and abandoned her, but she remained a saintly child all the same. Feast day, June 15. (See *Abandoned.*)

VICTIMS OF BETRAYAL

Epipodius (d. 178): Lived during the persecutions of Emperor Marcus Aurelius; native of Lyons; remained a single Christian; imprisoned for professing the faith; tortured and martyred; miracles reported at his tomb; remains preserved in the Church of St. John at Lyons (later renamed the Church of St. Irenaeus).

Epipodius was betrayed by a servant who revealed to the Roman authorities that he was a Christian. Despite his hiding in a nearby town, he was caught and imprisoned for three days. Epidopius was tortured and beheaded for his faith. Feast day, April 22.

Flora (d. 851): Little known about this woman; a Muhammadan through her father, but her mother was a Christian; betrayed by members of her family who were Muslims; died a martyr's death.

Flora's Muslim brother betrayed her after she was baptized. When he told authorities that she was a Christian, Flora went to her sister's house at Ossaria, where she hid from the persecutors. Her own sister, fearing that the authorities would harm her as well for harboring Flora, told her to leave.

Flora then returned to Córdoba and prayed for guidance at the Church of St. Sciscius. She finally gave herself up to the Muslim authorities, realizing that she could not hide forever. Still refusing to renounce her faith, Flora was put in a dungeon. After torture, she was beheaded with a sword.

Oswin (d. 651): Became King of Deira in 642 after the death of King Oswald. Oswald's brother Oswy took over as King of Bernicia. Suddenly, Oswy declared war on Oswin, wanting his share as well. Rather than fight, Oswin went into hiding at the home of Earl Hunwald at Gilling near Richmond, York. Hunwald betrayed him, and Oswin was murdered there by Ethelwin on orders from Oswy. Feast day, August 20 (see *Victims of Torture.*)

Philip Howard (d. 1595): Son and heir of Thomas Howard, Fourth Duke of Norfolk. After Queen Elizabeth ordered Thomas's death in 1572, she refused to allow Philip his rightful place as heir to his father. After his reconciliation with the Catholics in 1584, he was again betrayed by the leaders of England. He fled from London but was captured at sea and imprisoned in the Tower of London. Imprisoned for six years, he died on October 19, 1595. Feast day, October 19. (See *Falsely Accused.*)

Pulcheria (399-453): Daughter of Emperor Arcadius and Empress Eudoxia; her mother had died when she was five years old and her father when she was nine. Pulcheria was then placed in an orphanage. Her brother Theodosius II became Emperor at age seven, but because of his age the empire was really ruled through the guardianship of Anthimus. When Anthimus died, Theodosius was still only thirteen. Pulcheria took over as "Augusta" and served as her brother's partner in ruling the empire. Later on, Theodosius married Eudocia and proclaimed her as "Augusta." Eudocia betrayed her sister-in-law by supporting Nestorianism and through pressuring the right people to have Pulcheria banished from the court. Pulcheria was recalled when Eudocia was exiled to Jerusalem because of infidelity to Theodosius. Feast day, September 10. (See *Empresses.*)

VICTIMS OF CHILD ABUSE

Alodia (d. 851): Treated cruelly by her stepfather, a Muhammadan who hated the Christian faith. Alodia's mother was a Christian and raised her to be such. Her first husband had also been a Muhammadan. Feast day, October 22. (See *Runaways.)*

Germaine Cousin (1579-1601): Germaine was unwanted as a child because she was born with a deformed right hand and was very sickly. Her father and his second wife hid her from others, making her sleep in an outside stable or under the family stairs, and fed her scraps of food consisting of bread and leftovers from meals. Germaine was eventually found dead under the stairs at the age of twenty-two. Feast day, June 15. (See *Abandoned*.)

Lufthild (d. c. 850): Little known of early life; raised by a stepmother who was cruel to her; moved away and dedicated herself to contemplative life; charitable to the poor; miracles attributed to her after death.

According to historical accounts, Lufthild was abused as a child by her cruel and jealous stepmother, who was envious of her piety and care for the poor. Lufthild either left home of her own accord or was thrown out by the stepmother. Feast day, January 23.

Nunilo (851): Born at Huesca during the reign of Spain's notorious persecutor, the Moor Abdur Rahman II; sister to the martyr Alodia; father a Muslim and mother a Christian; after Nunilo's father died, her mother married another Muslim; both sisters sacrificed offers of marriage and vowed their virginity to God; arrested with Alodia for practicing the Christian faith; beheaded on orders of Rahman.

Nunilo and her sister Alodia were treated cruelly by their stepfather after their mother remarried. Since he was Muslim and they were Christian, the sisters suffered greatly for their faith throughout their youth. Feast day, October 22.

VICTIMS OF JEALOUSY

Elizabeth, Queen of Portugal (1271-1336): Married at age twelve to King Denis of Portugal; known for her piety, gentleness, and charity to the poor; founded hospitals and shelters for wayward girls; husband often involved in bitter disputes with their son Alfonso; Elizabeth became known as "Peacemaker," for she would faithfully intercede on behalf of both husband and son to keep peace in the family.

Once when King Denis thought Elizabeth was favoring Alonso over him, he had her exiled. After Denis died in 1325, Elizabeth became a Franciscan tertiary and dedicated her life to serving others. Feast day, July 4. (See *Falsely Accused, Queens, Tertiaries*.)

Hedwig, Queen of Poland (1371-99): Born the daughter of King Louis, nephew and successor to Casimir the Great; after Louis died, Hedwig was named to lead Poland at age thirteen; known as a beautiful lady; marriage to William Duke of Austria, prearranged since she was four, never took place; instead, Hedwig married Duke Jagiello of Lithuania at thirteen, the union causing an alliance between Poland and Lithuania that would last four hundred years; Jagiello changed his name to King Ladislaus II of Poland after unification of the empire; Hedwig help convert Ladislaus; generous to the sick and poor, she died in childbirth.

Hedwig's husband was very jealous of her beauty. He was also stubborn and irritable. Hedwig's Christian faith and piety contributed to Ladislaus's conversion and baptism in 1383. Venerated in Poland on February 28; universal feast day not yet established.

VICTIMS OF PHYSICAL ABUSE

Fabiola (d. 399): Married to a Roman patrician who was cruel and unfaithful to her; rumors that he beat her on occasion, so violent and unpredictable his behavior; granted a divorce, Fabiola later remarried but, repenting the sin while her first husband was still living, made public penance at the Lateran basilica. Feast day, December 27. (See *Difficult Marriages*.)

Godelière (Godaleva) (1049-70): Born at Londefort-lez-Boulogne of noble family; devoted to the poor; married Flemish lord Bertolf of Ghistellas at age eighteen; rejected by mother-in-law, who beat Godelière during her son's absences; eventually murdered by servants of Bertolf; miracles attributed to her after death, including curing blindness of Bertolf's daughter.

Because of the jealousy of her mother-in-law, Godelière was abused when given over to her care:, locked up in a small cell, given little to eat, she was also mentally abused by the woman, who wanted to get rid of her. Trying to ruin her reputation, she spread scandalous rumors about Godelière. Later husband Bertolf also had designs on her life; he had two servants drown her in a pond on his property. Away from home at the time, he avoided conviction for the crime. Godelière is also invoked for throat ailments, for she was drowned by having a thong drawn tight around her neck before submerging in water. Her feast is celebrated on July 6.

Margaret the Barefooted (1325-95): Born to a poor family in San Severino, Italy; married at age fifteen; abused by husband; went without shoes to identify with the poor; begged food for the sick and poor; after her husband died, lived a life of prayer and penance; died on August 5, buried in the Church of St. Dominic; remains transferred in 1920 to church at Cesolo.

Margaret was severely abused by her husband, who jeered at her for going without shoes and looking like a beggar. It is reported that he physically abused and possibly molested her. Feast day, August 27.

Monica (331-87): Mother of St. Augustine of Hippo; she married a citizen of Tagaste named Patricius, a pagan with an unruly character and violent temper; mentally abused by Patricius, who teased her about her Christian piety. It is not clear whether Patricius ever beat Monica; local witnesses claimed he never laid a hand on her. Perhaps that is why Monica is patron of victims of physical abuse. In spite of her husband's violent temper, her Christian influence prevented physical abuse and eventually led to his conversion in 370. (See *Alcoholism, Difficult Marriages, Mothers, Victims of Unfaithfulness, Widows.*)

Pharaïldis (d. c. 740): Although forced to marry a wealthy nobleman, she obeyed her parents and made the best of the prearrangement. She was physically and verbally abused by her husband, perhaps out of frustration because of her secret vow of virginity, kept until she was widowed; she remained a virgin the rest of her life. Venerated in her native Flanders, she is also known as Varelde, Verylde, or Veerle. Feast day, January 4. (See *Difficult Marriages.*)

VICTIMS OF RAPE

Agatha (d. 251): Subject to extreme torture and martyrdom at the hands of brutal Quintianus, governor of her region, she refused to have intercourse with him, having made a childhood vow to keep her virginity for God. Enraged, Quintianus tried to seduce her to no avail; she died in prison, her virginity intact. Feast day, February 5. (See *Nurses.*)

Agnes (d. c. 304): Born in a wealthy Roman family; known for her beauty, but consecrated virginity to God; because of her innocence, her symbol is a lamb; buried on the Via Nomentana.

Agnes was sent by Emperor Diocletian to a house of prostitution because she refused the advances of his servants. There, she remained firm in her faith, martyred at age ten or twelve for preserving her virginity. Some believe she was stabbed in the throat. Agnes is also the patron of young girls. Her feast day is January 21.

Dymphna (d. 650): Beautiful daughter of a pagan king and Christian queen in Ireland. After her mother died, the king sought another to marry who looked like her. Finding no one to meet the condition, he desired to marry his daughter Dymphna. She ran away from her deranged father through the help of the priest Gerebern, who took her to Gheel in Belgium. In time the king found Dymphna and demanded that she return to him. When she refused, he beheaded her, virginity intact. Feast day, May 15. (See *Mental Illness, Runaways.*)

Maria Goretti (1890-1902): Born in Corinaldo, Ancona, Italy, on October 16; her farmworker father moved his family to Ferriere di Conca, near Anzio; after his early death, Maria helped support the family as a young girl; known for acts of penance and mortification; killed by a would-be rapist she forgave; canonized by Pope Pius XII in 1950 for her purity as model for youth.

Maria was murdered by Alexander Serenelli (son of another worker), who had lived with the Goretti family. When she fought off his sexual advances in her home, he stabbed her. She died several hours later. Alexander repented after Maria appeared to him in a vision; he was present for her canonization. Feast day, July 6.

Potamiaena (d. c. 202): Slave girl given the chance to be set free if she gave up her virginity to her master; she refused and was later martyred.

After the prefect in Alexandria failed to convince her to give up her chastity, Potamiaena was ordered to be lowered into a cauldron of boiling pitch. She was supposed to be stripped of her clothes before death but pleaded to remain clothed. The prefect granted her request, and she was led to death by executioner Basilides, so moved by her faith that he converted, was baptized in prison and then beheaded. Potamiaena's feast is celebrated June 28.

Solangia (d. 880): Born to a family of vinegrowers at Villemont, near Bourges, France; took a vow of chastity at an early age; tended pastures and animals at the family's farm, guided by a bright star overhead each time she took up daily prayers; known for healings and cures; nearly raped and killed by traveling stranger; also known as "St. Geneviève of Berry."

Solangia was a near-rape victim by the son of the Count of Poitiers, who made advances after dismounting his horse. Solangia succeeding in fleeing, he later caught up with her and cut off her head with his knife. Legend reports that Solangia lived long enough to pick up her head and carry it to the church cemetery of St. Martin-du-Cros, where an altar was later erected in her memory (1281). Feast day, May 10.

VICTIMS OF TORTURE

Agatha (d. 251): Imprisoned for refusing the sexual advances of Quintianus, governor of her region. She was severely tortured during her confinement. Quintianus starved her and had her breasts cut off. When this did not cause death, he had her thrown in hot coals with broken pieces of pottery. Sent back to prison, she finally died a martyr's death. Feast day, February 5. (See *Victims of Rape, Nurses*.)

Alban (d. 209): First Christian martyr of Great Britain; charitable acts noted by Venerable Bede (673-735) in his Ecclesiastical History; courageous in faith; miraculously parted a river and walked across on dry land; beheaded for the faith on July 2 along with his planned executioner, converted after the river experience; remains at a monastery in the sty of St. Albans, some twenty miles north of London.

Alban was tortured for harboring a priest during the persecutions of Emperor Diocletian. His feast day is June 22.

Armogastes (d. c. 455): Cruelly tortured for his faith; bound by cords around his head and legs; later, suspended upside down for a long time; still his faith remained firm. Feast day, March 29. (See *Poverty.*)

Bibiana (date unknown): Little known of her life; reportedly a native of Rome, daughter of Flavian and Dafrosa, both ardent Christians; Flavian was burned in the face with a hot iron, his wife eventually beheaded; Bibiana and sister Demetria were denied all possessions by persecutors; they fasted, prayed, and remained steadfast in their faith.

Bibiana (or Viviana) was tortured for loyalty to her faith. She was tied to a pillar and whipped with scourges loaded with lead. After death, her body was left exposed for two days so that dogs might come and eat the remains, but they refused to come near. Feast day, December 2.

Blandina (d/ 177): Tortured by Roman persecutors of her time; her whole body beaten and broken, she was scourged, chewed by wild beasts in the amphitheater, and finally burned. Feast day, June 2. (See *Falsely Accused.*)

Charles Lwanga and Companions (d. 1886): Worked at court of King Mwanga of Uganda; succeeded Joseph Mkasa, a Catholic who exposed Mwanga's homosexual activities with children and his murder of Protestant missionary James Hannington; part of the "Martyrs of Uganda"; year after Lwanga's death, over five hundred Baganda people were baptized; catechumens rose from eight hundred to three thousand; canonized by Pope Paul VI in 1964.

Charles Lwanga was burned to death for his faith, and twenty-one other Christians lost their lives by fire or decapitation. Feast day, June 3.

Edmund (d. 870): Martyr; became King of East Anglia at age fifteen in 855; known for fairness and justice to all; attacked by Danish invaders in 866, taken captive and sent to Hinguar; buried at Hoxne but remains transferred to Beodriesworh (St. Edmundsbury); Benedictine abbey of St. Edmundsbury founded over his grave.

Edmund was severely tortured by Danish conquerors for refusing to renounce his faith: restrained in chains, beaten with clubs, and tied to a tree, where tormentors tore his flesh with whips; later, arrows were shot into his body, and he was decapitated. Throughout his martyrdom, Edmund called the name of Jesus, firm in his faith. Feast day, November 20.

Epipodius (d. 178): Tortured and martyred for his faith; under the cruel persecutions of Roman Emperor Marcus Aurelius, he was hit in the mouth until he bled, then stretched out on a rack. Remaining firm in his faith, he was punctured in the side with iron claws. Finally, the governor of his region had him beheaded. Feast day, April 22. (See *Victims of Betrayal.*)

Eulalia of Merida (d. 304): Persecuted under Roman judge Dacian, who served Emperor Diocletian. Eulalia's body was torn with iron hooks, then her wounds were burned with flaming torches in order to extend her pain. Smoke and flames eventually caused her death. Feast day, December 10. (See *Sailors*.)

Eustachius (d. c. 118): Roman general who converted to Christianity during a hunting trip, according to legend. Eustachius and his family were roasted to death for refusing to give up their Christian faith. Feast day, September 20. (See *Hunters*.)

Genesius (third century): Converted to Christ during a satirical play before Emperor Diocletian, he boldly went up to him and professed his faith. Diocletian ordered that he be tortured for disrespect to the Roman Gods. Genesius was eventually beheaded by Plautian, Roman prefect of the praetorium. Feast day, August 25. (See *Actors, Comedians*.)

Hugh the Little (d. 1255): Son of a widow, kidnapped, tortured and killed as a child of nine; in the story (retold by Chaucer), he was lured to the home of a man named Koppin (or Jopin), imprisoned for a month, scourged, crowned with thorns, and crucified by his killer as a mockery of the suffering and death of Jesus. Arrested and executed with eighteen others, Koppin told a fantastic story that the murder was a Jewish ritual. Many local Jews were arrested, but most were released through Franciscan intercession. When Hugh's body was recovered from the well, miracles were reported. Feast day, August 27.

James Intercisus (d. 421): Military officer for King Yezdegerd I of Persia; abandoned his Christian faith for the king; condemned by his family, he repented when the king died and declared himself Christian to the new king, Bahram; tortured and martyred for the faith.

Intercisus is Latin for "cut to pieces." James's fingers were cut off and his limbs severed; cut into twenty-eight pieces, he persevered to death by beheading. This martyr's feast day is November 27.

John Rigby (1570-1600): Tortured and hanged for refusing to renounce his Catholic faith in Protestant-dominated England. Before his death, he was dismembered and disemboweled. Executioners pulled out his heart and cut off his head, scattering body parts around Southwark. Feast day, June 21. (See *Bachelors*.)

Julia (d. sixth century): Martyr of Corsica; sold into slavery to a Syrian merchant named Eusebius; pressured to sacrifice to local gods, she heroically refused and was crucified for her faith; body eventually transferred to Brescia; declared patroness of Corsica.

Julia was beaten on orders of the governor, had her hair torn out, and was eventually crucified. Feast day, May 22.

Julitta (d. c. 303): Widow and martyr of Caesarea in Cappadocia; under the reign of Diocletian, refused to worship the god Zeus/Jupiter; a judge condemned her to death by burning; legend claims that where her body was buried a miraculous spring of water gushed forth, curing the sick and preserving the health of those who entered it.

Julitta suffered torture and death under the persecutions of Emperor Diocletian. After refusing to pay honor to the Roman god, Julitta was led to a burning fire and bravely walked through it of her own accord. She was never burnt but died of smoke inhalation instead. Feast day, July 30.

Julitta and Cyriacus (d. 304): Besides watching her small son killed in Tarsus by Governor Alexander, this Julitta was herself sentenced to death. She had her sides torn with hooks and was eventually beheaded. Feast day, June 16. (See *Death of Children*.)

Mamas (d. 275): Born in prison to Rufina, awaiting death because of her faith; she made arrangements for a Christian widow, Amya, to raise the child; after Amya died, Mamas went about converting others; was tortured for refusing to pay honor to Roman gods, his flesh torn with scourges; later attempts to burn or drown him failing through miraculous interventions, he finally died by the sword. Feast day unknown. (See *Guardians, Orphans*.)

Margaret Ward (d. 1588): Born at Congleton, Cheshire, England, a gentlewoman who helped the priest Richard Watson during his imprisonment in London; arrested for helping him to escape from Bridewell, she was offered freedom if she would ask the Queen's pardon but refused and was hanged; canonized by Pope Paul VI in 1970.

Margaret was chained during eight days in prison. When her chains were removed, torturers hung her by the hands for so long that she became paralyzed. She was hanged, drawn, and quartered at Tyburn on August 30, 1588. No universal feast day has yet been established.

Pantaleon (d. c. 305): Legendary life; born in Nicomedia and became physician to Emperor Maximian; lost his faith after enjoying court life; reconverted, serving the poor and sick with charity and compassion; donated his time and gave away his possessions; called the Great Martyr and Wonder Worker in the East; blood said to liquefy on his feast day.

Pantaleon was martyred under Emperor Diocletian, beheaded after six other attempts to kill him miraculously failed, including burning, drowning, wild beasts, the wheel, and the sword. Feast day, July 27.

Pelagius (d. 925): Boy martyr from Asturias, Spain; refused to renounce Christian faith during persecutions of Muslim Abd-ar-Rahman III; first racked on an iron horse and tortured, then suspended from the gallows and dismembered. Feast day, June 26. (See *Abandoned*.)

Regina (d. 251): Daughter of Clemens, a pagan citizen of Alise in Burgundy, she was tortured under Prefect Olybrius of Gaul when she refused to marry him because of her vow of virginity. Using her Christian faith as an excuse for persecution, the prefect had Regina whipped and burned with pincers and iron combs. Feast day, September 7. (See *Poverty*.)

Richard Gwyn (1537-84): A married Welsh Protestant with six children, he left teaching at Overton, Flintshire, when he became a Catholic. Arrested at Wrexham, Wales, he was imprisoned at Ruthin and tortured for his faith before being hanged, drawn, and quartered at Wrexham. He is considered the first Welsh Martyr of Queen Elizabeth's reign. Feast day, October 17. (see *Parents of Large Families*.)

Sabas (d. 372): Also known as "Sabath the Goth"; converted to Christianity as a youth. served as lector or cantor for the priest Sansala; taken captive and tortured for his faith during Roman persecutions; remained firm in faith until martyrdom.

Sabas was tortured in various ways: dragged on the ground and whipped with sticks; stretched on a rack for the duration of a night; suspended from a beam and stabbed with a javelin; and finally drowned at Targoviste, northwest of Bucharest in Romania. Feast day, April 12.

Simon of Trent (1472-75): Italian child reportedly kidnapped by a Jewish doctor, crucified out of hatred for Christ, and thrown in a canal; crime admitted under torture, but there was no proof that the Jews of Trento were involved in a conspiracy or that the crime was committed for ritualistic reasons; miracles reported at Simon's tomb at St. Peter's Church. Simon suffered agonizing pain as his torturers gagged, whipped, and finally crucified him, pierced through with awls and bodkins; occurrence on Good Friday, 1475. Feast day, March 24. (See *Kidnap Victims*.)

Theodota (d. 304): A wealthy woman from Nicaea, according to legend; martyred for her faith after refusing marriage to a Roman pagan.

Theodota was reportedly murdered because she refused to marry the prefect Leucatius. Angered by her rejection, Leucatius condemned her and her three children before Nicetius, proconsul in Bithynia, as Christians during Diocletian's persecutions, and she and the children were burned at the stake. Feast celebrated August 2.

Victor of Marseilles (d. 304): Christian officer of the Roman army according to legend; arrested by authorities when his true faith was revealed during the persecutions of Emperor Maximian; cruelly martyred and thrown into the sea; recovered relics placed in a Benedictine abbey at Marseilles but later removed or destroyed.

Victor was to encounter extreme suffering for proclaiming his faith and refusing to worship Roman gods. He was beaten, imprisoned, stretched on a rack, his foot cut off, his body crushed by a millstone and beheaded. Finally he was cast into the sea with three other martyrs. Feast day, July 21.

William of Norwich (1132-44): A tanner's apprentice in England, apparently murdered by ritual torture and crucifixion after being kidnapped, allegedly by two Jews. The killers pierced his side, punctured his head with thorns, and ultimately crucified him. He was only twelve years old at the time of his martyrdom. There is no proof that the crime was committed for hatred of Christ, but many miraculous intercessions were reported after the death. Feast day, March 24. (See *Kidnap Victims.*)

VICTIMS OF UNFAITHFULNESS

Catherine of Genoa (1447-1510): Married to Julian Adorno at age sixteen, she suffered greatly because he was careless, a spendthrift, possessed a quick and violent temper, and admitted being unfaithful to her. They had no children. After Catherine converted Julian, they agreed to live celibate lives and dedicated themselves to the sick and the poor. Both became Franciscan tertiaries and worked in a hospital the rest of their lives. Feast day, September 15. (See *Childless, Difficult Marriages.*)

Elizabeth of Portugal (1271-1336): Married to King Denis of Portugal at age twelve; served as peacemaker in quarrels between her husband and son Alfonso; when Denis thought she was favoring Alfonso for the throne, he had Elizabeth exiled. She was not allowed to return until Denis died in 1325. Feast day, July 4. (See *Tertiaries, Victims of Jealousy.*)

Fabiola (d. 399): Married to a Roman patrician who was unfaithful to her, she obtained a divorce and married another. Feast day, December 27. (See *Difficult Marriages.*)

Gengulphus (d. 760): Also known as Gengoul; Burgundian knight known for his virtuous life and even temper; married an unfaithful woman; lived as a recluse after retirement, helping the needy, doing penance; especially admired in Holland, Belgium, Savoy.

Gengulphus, hurt and shamed by the actions of his beloved wife, left her to be cared for by servants and moved alone to his castle in Avallon. He was reportedly killed in bed by his wife's lover at her instigation. Feast day, May 11. (See *Difficult Marriages.*)

Monica (331-87): Wife of Patricius and mother of St. Augustine of Hippo; reportedly, Patricius lived a wild life, was unfaithful to Monica and also short-tempered. She patiently put up with his shortcomings until he was converted to the faith in 370. Feast day, August 27. (See *Difficult Marriages, Victims of Physical Abuse.*)

WIDOWS

Adelaide (d. 999): Her first husband (Lothaire of Italy) died after having given her one child, Emma. She married Otto the Great of Germany a year later and bore five more children. Feast day, December 16. (See *Empresses*.)

Angela of Foligno (1248-1309): Born in Foligno, Italy; married a wealthy man and bore several children; led a frivolous, worldly life the first years of marriage; repented her past, made reparation, and became a Secular (lay or tertiary) Franciscan about 1285; known for great prayer and penance; experienced supernatural visions but remained humble and simple; received mystical marriage from our Lord, bore stigmata, and died on January 4; her remains are located at the Church of St. Francis in Foligno; miracles reported from her intercession; cult confirmed by Pope Innocent XII.

Angela bore a heavy cross when her husband and mother both died. She was to know further sorrow in seeing her children precede her in death. Aided by Franciscan Friar Arnold, Angela resigned her trials to the will of God and continued her life of prayer, reparation, and mystical union with the Lord. Feast day, February 28.

Anne Line (d. 1601): Married to Roger Line of Ringwood, England; Roger died abroad in Flanders in 1594; Anne dedicated the rest of her life to helping those persecuted for their faith. Feast day, February 27. (See *Converts*.)

Blaesilla (d. 383): Little known of her life; daughter of St. Paula; widowed young; practiced prayer and devotions; cured of a fever after converting to the faith; highly praised by St. Jerome (who knew her mother) studied Hebrew and encouraged Jerome to translate Ecclesiastes; died at Rome at the age of twenty.

Blaesilla became a widow in her teens after only seven months of marriage. Feast day, January 22.

Catherine of Genoa (1447-1510): Married Julian Adorno at the age of sixteen; suffered greatly because he was careless, a spendthrift, had a quick and violent temper, and admitted being unfaithful; they had no children; after Catherine converted Julian, they agreed to live celibate lives and dedicated themselves to the sick and poor; both became tertiaries and worked in a hospital the rest of their lives; Julian died in 1497.

After she became a widow, Catherine found a spiritual director, Don Cattaneo Marabotto, to guide her inner life; at this time she received mystical visions and wrote her famous discourses, *Dialogue Between the Soul and the Body* and *Treatise on Purgatory*. Feast day, September 15. (See *Difficult Marriages*.)

Dorothy of Montau (1347-94): Born in Prussia; married wealthy swordsman Albrecht of Danzig when she was seventeen and bore him nine children; he fell ill and died when she was on Pilgrimage to Rome, and she finished her days in a hermitage. Feast day, October 30. (See *Death of Children*.)

Elizabeth of Hungary (1207-31): Married Landgrave Ludwig in 1221 and bore four children. Ludwig died of plague while on crusade with Emperor Frederick II. Feast day, November 19. (See *Bakers*.)

Elizabeth of Portugal (1271-1336): Married King Denis of Portugal at age twelve; Denis died in 1325, and Elizabeth became a Franciscan tertiary. Feast day, July 4. (See *Victims of Jealousy* and *Victims of Unfaithfulness*.)

Fabiola (d. 399): Married and divorced; remarried, but her second husband died; after his death, dedicated her life to serving the sick and poor; dear friend of St. Jerome, visiting him in Bethlehem and eventually moving to a hospice under authority of St. Paula. Feast day, December 27. (See *Difficult Marriages*.)

Felicity (d. second century): Martyred with seven sons under persecution of Roman Emperor Antoninus; lost her husband early, thereafter dedicating her life to prayer, good works and fasting; instrumental in converting many pagans from false gods. Feast day, July 10. (See *Death of Children*.)

Hedwig (1174-1243): Daughter of Count Berthold IV and Queen of Poland; married Henry I of Silesia at age twelve; many tragedies during the marriage; of seven children, three died at birth and three passed away later; Henry wounded in 1227 and later imprisoned; with many concessions, she bargained for his release; on Henry's death, Hedwig went to a convent at Trebnitz to finish her life in poverty and charity. Feast day, October 16. (See *Silesia*.)

Helen of Sköfde (d. c. 1160): Daughter of a noble family; married young, but her husband died shortly after; spent the rest of her life in service to the poor; later, suffered more heartache when her daughter's husband was killed by his own servants. Feast day, July 31. (See *Falsely Accused*.)

Ida of Herzfeld (d. 825): Great-granddaughter of Charles Martel; grew up in Charlemagne's court; married Lord Egbert but widowed early; founded a church at Hofstadt in Westphalia, moving later to Herzfeld; suffered great illness in her last days; buried in the cemetery of a convent she founded.

Emperor Charlemagne arranged Ida's marriage to Egbert. Their marriage was filled with faith, and they practiced virtue to a heroic degree before Ida was left a widow at an early age. Thereafter she increased her acts of prayer, penance, and charity; she moved to Herzfeld when son Warin became a monk. Feast day, September 4.

Ivetta of Huy (d. 1158-1228): Sometimes called Jutta; married at the tender age of thirteen, she would bear three children before her husband died and left her a widow at age eighteen. Feast day not yet established. (See *Parents of Large Families*.)

Julitta (d. c. 304): Died a martyr's death under the reign of Emperor Diocletian. After her husband died she left Iconium and relocated in Isauria, taking her three-year-old son Cyriacus (Quiricus); authorities discovered her Christian faith and arrested her; her son taken when she was thrown into prison; was to witness Cyriacus's death at the hands of her persecutors, but remained firm in her faith when tortured and beheaded. Feast day, June 16. (See *Victims of Torture*.)

Ludmila (860-921): Married to Borivoj, Duke of Bohemia; converted to Christianity with her husband, who was baptized by St. Methodius in 871; returned to Prague when Borivoj died at age thirty-five, raising her children and grandson St. Wenceslaus as upright and pious Christians. Feast day, September 16. (See *Bohemia; Duchesses*.)

Macrina the Elder (d. c. 340): Married saint who lived seven years in hiding at Pontus during the persecutions of Diocletian; had several famous grandchildren: Basil the Great (329-79), Gregory of Nyssa (330-95), Peter of Sebaste (340-91), and Macrina the Younger (330-79); influenced the learning of those saintly descendants.

Macrina survived her husband, but the exact date of her death is not recorded. Feast celebrated January 14.

Margaret of Scotland (1045-93): Apparently born in Hungary to Prince Edward d'Outremer and Princess Agatha; famed for penance, mortification, and devotion; founded Holy Trinity Church at Dunfermline as Queen of Scotland; served the poor and promoted justice; died At Edinburgh Castle; canonized by Pope Innocent IV in 1250.

Margaret married King Malcolm and bore eight children. Malcolm and a son were killed in 1093, tricked and murdered at Ainwick Castle. Margaret suffered great loneliness without Malcolm, and was bedridden with illness toward the end of her life. She was declared patroness of Scotland by Pope Clement X in 1673. Her feast day is November 16.

Margaret the Barefooted (1325-95): Born in poverty in Italy; married at age fifteen, she bore the ill treatment of her husband patiently and gave food to the needy, even going barefoot to identify with the poor; her husband was embarrassed by her actions but after his death Margaret continued to practice her faith with conviction and determination. Feast day, August 27. (See *Difficult Marriages; Victims of Physical Abuse*.)

Matilda (d. 968): Daughter of Count Dietrich of Westphalia and Reinhild of Denmark; married Henry, son of Duke Otto of Saxony; bore five children: Otto (later emperor), Henry the Quarrelsome, St. Bruno (who married Louis IV of France), and Hedwig (mother of Hugh Capet); her husband dying in 955 as she had prophesied, as a widow she built three convents and a monastery, running the empire until son Otto took over in 962 and then retiring to the convent she had built at Nordhausen. Feast day, March 14. (See *Death of Children, Falsely Accused*, and *Queens*.)

Monica (331-87): Mother of St. Augustine of Hippo, married to a pagan named Patricius, whom she helped convert to the Christian faith in 370; widowed in 370, she prayed for many years for her son to convert as well; this finally happened in 386 when Augustine embraced Christianity at Milan, baptized in 387. Monica lived with Augustine and his son Adeodatus at Cassiciacum, dying at Ostia while awaiting a ship to take them back to Africa. Feast day, August 27. (See *Difficult Marriages* and *Mothers*.)

Pharaïldis (d. 740): Forced to marry a wealthy nobleman, she obeyed her parents and made the best of this prearranged affair; physically and verbally abused by her husband, perhaps out of frustration because of her secret vow of virginity to God; this she kept until she was widowed, and Pharaïldis remained a virgin the rest of her life. Feast day, January 4. (See *Difficult Marriages*.)

WIDOWERS

Edgar, King of England (944-75): Nicknamed "The Peaceable"; succeeded King Eadwig in 959; married Ethelfleda ("The Duck"), who bore him a son, the future St. Edward; second marriage to Ethelfrida, who bore two sons, one of whom died young; rumored to have raped the future St. Wilfreda, resulting in fathering of St. Edith of Wilton; severe acts of penance, including a seven-year delay for his coronation imposed by St. Dunstan; eventually restored secular clergy, promoted ecclesiastical reform, and inspired spiritual renewal among clergy and religious; died after a two year reign as king; buried in a high altar at the Abbey of Glastonbury; miraculous intercessions reported after death.

Edgar's first wife, named The Duck because of her pale complexion, died after childbirth. Then he married the daughter of Ordgar, Earl of Devon. Although he is declared a saint, his feast day is not yet approved.

Thomas More (1478-1535): Married Jane Holt in 1505; they had four children: Margaret, Elizabeth, Cecily, and John. By the time the eldest child was five, Jane died. Thomas then married Alice middleton, seven years older than his thirty-four years. She was considered a good stepmother to the children, whom she and Thomas brought up to be good solid Christians. Feast day, June 22, (See *Lawyers*.)

WOMEN IN LABOR

Anne (first century B.C.): According to the apocryphal *Protevangelium of James*, the barren wife of Joachim. After a visit from an angel, Anne's prayers were answered, for she conceived a child at about the age of forty. The child was Mary, the mother of Jesus. Feast day, July 26. (See *Cabinetmakers*.)

YOUNG BRIDES

Adelaide (d. 999): Bore six children through two marriages: Emma with Lothaire (first husband), and with Otto the Great of Germany: Otto II, Henry, Bruno, and two daughters who became nuns. Feast day, December 16. (See *Empresses*.)

Blaesilla (d. 383): Married at nineteen or twenty to Furius, son of Titiana; widowed after only seven months of marriage. Feast day, January 22. (See *Widows*.)

Catherine of Genoa (1447-1510): Married Julian Adorno at age sixteen and suffered greatly because of his careless and spendthrift ways; they had no children; after Catherine converted Julian, they agreed to live celibate lives and dedicate themselves to the sick and poor. Feast day, September 15. (See *Difficult Marriages*.)

Clotilde (474-575): Wife of Clovis, king of the Salian Franks; married at age eighteen; bore five children, two of whom were killed by younger brother Clotaire. Feast day, June 3. (See *Death of Children*.)

Delphina (d. 1360): Married St. Elzear when both were about sixteen years old. Feast day, September 27. (See *Tertiaries*.)

Dorothea of Montau (1347-94): Married wealthy swordsman Albrecht of Danzig; the couple had nine children before Albrecht's death in 1370. Feast day, October 30. (See *Death of Children, Difficult Marriage*, and *Parents of Large Families*.)

Elizabeth of Hungary (1207-31): Married Ludwig in 1221 at age fourteen; couple had four children. Feast day, November 17. (See *Bakers*.)

Elizabeth of Portugal (1271-1336): Married at age twelve to King Denis of Portugal, thus becoming a queen in early teens. Feast day, July 4. (See *Victims of Jealousy* and *Victims of Unfaithfulness*.)

Hedwig (1174-1243): Daughter of Count Berthold IV, she would become Queen of Poland through marriage to Henry I of Silesia in 1186, when she was twelve years old and he was eighteen; they would have seven children, three of whom died in childbirth; widowed in 1238, she moved to a monastery at Trebnitz to finish her days in prayer and works of charity. Feast day, October 16. (See *Silesia*.)

Ida of Herzfeld (d. 813): Married to Lord Egbert in Emperor

Charlemagne's court; the couple lived a life of great faith and virtue; widowed at a very young age, she devoted the rest of her life to prayer, penance, and charity to the poor. Feast day, September 4. (See *Widows.*)

Margaret the Barefooted (1325-95): Born poor at San Severino, Ancona, Italy, she married at the age of fifteen. Feast day not yet established. (See *Difficult Marriages, Victims of Physical Abuse*, and *Widows*.)

YOUNG GROOMS

Louis IX (1215-70): King of France, married Margaret, daughter of the count of Provence, at the age of nineteen; they would eventually have eleven children (five sons, six daughters); favorite son, young Louis, died at age sixteen. Feast day, August 25. (See *Crusaders*.)

Nicholas of Myra (see *Russia* under "Countries and Nations").

YOUTH

Aloysius Gonzaga (1568-910): Born to a noble family in Lombardy; chose religious life during youth; educated in Florence; joined the court of the Duke of Mantua; suffered a failed kidney, which weakened him for life; great practice of penance and prayer; taught catechism to the poor; joined the Jesuits in 1585 at Rome; worked in a hospital there after plague hit the city; died of plague himself on June 21 while serving the sick; canonized in 1726 by Pope Benedict XIII.

Aloysius taught catechism to the poor children of Castiglione, a model of pious living and virtue, especially influential with youth, for he himself was a young man. Aloysius was declared protector of young students by Pope Benedict XIII and patron of Catholic youth by Pope Pius XI. Feast day, June 21.

Gabriel of the Sorrowful Mother (1838-62): Ideal role model for well-behaved, pious young people, he was eleventh in a family of thirteen children. Although not endowed with any unusual mystical favors as a child, Gabriel was even-tempered and considerate. He was a good student and sociable with all. After entrance into a religious order, Gabriel continued to do average everyday things with extraordinary effort. His philosophy was centered on doing one's daily duty — however small or mundane — cheerfully and to the best of one's ability because that showed perfect obedience to God's will. Feast day, February 27. (See *Clerics*.)

John Berchmans (d. 1621): Famous for the prophetic words he once uttered about himself: "If I do not become a saint when I am young, I shall never become one." True to his word, he was to die at the tender age of twenty-two, immediately recognized as a saint by all his Jesuit peers. In fact, he is known today as one of the "three notable young saints" of the Jesuit order, the others being St. Aloysius Gonzaga (1568-91) and St. Stanislaus Kostka (1550-68). Feast day, November 26. (See *Altar Boys*.)

IV. Our Lady as Patron Saint

The Blessed Virgin Mary is perhaps the most popular patron saint (or patroness) in the history of the Church. She is the object of invocation for many different needs or conditions: grave sickness or illness; protection from evil; mediation in prayer between the faithful and Jesus Christ; conversions and reconciliations; etc. She is also the object of countless visions and apparitions which span the centuries throughout the world.

In most cases, these supernatural appearances occur in order to teach or inspire the faithful, to protect them from danger, to announce a future providential plan, or to comfort and reassure. Only rarely does Mary appear without some verbal messages or lessons (Our Lady's appearance in Knock, Ireland in 1879 was an exception). Even in that case, however, the Virgin gave silent messages within the context of further images related to the Book of Revelation: Jesus as the Lamb of God, John the Evangelist, Joseph, a cross, an altar, and so on.

Clearly, Our Lady does not appear exclusively to prove the reality of her heavenly existence. Rather, she comes to point the way to her Son in the forms of images, messages, prophecies, warnings, and/or truths which are revealed in the Gospel.

One of the ways in which faithful Catholics pay homage to Mary is through the numerous shrines dedicated to her throughout the world. For those who may be unfamiliar with these sites of devotion, a shrine is a particular sacred place which is built by and for the faithful in order that they may venerate or pray to the particular saint of their devotion. A shrine is sacred because it usually identifies the place of a saint's tomb, relics, statue, image, apparition, or some other memorable experience which took place in that location.

Although proper Church authorities must investigate the messages, favors, or reported apparitions surrounding each shrine, nevertheless it is not the hierarchical Church which establishes a shrine in the first place; rather, it is formed out of the devotions and spontaneous acclamations of the faithful who witness to something extraordinary or inspiring concerning the saint and the subsequent site in question.

After the newness or emotional fervor surrounding a site dies down, if the shrine is authentic there will develop over the course of time a powerful tradition among the faithful to visit the sacred site and preserve its memory. It is usually only after many years of continued devotion by the faithful and subsequent investigations by the Church that a shrine will enter the Church annals as a sacred, authentic site.

The number of Marian shrines that span the globe are too numerous to include in this work. Indeed, there are literally hundreds of such places throughout the world. Here you will find the more popular shrines and types of devotion practiced in honor of the Blessed Virgin. Some of these are not yet approved or thoroughly investigated by the Church, but they are at least given local approval or show favorable signs from various Church authorities. Therefore, I have included these with the traditional ones for the sake of expanding our understanding and information concerning Marian devotional practices today.

Devotions, Images, Shrines: Countries and Places

BASILICA OF ST. MARY MAJOR: Located in Rome on the Esquiline Hill, this basilica was built in 366. After the Council of Ephesus (431) proclaimed Mary as the Mother of God, Pope Sixtus III dedicated this basilica to Mary in 435. It is the third of the Roman patriarchal basilicas and the oldest one in Western Christendom built in honor of Mary.

THE HOLY MOUNTAIN OF OUR LADY: Also known as Mount Athos, a site in Greece containing three sacred shrines of the Blessed Virgin: Our Lady of Iviron (at Iviron), the Three-Handed Virgin (at Khilandar), and the Consoling Virgin (at Vatopedi).

IMMACULATE HEART OF MARY (see *Sacred Heart of Mary*).

MADONNA OF SAINT LUKE: Also known as Our Lady of Rome, this image of Mary was found in the chapel of the Church of St. Mary Major in Bologna. An ancient tradition claims that St. Luke himself painted this image of Mary.

MARY, QUEEN OF AFRICA: Crowned in 1954, this Marian statue is located in Koboho, Uganda. A cross and a crescent form a part of the image, which is venerated by Christians and Muslims alike.

NOTRE DAME CATHEDRAL OF PARIS: Built between 1163-1320, a beautiful cathedral dedicated to the Blessed Virgin Mary. The building has five aisles and is filled with sculptured works of the Madonna.

NOTRE DAME DE CHARTRES: A magnificent cathedral built in the twelfth and thirteenth centuries. An amazing display of architecture, stained glass windows, and Gothic design.

OUR LADY HELP OF CHRISTIANS: The devotional title of Mary honored in Australia and New Zealand. Mary has long been recognized for her role as a powerful intercessor before her Son, Jesus Christ. Because she is Mother of God and Mother of the Church (Pope Paul VI, November 21, 1964), Mary is entitled to intercede for the needs of the faithful and to protect them from all spiritual harm or danger.

OUR LADY IN AMERICA: See item at the end of this unit.

OUR LADY MEDIATRIX OF ALL GRACE: A title and privilege of the Blessed Virgin which many implore the world over, seeking her aid and protection in times of need. Pope Pius IX once declared in his bull defining the Immaculate Conception (1854) that "Mary intercedes with her Son, in all the power of her maternal prayer." Later, Pope Paul VI proclaimed in *Marialis Cultus* that Mary "has not abandoned her mission of intercession and salvation" for the children of God. The ancient Marian prayer *Sub tuum* of the third-century Church proclaimed the following: "We fly to your patronage, O holy Mother of God; despise not our petitions in our necessities, but deliver us always from all dangers, O glorious and blessed Virgin." Although Jesus remains our sole Mediator before the Father, Mary is likewise our mediator (mediatrix) to her Son. Indeed, the Second Vatican Council proclaimed Mary to be Advocate, Auxiliary, Adjutrix, and Mediatrix (*Lumen Gentium*, no. 62). Earlier, Pope Leo XIII in his encyclical *Octobri mense* (September 22, 1891) made this statement: "It may be affirmed with . . . truth and precision that, by the will of God, absolutely no part of that immense treasure of every grace which the Lord amasses . . . is bestowed on us except through Mary." The Office and Mass of Mary Mediatrix of All Graces was formed by Cardinal D.J. Mercier and approved by Pope Benedict XV in 1921.

OUR LADY OF AFRICA: A bronze, dark-colored statue representing the Immaculate Conception. It was first brought from France in 1840 and later transferred to a basilica in Algeria (1876). This statue was crowned by

Cardinal Lavigerie, founder of the White Fathers. Because of his love for the Blessed Virgin, Cardinal Lavigerie put his entire congregation under the protective mantle of Our Lady of Africa.

OUR LADY OF ALTÖTTING: A shrine located at Altötting, Bavaria, West Germany, some sixty miles east of Munich. The chapel of this black Madonna was originally part of the imperial palace in 877. The shrine was built in 1228 because of a local story reporting that a young child had drowned in a nearby river but was resurrected by the Virgin's intercession some three days after the drowning. Today, Our Lady of Altötting remains the Bavarian national shrine, visited annually by hundreds of thousands of pilgrims. The image is adorned with precious jewels and stones, and the Madonna herself is made of obsidian. Outside the shrine, dozens of wooden crucifixes are found, as pilgrims continue to make the stations of the cross around Our Lady of Altötting. Dozens of cures or protective favors have been claimed by the faithful because of Our Lady's intercession. Paintings representing these cures date back to the sixteenth century and are placed around the outside of the shrine.

OUR LADY OF BANDEL: A shrine founded by the Portuguese in 1596, Our Lady of Bandel is located in the city of Begal. The shrine houses a statue of Our Lady of Safe Travel.

OUR LADY OF BANDRA: A national shrine of India founded in 1640. Inside the shrine is a statue of Our Lady of the Mount, crowned in 1954.

OUR LADY OF BANNEUX: In 1933, the Blessed Virgin appeared to a young child at Banneux, Belgium, about fifteen miles from Liège. Mariette Beco, the visionary, received a total of eight apparitions between January 15 and March 2. The local bishop approved of these supernatural happenings from the beginning, but official approval came in 1949. The visions (which occurred each time about 7:00 P.M.) stressed that she was the "Virgin of the Poor" (January 19). During the apparitions, a miraculous spring came out of the ground and many healings were reported there. The Madonna requested more prayer from the people, stressing that she had come to comfort the sick and the poor. During one vision (March 2), the Blessed Virgin called herself the "Mother of the Savior, Mother of God." A chapel was built at the site to honor Our Lady's request. The messages were for all the people of the world, not just for Mariette or the local parish community.

OUR LADY OF BEAURAING: Thirty-three supernatural apparitions of the Blessed Virgin occurred between November 29, 1932 and January 3, 1933. The visionaries were five schoolchildren from two different families. The Blessed Virgin appeared by the road in a place near Beauraing, Belgium, referred to by the seers as "the Garden." Actually, this garden of the apparitions was located on the school playground. In these visions, Mary called herself "The Immaculate Virgin" (January 21, 1932) and the "Mother of God, Queen of Heaven" (January 3, 1933). Her messages concerned prayer, following the Gospel, the faith life, and the importance of the family. As with Banneux, Our Lady asked for a chapel to be built on the site of the apparitions (December 17, 1932), and she encouraged pilgrims to come from everywhere. She also indicated that she would help to convert sinners. The local bishop permitted a limited veneration in 1942 but gave his full approval for the authentication of this site in 1949. Since these apparitions occurred, two authenticated healings have taken place. Over 200,000 pilgrims visit the shrine every year.

OUR LADY OF COPACABAÑA: A Bolivian shrine that houses a Marian statue built by Indian fishermen in thanksgiving for Mary's protection. It is made of plaster and wood. Originally placed in a chapel near Lake Titicaca in northern Bolivia, it was later moved to a large church and was crowned in 1925.

OUR LADY OF CZESTOCHOWA: A miraculous icon brought to Czestochowa, Poland, by Prince Ladislaus Opolczyk for the monks of St. Paul in 1384. It was probably made between the fifth and eighth centuries. After it suffered damage through raiders in 1430, King Ladislas Jagiello had the icon restored by Austrian artists. Also known as the "Madonna of Czestochowa," the image shows Mary pointing her right hand to the Child Jesus held in her left arm. Many kings and high-ranking officials came and paid tribute to the Madonna. Miracles surrounding this icon began in 1402, and later the people identified this Marian image as the "Healer of the Sick, Mother of Mercy, and Queen of Poland." By 1957, over 1,500 healings were on record. The first public coronation of the icon occurred in 1717 with Pope Clement XI. By 1979, over two million pilgrims had visited Our Lady of Czestochowa. Today, over 10,000 altars around the world have duplicate images of this famous and miraculous icon.

OUR LADY OF EUROPE: This is the Marian title of devotion in Gibraltar. The title was formally recognized on May 31, 1979. Although a general statement about the love of the people of Gibraltar for Mary, it symbolizes all the characteristics and virtues of the Blessed Virgin which her people admire and respect.

OUR LADY OF FÁTIMA: Marian apparitions which occurred in 1917 at Fátima in the Diocese of Leiria, Portugal. In the summer of 1916, the Angel of Portugal's appearance preceded the Marian visitations to three young children of the village: Lucia dos Santos (age ten) and her two cousins, Francisco (age nine) and Jacinta Marto (age seven). The angel taught them a prayer to the Blessed Trinity. On Sunday, May 13, 1917, Our Lady appeared to all the children for the first time as they were resting from gathering their sheep at the Cova da Iria. Mary appeared in a flash of light, asking for prayer and the conversion of sinners to end World War I. She also told them she would reappear every month on the 13th. The apparitions continued every month through October 13, when the Virgin revealed herself as "Our Lady of the Rosary." During that last apparition, 30,000 people saw the sun spin, pulsate, and dance in the sky. Many claimed that it appeared to be falling toward the earth. Our Lady had predicted this sign as early as the first apparition (May 13). The Bishop of Leiria gave formal approval to the apparitions and messages on October 13, 1930, after years of intense investigations. He also approved pilgrimages to the site. Mary's messages at Fátima concerned the following statements: the need for more prayer, penance, conversion, fasting, and reconciliation; the need to pray the rosary more often; predictions and warnings about future wars (such as World War II) if her requests went unheeded; and the desire for Russia and then the world to be consecrated to her Immaculate Heart (these were first done by Pope Pius XII on October 31, 1942). A secret message was also given to the children, and they experienced a vision of heaven, hell, and purgatory. The secret of Fátima has never been revealed, although it is reported that Lucia (the only surviving seer) gave the message to Pope John XXIII. It is also claimed that Pope Paul VI and perhaps Pope John Paul II read this message as well. Many feel that it deals with a grave issue such as a third world war, Armageddon, or the Great Tribulation, and the Second Coming of Christ. Of course, these are mere conjectures without solid justification at this time. Pope John Paul II visited Fátima on May 13, 1982 to celebrate the sixty-fifth anniversary of Our Lady's first appearance. He attributed the Blessed Virgin's intercession and protection in saving his life after an attempted assassination the year before. John Paul also reconsecrated the world to Mary's Immaculate Heart.

OUR LADY OF GRACE (see *Our Lady of High Grace*).

OUR LADY OF GUADALUPE: One of the first of the "Marian-Age" apparitions occurred to a Mexican-Indian peasant named Juan Diego in 1531. The location was Tepeyac. One day while Juan was walking through the country on his way to a catechetical class, Our Lady appeared to him on the top of a hill. It was a significant time, for in 1521 the Spaniards had conquered Mexico and converted thousands to Christianity. At the site, Mary called herself the "Mother of the true God who gives life." She also requested that a shrine be built upon the site in honor of her appearance. Juan reported his vision to Bishop Juan de Zumárraga, who told him to ask for a sign from the Lady to confirm the authenticity of the apparition. The next time Juan Diego visited the hill, Mary appeared again. She left him a sign in response to the bishop's request: blooming roses blanketing the top of the hill in the middle of winter. Juan picked some of the roses and carried them in his *tilma* (cloak). When he appeared to the bishop, upon opening his cloak, the roses fell out and an image of Our Lady appeared in their place on the garment. This miraculous imprint still exists as the same clear image that was formed back in 1531. In 1979, Pope John Paul II made a pilgrimage to the Cathedral in Mexico City to honor Our Lady of Guadalupe. There he called Mary the "Star of Evangelization." Millions of pilgrims have visited the sacred shrine since the appearance of Our Lady.

OUR LADY OF GUADALUPE OF ESTREMADURA: A statue given to St. Leander of Seville by St. Gregory the Great. Although the more famous Lady of Guadalupe is known from the 1531 story of Juan Diego in Mexico City, this honorary title actually dates back to the eighth century.

OUR LADY OF HIGH GRACE: A devotional title given to Mary and particularly celebrated in the Dominican Republic. Mary is depicted in the Gospels by the Archangel Gabriel as being "full of grace" (Lk 1:28). Mary herself exclaimed that all generations would call her blessed and that God had done mighty things for her (Lk 1:48-49). Indeed, the deeply loved "Hail Mary" begins, "Hail Mary, full of grace, the Lord is with you." The last line implores Mary to "pray for us sinners now and at the hour of our death." Clearly, Mary's role as *Theotokos* (Mother of God or God-bearer) and the fact that she brought forth the Source of all our Grace — Jesus Christ — gives her the unique privilege of being a vehicle or aqueduct of that same grace to the faithful through her Son's hands.

OUR LADY OF HUNGARY: Also known as the "Great Lady of Hungary," Mary is invoked under this title in remembrance of King

Stephen (d. 1038), who once built a church at Szekesfehervar in honor of the Mother of God. Many kings of Hungary were crowned and buried at Szekesfehervar, and Stephen made it his permanent home.

OUR LADY OF JAPAN: Built in 1897, this Nagasaki shrine commemorates the seventeenth-century Japanese martyrs. The shrine was placed in a cathedral which was miraculously preserved through the atomic blasts of 1945 (only one chapel there was destroyed).

OUR LADY OF KEVELAER: A shrine containing a picture of Our Lady of Consolation at Luxembourg. Built near the Lower Rhine in Germany, it was relocated to Kevelaer by a soldier in 1642. Since that time, thousands have visited the popular shrine.

OUR LADY OF KNOCK: In 1879, the Blessed Virgin appeared to sixteen persons by the side of the church in Knock (Count Mayo), Ireland. The vision lasted between 7:30 and 9:30 P.M. on August 21. Mary appeared as a moving, lifelike light together with images of St. John the Evangelist, St. Joseph, a lamb on an altar, and a cross. She appeared with a crown on her head. This is one of the few Marian apparitions where no words or messages were spoken. Many feel that Our Lady appeared to comfort the people of County Mayo, the poorest district in all of Ireland. Others have interpreted the images to mean many things: St. John the Evangelist stresses the truth and power of the Gospel; St. Joseph stands for charity; the image of the cross represents sacrifice; the lamb on the altar recalls the holy Mass and the crucifixion and resurrection of our Lord. Thousands of cures have been reported from those who have visited the shrine. Pope John Paul II paid a visit to Our Lady of Knock on September 30, 1979 — 100 years after the apparition occurred. Today, the original church in Knock has been designated a basilica by the Holy Father. He gave a rose of gold to the new shrine.

OUR LADY OF LA SALETTE: On September 19, 1846, the Blessed Virgin appeared to Maximin Giraud (age eleven) and Melanie Calvat (age fourteen) while the two children were grazing sheep on a hillside near La Salette, France. Mary appeared with a crucifix hung from her neck, and she was crying. Bishop Bruillard of Grenoble declared the apparitions authentic. Soon, pilgrims flocked to La Salette from all over. The messages of Our Lady concerned trust in Jesus, the necessity of daily prayer, participation in the Eucharist, conversion, the signs of the times, and reconciliation with God.

OUR LADY OF LA VANG: The most famous shrine in Vietnam. According to reports, the alleged vision of the Blessed Virgin occurred at Hué in 1800. Since then, thousands of faithful pilgrims have visited this sacred site from all over the country.

OUR LADY OF LIMERICK: Crowned in 1954, this Marian statue was originally made in Flanders in 1622. It depicts the Madonna with Child. At a later date, the image was given to the care of the Rosary Confraternity of Limerick, Ireland. In 1816, it was placed in the Dominican church at Limerick and has remained there ever since.

OUR LADY OF LORETO: According to tradition, the Holy House of Nazareth (where Mary was born, grew up, and where she conceived Jesus) was miraculously transported to this site in Loreto, Italy, in 1291. This occurred by either land or sea after a temporary stop in Tersato in Dalmatia in 1291 and at Recanati in 1294. Archeological investigations of the small house in Loreto reveal that the stones match those of other houses unearthed in Nazareth from the first century. However, many believe that there is nothing miraculous about the house at all. There is some evidence that the stones were transported from Nazareth by military personnel during the times of the crusades to the Holy Land. The story is that zealous Christians wanted to protect the alleged Holy House from Muslims and all hostile invaders. At any rate, many Popes have visited this holy shrine through the centuries, including John XXIII (October 4, 1962) and John Paul II (September 8, 1979). The site was made into a basilica by the order of Pope Benedict XIII in 1728.

OUR LADY OF LOURDES: In 1858, the Blessed Virgin appeared in Lourdes (population 5,000) near the river Pau in the Pyrenees of France. The visionary was St. Bernadette Soubirous, a fourteen-year-old peasant girl from the country. One day Bernadette was looking for deadwood with two other friends. After her companions crossed a bridge and Bernadette remained behind, Our Lady appeared at the Grotto of Massabielle. Bernadette described her as a "lady in white" who smiled at her and prayed the rosary. There were eighteen apparitions between February 14 and March 25. She revealed herself as the "Immaculate Conception" (March 25), a significant title, for in 1954 Pope Pius XII defined the Immaculate Conception of Mary in dogmatic form; thus, the revelation to Bernadette was an affirmation of the dogma pronounced only four years earlier. The Blessed Virgin's messages also included a request for more prayer, penance, the conversion of sinners, and attendance at Mass. She asked for a chapel to be built upon the site of her appearance, a request that was soon to be granted. A miraculous spring came forth from the place of the site, and hundreds of healings have been reported ever since. An image of Our Lady was crowned in 1876, and in 1889 the Church of the Rosary was opened. Lourdes is one of the most popular Catholic shrines, visited by more than four million people each year.

OUR LADY OF LUJAN: A large basilica was built around this shrine in Argentina in 1904. It had been transported from Buenos Aires in 1630, a twenty-two-inch terra-cotta statue of the Immaculate Conception. Apparently, its arrival in Lujan is a mystery that no one has explained. Our Lady of Lujan is also fervently honored in Uruguay and Paraguay.

OUR LADY OF MADHU: This Marian shrine in Sri Lanka dates back to the seventeenth century. It is a center of devotion for both Christians and non-Christians.

OUR LADY OF MARIAZELL: This Austrian shrine dates back to the tenth century. Here at Mariazell, a statue of the Blessed Virgin was enshrined by the Benedictine Monastery in 1157.

OUR LADY OF THE MILK AND HAPPY DELIVERY: A shrine in St. Augustine, Florida. Originally built in the seventeenth century, it was rebuilt in 1915. Pregnant women have shown particular devotion to this shrine, as many favors have been granted.

OUR LADY OF MONTSERRAT: A ninth-century statue representing the Black Madonna, this image is venerated in Montserrat, Barcelona, Spain. It was originally found by local shepherds. Today the shrine is located at the Benedictine Abbey.

OUR LADY OF MOUNT CARMEL: The Order of Our Lady of Mount Carmel was founded in Palestine by St. Berthold in 1195. The Order claims to be linked with the hermits of the area who date back to the time of the prophet Elijah. As early as the fifth century, the Blessed Virgin was honored in the area. By the twelfth century, it was a crucial site of Marian devotion. The Brothers of the Blessed Virgin Mary of Carmel (the Brother Hermits) declared Mary their protectress. They had been in the area since at least 1220, when a church was built there in her honor. Carmel is the spiritual location of all members who choose to follow the example of Mary in their particular religious vocation.

OUR LADY OF MOUNT CARMEL AT AYLESFORD: In 1241, a Carmelite friary was established at Aylesford, England. At the same time, a Marian statue was placed there for devotion. Although many favors were granted through the Blessed Virgin's intercession, the friary was dissolved in 1538. In 1949, it was reestablished. Our Lady Guardian of the Carmelites is the statue dedicated to the Madonna. The friary also houses the relics of St. Simon Stock.

OUR LADY OF NAZARETH: Great devotion to this statue grew in the city of Belem, Brazil, after it was found by two hunters under a palm tree in the northern part of the country.

OUR LADY OF PEACE: The devotional title given to the Blessed Virgin in El Salvador. It was formally proclaimed on October 10, 1966. The Blessed Virgin has often been implored for peace and reconciliation among men and with God. Our Lady is known as the Queen of Peace in many parts of the world. The tradition stems back to the fourth century as an indication of her preeminence and power. In the Liturgy of the Hours, the title "Hail Holy Queen, Queen of Heaven" is used. In our Litany of the Blessed Virgin, Mary is invoked as "Queen of Peace." Recently, the Blessed Virgin has been declared "Queen of Peace" in the Marian apparitions reported at Medjugorje, Yugoslavia (1981-present). Many of the faithful implore Mary for peace in the world in order to avert war and catastrophe.

OUR LADY OF PERPETUAL HELP: Located in Rome, this shrine was founded at the Church of St. Alphonsus Liguori (Doctor of the Church). At this site is one of the most famous paintings in the history of the Church, a fourteenth-century icon made on walnut wood, perhaps originating on Crete.

OUR LADY OF POMPEII: A lawyer from Brindisi, Italy, Bartolo Longo moved to Pompeii in 1872 to work for the Countess Marianna Farnaro di Fusco. A devout Catholic, Bartolo sought to spread devotion of the rosary among the people. He received a picture of the Blessed Virgin from Sister M. Concetta di Litala at the Monastery of the Rosary at Porta Medina. Thereafter, he recited his rosary in front of that picture. It depicted Our Lady of the Rosary, St. Dominic, and St. Catherine of Siena. In 1875, Bartolo placed this picture in a small chapel but later received permission from the Bishop of Nola to build a new church in honor of Mary. Miracles were reported from visitors thereafter. Soon Bartolo formed a confraternity in honor of Our Lady. He also formed many new organizations around

Pompeii: orphanages, the Sons of Prisoners, the Daughters of Prisoners, the Daughters of the Holy Rosary, and Dominican tertiaries. The devotional title of Our Lady was to be known under the name of Queen of Victories. The picture went through several restorations: in 1875, 1879, and 1965. After it stayed some time in Rome, Pope Paul VI ordered the picture back to its place in Pompeii. Pope John Paul II visited the shrine in 1979, and Bartolo Longo was beatified by the same Holy Father in 1980 as "the man of the Madonna" and "the Apostle of the Rosary."

OUR LADY OF PONTMAIN: On January 17, 1870, two children (Eugene and Joseph Barbarette) claimed to have experienced an apparition of the Virgin Mary at 6:00 P.M. over their family barn in France. The Franco-Prussian War (1871) was about to bring sorrow and death upon thousands of French citizens. The lady appeared in a dark-blue robe and was encircled with stars. Both the father and mother saw nothing upon visiting the site and accused their children of lying or dreaming. Later on, the boys saw Mary again, but nobody else did. The Sisters of their school came to investigate the site, but nothing was seen. However, two other children with the Sisters saw the same image as Eugene and Joseph. Believing the children, local pastor Father Guerin led a large group of people at the site in the Rosary; they also sang the Magnificat. The messages to Eugene and Joseph centered on the need for more prayer and trust in God. The Virgin, once smiling, appeared sad at the state of the world. The visions and messages lasted that night for two hours.

OUR LADY OF RANSOM: The Blessed Virgin Mary appeared in Spain on August 10, 1218, to St. Peter Nolasco. Mary's appearance and subsequent blessing resulted in the foundation of the Order for the Redemption of Captives. She is called Our Lady of Ransom because of her protection from foreign invaders in Spain and her intercession against religious error through the country. England also invokes Our Lady of Ransom against religious heresies in her country. Many today ask Our Lady of Ransom to "free" us from the bondage of sin. The feast was granted in Spain in 1680 and was extended throughout the world in 1696.

OUR LADY OF SAFE TRAVEL: This statue reportedly was transported from Mexico to Manila, Philippines, in 1626. After being moved to several different locations, it was brought back to Manila and crowned in 1929. Later, it was returned to Antipolo, where it is usually kept.

OUR LADY OF SHONGWENI: This is a statue of Mary under the title of Mary Mediatrix of All Grace. It is located upon a hill near Durban in South Africa.

OUR LADY OF SORROWS: A devotion to Mary which focuses upon her trials, sorrows, and tribulations concerning the suffering and death of her Son and the sinful nature of all of God's children. This particular devotion was first established with Blessed Henry Suso (1295-1366). With the *Five Joys of Mary* already a practiced Catholic devotion, Henry included the *Five Sorrows of Mary* to emphasize the sad and tearful nature of the Madonna.

Later on, the Five Joys and Sorrows were extended to Seven Joys and Sorrows of Mary. This increase reflected the seven Hours of the daily Office and the seven joys of Mary. The sorrows traditionally represented include meditation upon the following scenes: 1) Jesus being arrested and struck; 2) Jesus being led to Pilate for condemnation; 3) Jesus' condemnation before Pilate and the Jewish people; 4) Jesus being nailed to the Cross; 5) Jesus dying upon the Cross and giving up His spirit; 6) Jesus being taken down from the Cross; and 7) Jesus' wrapping and burial in the tomb. Other sorrows were often included for additional meditations: the prophecy of Simeon, the massacre of the innocents, the flight to Egypt, Jesus being lost in Jerusalem, etc. Starting in 1482, a parish priest from Flanders, Fr. John de Coudenberghe, preached a devotion to the Seven Sorrows of Mary which has remained fixed since that time: 1) the prophecy of Simeon (Lk 2:34-35); 2) the flight into Egypt (Mt 2:13-21); 3) the loss of Jesus for three days (Lk 2:41-50); 4) the ascent to Calvary (Jn 19:17); 5) the crucifixion and death of Jesus (Jn 19:18-30); 6) Jesus taken down from the cross (Jn 19:39-40); and 7) Jesus being laid in the tomb (Jn 19:40-42). This fixed devotion brought about the *Confraternity of Our Lady of Sorrows*, which was later approved by the Pope.

OUR LADY OF TEARS: A statue of the Blessed Virgin in Syracuse, Sicily, which has cried human tears many times (first on August 29 and September 1, 1953). The image depicts the Immaculate Heart of Mary. The first reported incident (witnessed by 188 people) occurred at the home of Angelo Jannuso and Antonina Giusto (11 Garden Street in Syracuse) in the picture above their bed. The image of the weeping Madonna was photographed as well. Soon after, samples of the tears were taken and examined by medical authorities. They concluded that the fluid was indeed that of human tears. Our Lady of Tears (or the Weeping Madonna of Sicily) receives at least one million pilgrims every year.

OUR LADY OF THE ASSUMPTION: A title and role of Mary especially honored in the countries of India and Paraguay. In 1950, Pope Pius XII declared as dogma that Mary was spared a physical death and taken up to heaven body and soul immediately at the end of her earthly life. This belief centers on the fact that Mary was immaculately conceived and lived a life free from all sin. If this is the case, then a sinless body should not be subjected to the sting of physical death and corruption. The dogma of the Assumption is only fitting: the Mother of God, like her Son, was preserved from sin her entire life and should be exempt from normal human corruption of body and soul. Devotion to Our Lady of the Assumption gives hope for all believers that one day we too will overcome death, be created anew, and live an eternal life with God in heaven. Then there will be no more sorrow, tears, suffering, or corruption, but only everlasting happiness and peace in the Lord.

OUR LADY OF THE CAPE: A place of devotion to the Blessed Virgin Mary since 1879 at the Canadian parish of St. Mary Magdalen. That year, the French priests Frs. Desilets and Duguay left their native home for the new world of Quebec, Canada. They were particularly fond of spreading devotion to the Rosary. When they decided to enlarge their parish church on the St. Lawrence River, the necessary stones for its foundation were located on the other side. Unable to move the stones to their desired location because the river (over a mile wide) was not frozen, they needed ice to cross in order to get the stones to their destination. Turning to Mary, the two priests promised that they would not destroy the old church of the parish but would dedicate it to Our Lady if she would help. Their prayers were answered, for an ice bridge across the St. Lawrence was soon formed — long enough for the people of the parish to transport the stones across the frozen river to the other side. Subsequently, they named the miraculous bridge the "Bridge of Rosaries." Other miracles took place. Three witness (Fr. Desilets, Fr. Frederick, O.F.M., and a handicapped man) saw the new statue of Mary with an image of the Miraculous Medal move, including her eyes. Today, a million people visit the shrine of Our Lady of the Cape. A large basilica has been built there to honor the Virgin (1964).

OUR LADY OF THE HERMITS: A Marian statue located in a well-known Benedictine Monastery in Switzerland. It is claimed that this shrine was very dear to St. Meinrad (d. ninth century).

OUR LADY OF THE IMMACULATE CONCEPTION: An honorary title of Our Lady used the world over, it invokes the Blessed

Virgin as the one chosen by God to be born free of all sin (the only human ever to be granted this grace besides Jesus Christ Himself). Pope Pius IX, in 1854, proclaimed the dogma of the Immaculate Conception. Through this dogma the Church expresses the belief that Mary was not only conceived without Original Sin — she was also preserved from all sin throughout her earthly life. This belief resulted in the dogma of the Assumption (Pope Pius XII, 1950), whereby the Church states that the Blessed Virgin was spared bodily death by being immediately "assumed" or taken up into heaven at the end of her earthly life. We honor this state of Our Lady's humanity — freedom from sin — in order to invoke her protection and intercession concerning our own efforts to overcome our struggles with imperfections and sin.

OUR LADY OF THE MIRACULOUS MEDAL: In 1830, the Blessed Virgin appeared to St. Catherine Labouré (age twenty-four) in the chapel of the motherhouse of the Daughters of Charity in Paris, France. The place is often known as the "Rue de Bac" because Bac is the street name of the site. The Blessed Virgin appeared to Catherine on July 18-19 and November 27. She appeared hovering over a globe of the world, with arms extended and rays of light beaming from her hands. Catherine saw a message in the vision which read, "Mary conceived without sin, pray for us who have recourse to you." This concept of Mary conceived without sin influenced the Church's dogma of the Immaculate Conception, pronounced by Pope Pius IX in 1854. Another image represented the letter "M" on top of a cross which was placed over the hearts of Jesus and Mary. Our Lady then told Catherine, "Have a medal struck on this model." Millions of medals have since been made, bringing hundreds of blessings and graces to the faithful. The sign of the Miraculous Medal reveals a trust in providence and protection under the mantle of Mary and her Son, Jesus Christ.

OUR LADY OF THE PILLAR OF SARAGOSSA: Legend claims that this statue in Zaragoza, Spain, dates back to the time of the Blessed Virgin herself. Supposedly, Mary placed the statue in a shrine at the request of St. James the Apostle.

OUR LADY OF THE ROSARY: Practiced the world over, the prayer of the Rosary is a means of devotion to both Mary and her Son. The Rosary began to take shape in twelfth-century devotions to the *five joys* of Mary: the Annunciation, the Nativity, the Resurrection, the Ascension, and the Assumption. Afterwards, the five joys were extended to the *seven delights*. This in turn became a part of the expanded *fifteen joys* in response to the fifteen decades of the Psalter (150 psalms=150 Hail Marys). Franciscans and Servites were the first religious groups to spread devotion to the *five sorrows* of Our Lady in the thirteenth-fourteenth centuries. As Marian spirituality developed, the five sorrows became *seven sorrows*. It wasn't until the fifteenth century that a Dominican named St. Alban added ". . . and blessed is the fruit of your womb, Jesus Christ, whom at the announcement of the angel you conceived by the Holy Spirit," etc., to the end of the 150 Hail Marys of the Rosary. In 1464, the Dominican Blessed Alan of Roche began spreading devotion to the Rosary, adding the "new Psalter of the Virgin." It was Alan who separated the Rosary into the three categories of mysteries that we are familiar with today: the joyful (Incarnation), the sorrowful (Passion), and the glorious (Resurrection). Soon thereafter, confraternities of the Rosary began to spread throughout the world (the first in 1475 by the Dominicans at Cologne). Pope Paul VI has called the Rosary a "compendium of the entire Gospel."

OUR LADY OF THE SNOW: A feast celebrating the dedication of the third patriarchal basilica within the walls of Rome. The basilica was founded by Pope Liberius in the fourth century, and it was restored and consecrated to the Virgin Mary by Pope Sixtus III (435). This basilica is now known as St. Mary Major, the first great church in Rome dedicated to Our Lady. A popular tradition claims that after an invocation of the Blessed Virgin a miraculous snowfall occurred at this basilica in the middle of summer. At time of Pope Liberius, it is reported that Mary appeared to a patrician named John, who financed and planned the building of the basilica because Mary requested it. Many claim that this story is mere legend.

OUR LADY OF THE TURUMBA: This statue of Our Lady was found in the eighteenth century in water near Pakil on the Laguna de Baie, Philippines. The word "Turumba" is also the name of a Marian song sung by the people in the church where her statue now rests.

OUR LADY OF VICTORY: In 1692, Diego Vargas built a shrine in honor of Our Lady for his victory in Santa Fe, New Mexico. Also known as *La Conquistadora*.

OUR LADY OF WALSINGHAM: A shrine dedicated to the Annunciation. It was founded in the twelfth century at Walsingham, England, and built to imitate the Holy House of Nazareth. It was destroyed in 1738, but a new site was built close by in 1934. A statue of Mary with Jesus on her knees was crowned in 1954.

OUR LADY WHO APPEARED: In 1719, a headless wooden statue was found by fisherman in a river in Brazil. A head was later made and placed on it. The statue eventually made it to the local village church, where it was kept and honored. Shortly thereafter, this statue was moved to a church in nearby Sao Paulo. Many favors were reported through this image of the Madonna. In 1929, it was given the title Our Lady Who Appeared. Since then, the Blessed Virgin under this title has been the patroness of Brazil.

SACRED HEART OF MARY: The Sacred Heart of Mary has long been an object of devotion throughout the world. It is a particularly favored devotion of the Philippines. The connection with Mary's Sacred Heart is really a reflection of her Immaculate Heart, whereby the faithful look to her physical heart as a sign and symbol of her compassion and sinlessness. The first formal approval of this devotion occurred in 1805, when Pope Pius VII gave permission for the feast of the Pure Heart of Mary. Devotion to the Immaculate Heart became a worldwide phenomenon with the messages and apparitions of Our Lady at Fátima, 1917. These appearances were later approved by the Holy See. On October 31, 1942, Pope Pius XII consecrated the entire world to Mary's Immaculate Heart. Some of the requirements for consecration to the Sacred or Immaculate Heart are: living good Christian lives, attending Mass frequently, praying the Rosary, and frequent and reverent partaking of the Holy Eucharist.

ST. MARY OF THE HURONS: A shrine built in Canada by Fr. Jérôme Lalemant, S.J., for the Huron Indians in 1639. Destroyed in 1649 by the Iroquois, it was rebuilt in 1925 and pays tribute to the martyrs John de Brébeuf and Gabriel Lalemant.

VIRGIN OF CHARITY: At a church in Santiago del Prado, El Cobre, Oriente, the faithful venerate a statue of *La Virgen de la Caridad* found in the Bay of Nipe about 1605, also called the Virgin of El Cobre, declared the patroness of Cuba by Pope Benedict XV in 1916; feast day, September 8.

OUR LADY IN AMERICA
The Blessed Virgin Mary has always been the object of devotion for a various peoples throughout the different countries of the world. The titles or "litanies" express a variety of devotional aspects of Our Lady's privileges, virtues, or intercessory powers.

What is not generally known, however, is the fact that Mary is the object of many other devotions in the United States under diverse names or titles. Although many of these shrines or traditional devotion sites have not been officially investigated or accepted by the Church universal, I have included here those that are approved at least on a diocesan or regional level. Note that many of these titles involve traditions unrelated to the states per se, but instead focus upon individual or group experiences of the Blessed Virgin's favors or intercessory powers.

The specific titles chosen for these devotional aspects of the Blessed Virgin Mary may often seem unclear or confusing. At times the particular title reflects nothing more than a name of the area where Marian devotion in general is especially strong: "Our Lady of the Kodiak and the Islands" in Alaska is one such example. In other cases, the title expresses a particular experience of a vision or apparition of Mary: "Our Lady of the Snows" in Utah and "Our Lady of Lourdes" in Tennessee fall under this category. Another remembers favors once received: "Our Lady of Perpetual Help" in New Hampshire emphasizes this role. Finally, some titles represent privileges or honors bestowed upon the nature and person of the Blessed Virgin: "Our Lady of the Assumption" in Maryland and "Our Lady of the Annunciation" in Texas come to mind.

In the examples of the individual states of North America, the titles may have nothing to do with something that occurred in those particular states; rather, they express a devotion of another time, place, or condition. This peculiar aspect of Marian devotion and titles expresses the fact that traditional beliefs and values are carried on through the faith of every generation of believers, whether they be recent or from the distant past. This continuity with past and present is a distinguishing mark of the Roman Catholic Church, and it is best seen through the unbroken faith of a two-thousand-year tradition.

ALABAMA: *Our Lady of the Gulf*
ALASKA: *Our Lady of the Kodiak and the Islands*
ARIZONA: *Our Lady of the Highways*
ARKANSAS: *Our Lady of the Holy Souls*
CALIFORNIA: *Our Lady of the Wayside*
COLORADO: *Immaculate Mary*
CONNECTICUT: *Notre Dame of Easton*
DELAWARE: *Our Lady of Mercy*
FLORIDA: *Our Lady of La Leche*
GEORGIA: *Immaculate Heart of Mary*
HAWAII: *Star of the Sea*
IDAHO: *Our Lady of Limerick*
ILLINOIS: *Our Lady of the Universe*

INDIANA: *Our Lady of Providence*
IOWA: *St. Mary of Nazareth*
KANSAS: *Mary Queen of Angels*
KENTUCKY: *Mother of God*
LOUISIANA: *Our Lady of Prompt Succor*
MAINE: *Our Lady of Peace*
MARYLAND: *Our Lady of the Assumption*
MASSACHUSETTS: *Our Lady of the Incarnation*
MICHIGAN: *Gate of Heaven*
MINNESOTA: *Mother of the Church*
MISSISSIPPI: *Our Lady of Sorrows*
MISSOURI: *Our Lady of Calvary*
MONTANA: *Our Lady of the Pines*
NEBRASKA: *Our Lady of the Presentation*
NEVADA: *Our Lady of Las Vegas*
NEW HAMPSHIRE: *Our Lady of Perpetual Help*
NEW JERSEY: *Our Lady of Fátima*
NEW MEXICO: *Our Lady of Guadalupe*
NEW YORK: *Mary Help of Christians*
NORTH CAROLINA: *Our Lady of the Holy Rosary*
NORTH DAKOTA: *St. Mary, Queen of Peace*
OHIO: *Our Lady of Consolation*
OKLAHOMA: *Queen of All Saints*
OREGON: *Our Lady of the Woods*
PENNSYLVANIA: *Our Lady of the Miraculous Medal*
RHODE ISLAND: *Our Lady of Mount Carmel*
SOUTH CAROLINA: *St. Mary the Virgin Mother*
SOUTH DAKOTA: *Our Lady of the Prairie*
TENNESSEE: *Our Lady of Lourdes*
TEXAS: *Our Lady of the Annunciation*
UTAH: *Our Lady of the Snows*
VERMONT: *Our Lady of Grace*
VIRGINIA: *Queen of the Apostles*
WASHINGTON: *Our Lady of Good Help*
WASHINGTON, D.C.: *Our Immaculate Queen*
WEST VIRGINIA: *Our Lady of Victory*
WISCONSIN: *Our Lady of the Americas*
WYOMING: *St. Mary of the Valley*

TITLES OF THE BLESSED VIRGIN MARY

Adam's Deliverance
Advocate of Eve
Advocate of Sinners
All Chaste
All Fair and Immaculate
All Good
Aqueduct of Grace
Archetype of Purity and Innocence
Ark Gilded by the Holy Spirit
Ark of the Covenant
Blessed Among Women
Bridal Chamber of the Lord
Bride of Christ
Bride of Heaven
Bride of the Canticle
Bride of the Father
Bride Unbrided
Cause of Our Joy
Chosen Before the Ages
Comfort of Christians
Comforter of the Afflicted
Conceived Without Original Sin
Consoler of the Afflicted
Co-Redemptrix
Court of the Eternal King
Created Temple of the Creator
Crown of Virginity
Daughter of Men
David's Daughter
Deliverer of Christian Nations
Deliverer From All Wrath
Destroyer of All Heresies
Dispenser of Grace
Dwelling Place for God
Dwelling Place Meet for God
Dwelling Place of the Illimitable
Dwelling Place of the Spirit
Earth Unsown
Earth Untouched and Virginal
Eastern Gate
Ever Green and Fruitful
Ever Virgin
Eve's Tears Redeeming
Exalted Above the Angels
Fleece of Heavenly Rain
Flower of Jesse's Root
Formed Without Sin
Forthbringer of God
Forthbringer of the Ancient of Days
Forthbringer of the Tree of Life
Fountain of Living Water
Fountain Sealed
Free From Every Stain
Full of Grace
Garden Enclosed
Gate of Heaven
God's Eden
God's Olive Tree
God's Vessel
Handmaid of the Lord
Healing Balm of Integrity
Health of the Sick
Helper of All in Danger
Holy in Soul and Body
Hope of Christians
House Built by Wisdom
House of Gold
Immaculate
Immaculate Conception
Immaculate Heart
Immaculate Mother
Immaculate Virgin
Incorruptible Wood of the Ark
Inventrix of Grace
Inviolate
Joseph's Spouse
Kingly Throne
King's Mother

Lady Most Chaste
Lady Most Venerable
Lady of Good Help
Lady of Grace
Lady of Mercy
Lady of Peace
Lady of Perpetual Help
Lady of the Rosary
Lady of Sorrows
Lady of Victory
Lamp Unquenchable
Life-giver to Posterity
Light Cloud of Heavenly Rain
Lily Among Thorns
Living Temple of the Deity
Loom of the Incarnation
Marketplace for Salutary Exchange
Mediatrix
Mediatrix and Conciliatrix
Mediatrix of All Graces
Mediatrix of Salvation
Mediatrix to the Mediator
Minister of Life
Mirror of Justice
More Beautiful Than Beauty
More Glorious Than Paradise
More Gracious Than Grace
More Holy Than the Cherubim,
Morning Star
the Seraphim, and the
Mother and Virgin
Entire Angelic Hosts
Mother Most Admirable
Mother Most Amiable
Mother Most Chaste
Mother Most Pure
Mother Inviolate
Mother of Christians
Mother of Christ's Members
Mother of the Church
Mother of Divine Grace
Mother of God
Mother of Good Counsel
Mother of Jesus Christ
Mother of Men
Mother of the Mystical Body
Mother of Our Head
Mother of Our Creator
Mother of Our Savior
Mother of Wisdom
Mother Undefiled
My Body's Healing
My Soul's Saving
Mystical Rose
Nature's Re-Creation
Nature's Restoration
Neck of the Mystical Body
Never-Fading Wood
New Eve
Nourisher of God and Man
Olive Tree of the Father's
Only Bridge of God to Men
Compassion
Our Own Sweet Mother
Paradise Fenced Against the Serpent
Paradise of Innocence and
Paradise of the Second Adam
and Immortality
Paradise Planted by God
Patroness and Protectress
Perfume of Faith
Preserved From All Sin
Protectress From All Hurt
Queen of All Saints
Queen of Angels
Queen of Creation
Queen of Heaven
Queen of Heaven and Earth
Queen of Martyrs
Queen of Peace
Queen Unconquered
Refuge in Time of Danger

Refuge of Sinners
Reparatrix of Her Parents
Refuge of Sinners
Rose Ever Blooming
Scepter of Orthodoxy
Second Eve
Sister and Mother
Source of Virginity
Star of the Sea
Suppliant for Sinners
Surpassing the Heavens
Sweet Flowering and Gracious
    Mercy
Temple Divine
Temple of the Lord's Body
Tower of David
Tower Unassailable
Treasure of Immortality
Undefiled Treasure of Virginity
Unlearned in the Ways of Eve
Unplowed Field of Heaven's Bread
Vessel of Honor
Victor Over the Serpent
Virgin Inviolate
Virgin Most Merciful
Virgin Most Prudent
Most Venerable
Wedded to God
Workshop of the Incarnation

Reparatrix
Reparatrix of the Lost World
Rich in Mercy
Sanctuary of the Holy Spirit
Seat of Wisdom
Singular Vessel of Devotion
Spiritual Vessel
Spotless Dove of Beauty
Star That Bore the Sun
Surpassing Eden's Gardens
Surpassing the Seraphim
Tabernacle of God
Tabernacle of the Word
Temple Indestructible
Throne of the King
Tower of Ivory
Treasure-house of Life
Treasure of the World Undefiled
Undug Well of Remission's
    Waters
Unwatered Vineyard of
    Immortality's Wine
Virgin of Virgins
Virgin Most Faithful
Virgin Most Powerful
Virgin Most Pure
Virgin Mother
Woman Clothed With the Sun

V. Appendix A:
Symbols of the Patron Saints

Agatha (date unknown): tongs, veil

Agnes (d. c. 304): lamb

Ambrose (c. 340-97): bees, dove, ox, pen

Andrew (first century): transverse cross

Anne, Mother of Jesus (first century): door

Anthony of Padua (1195-1231): Infant Jesus, bread, book, lily

Augustine of Hippo (354-430): dove, child, shell, pen

Bartholomew (first century): knife

Benedict (c. 480-547): broken cup, raven, bell, crosier, bush

Bernard of Clairvaux (1090-1153): pen, bees, instruments of the Passion

Bernardine of Siena (1380-1444): tablet or sun inscribed with IHS

Blaise (d. 316): wax, taper (candle), iron comb

Bonaventure (1221-74): communion, ciborium, cardinal's hat

Boniface (974-1009): oak, ax, book, fox, scourge, fountain, raven, sword

Bridget of Sweden (1303-73): book, pilgrim's staff

Catherine of Ricci (1522-90): ring, crown, crucifix

Catherine of Siena (1347-80): stigmata, cross, ring, lily

Cecilia (date unknown): organ

Charles Borromeo (1538-84): communion

Christopher (d. c. 251): giant, torrent, tree, Child Jesus on shoulder

Clare of Assisi (1194-1253): monstrance

Cosmas (d. 303) and Damian (d. 303): a phial, box of ointment

Dominic (1170-1221): rosary, star

Elizabeth of Hungary (1207-31): alms, flowers, bread, the poor, a pitcher

Francis of Assisi (1182-1226): wolf, birds, fish, skull, the stigmata

Francis Xavier (1506-52): crucifix, bell, vessel

Geneviève (c. 422-500): bread, keys, herd, cattle

George (d. c. 303): dragon

Gertrude (c. 1256-1302): crown, taper, lily

Gregory I, the Great (c. 540-604): tiara, crosier, dove

Helena (c. 250-330): cross

Ignatius of Loyola (1491-1556): communion, chasuble, book

Isidore (c. 560-636): bees, pen

James the Greater (d. 42): pilgrim's staff, shell, key, sword

James the Less (d. 62): square rule, halberd, club

Jerome (c. 342-420): lion

John Berchmans (1599-1621): Rule of St. Ignatius, cross, rosary
John Chrysostom (c. 347-407): bees, dove, pen
John of God (1495-1550): alms, a heart, crown of thorns
John the Baptist (first century): lamb, head on a platter, animal skin
John the Evangelist (c. 6-104): eagle, chalice, kettle, armor
Joseph, spouse of Mary (first century): Infant Jesus, lily, rod, plane, carpenter's square
Jude (first century): sword, square rule, club
Justin Martyr (c. 100-65): ax, sword
Lawrence (1559-1619): cross, book of the Gospels, gridiron
Leander of Seville (c. 534-600): a pen
Liborius (fourth century): pebbles, peacock
Louis IX of France (1214-70): crown of thorns, nails
Lucy (d. 304): cord, eyes on a dish
Luke (first century): ox, book, brush, palette
Mark (first century): lion, book
Martha (first century): holy water sprinkler, dragon
Matilda (c. 895-968): purse, alms
Matthew (first century): winged man, purse, lance
Maurus (d. c. 287): scales, spade, crutch
Michael: scales, banner, sword, dragon
Monica (c. 331-87): girdle, tears
Nicholas (d. c. 350): three purses or balls, anchor, boat, child
Patrick (c. 389-461): cross, harp, serpent, baptismal font, demons, shamrock
Paul (d. c. 67): sword, book or scroll
Peter (d. c. 64): keys, boat, cock
Philip the Apostle (first century): column
Rita of Cascia (1381-1457): rose, crucifix, thorn
Roch (1295-1378): angel, dog, bread
Rose of Lima (d. 1586): crown of thorns, anchor, city
Sebastian (d. c. 288): arrows, crown
Teresa of Ávila (1515-82): heart, arrow, book
Thérèse of Lisieux (1873-97): roses entwining a crucifix
Thomas Aquinas (c. 1225-74): chalice, monstrance, dove, ox
Thomas the Apostle (first century): lance, ax
Vincent de Paul (1580-1660): children
Vincent Ferrer (1350-1419): pulpit, cardinal's hat, trumpet, captives

VI. Appendix B:
Feast Days of the Patron Saints

(Note that the following information is not exclusively restricted to the patron saints, although many of them are included here).

1. SAINTS IN THE ROMAN CALENDAR

Since the time of the Second Vatican Council (1962-65), the universal Church calendar has undergone major changes which are reflected today in the Roman Rite. His Holiness Pope Paul VI approved of these changes in 1969. The newly revised calendar includes additional saints who have been added to the Church's feast celebrations; other names have been removed altogether for the following reasons: 1) there is not enough historical basis concerning their lives to justify their admittance into the liturgical celebrations; or 2) they lack a universal significance. The omissions have nothing to do with the lack of heroic virtue or the reputation for sanctity.

Those feasts which have been removed from the revised Roman Calendar are as follows:

JANUARY: 5, Telesphorus; 11, Higinus; 19, Marius, Martha, Audifax, Abachum; 21, Agnes.

FEBRUARY: 6, Dorothy; 15, Faustinus & Jovita.

MARCH: 4, Lucius; 10, The 40 Holy Martyrs.

APRIL: 17, Anicetus; 22, Soter & Caius; 26, Cletus & Marcellinus.

MAY: 12, Domitilla; 14, Boniface; 25, Urban I; 30, Eleutherius, Felix I.

JUNE: 12, Basilides, Cyrinus, Nabor & Nazarius; 15, Modestus & Crescentia.

JULY: 10, Seven Holy Brothers; 11, Pius I; 17, Alexius; 18, Symphrosa & her seven sons; 20, Margaret of Antioch; 26, Victor I, Innocent I.

AUGUST: 20, Hippolytus; 26, Zephrynus.

SEPTEMBER: 1, Twelve Holy Brothers; 16, Lucy, Gemianus; 19, Companions of St. Januarius.

OCTOBER: 5, Placid & Companions; 8, Sergius; 21, Ursula & Companions; 26, Evaristus.

NOVEMBER: 10, Tryphon, Respicius & Nympha; 25, Catherine of Alexandria.

DECEMBER: 4, Barbara.

There are four divisions or ranks of liturgical ceremonies representing the various feast days in the Roman Calendar: *solemnities* (those of greatest importance and universal significance); *feasts* and *memorials* (second and third-class feasts which are universally observed); and *optional memorials* (feast days of lesser significance). The optional memorials are celebrated by choice. Included here are only the universal liturgical celebrations found in the first three ranks.

2. HOLY DAYS OF OBLIGATION

The Solemnity of Mary (January 1)
Ascension Thursday (40 days after Easter)
The Assumption (August 15)
All Saints' Day (November 1)
The Immaculate Conception (December 8)
Christmas (December 25)
All Sundays of the Year

3. SOLEMNITIES

Mary, Mother of God (January 1)
Joseph, husband of Mary (March 19)
The Annunciation (March 25)
Resurrection (Easter Sunday)
Ascension (40 days after Easter)
Pentecost (50 days after Easter)
Corpus Christi (Second Sunday after Pentecost)
Sacred Heart (Friday after Corpus Christi)
John the Baptist's Birthday (June 24)
The Apostles Peter & Paul (June 29)
The Assumption (August 15)
All Saint's Day (November 1)
Christ the King (Last Sunday of Ordinary Time)

4. FEASTS

Conversion of St. Paul (January 25)
Presentation of Our Lord (February 2)
Chair of St. Peter (February 22)
Mark the Evangelist (April 25)
The Apostles Philip & James (May 3)
Matthias the Apostle (May 14)
The Visitation (May 31)
The Apostle Thomas (July 3)
The Apostle James (July 25)

The Transfiguration (August 6)
Lawrence the Martyr (August 10)
The Apostle Bartholomew (August 24)
Birth of Mary (September 8)
Triumph of the Cross (September 14)
The Apostle Matthew (September 21)
The Archangels: Michael, Gabriel, Raphael (September 29)
Luke the Evangelist (October 18)
The Apostles Simon & Jude (October 28)
Dedication of St. John Lateran (November 9)
The Apostle Andrew (November 30)
Stephen the Martyr (December 26)
The Apostle John (December 27)
The Holy Innocents (December 28)
The Holy Family (Sunday after Christmas)
Baptism of the Lord (Sunday after January 1)

5. MEMORIALS (Obligatory)

JANUARY: 2, Basil the Great; Gregory Nazianzen; 4, Elizabeth Seton; 5, John Neumann; 17, Anthony; 21, Agnes; 24, Francis de Sales; 26, Timothy & Titus; 31, John Bosco.

FEBRUARY: 5, Agatha; 6, Paul Miki & Companions; 10, Scholastica; 14, Cyril & Methodius; 23, Polycarp.

MARCH: 7, Perpetua & Felicity, Thomas Aquinas.

APRIL: 30, Catherine of Siena.

MAY: 2, Athanasius; 26, Philip Neri.

JUNE: 1, Justin Martyr; 3, Charles Lwanga & Companions; 5, Boniface; 11, Barnabas; 13, Anthony of Padua; 21, Aloysius Gonzaga; 28, Irenaeus.

JULY: 11, Benedict; 14, Bonaventure; 22, Mary Magdalene; 26, Joachim & Anne; 29, Martha; 31, Ignatius of Loyola.

AUGUST: 1, Alphonsus Liguori; 4, John Vianney; 8, Dominic; 11, Clare; 20, Bernard; 21, Pius X; 22, Queenship of Mary; 27, Monica; 28, Augustine; 29, Beheading of John the Baptist.

SEPTEMBER: 3, Gregory the Great; 9, Peter Claver; 13, John Chrysostom; 15, Our Lady of Sorrows; 16, Cornelius; 27, Vincent de Paul; 30, Jerome.

OCTOBER: 1, Thérèse of Lisieux; 2, Guardian Angels; 4, Francis of Assisi; 7, Our Lady of the Rosary; 12, Cyprian; 15, Teresa of Ávila; 17, Ignatius of Antioch.

NOVEMBER: 4, Charles Borromeo; 10, Leo the Great; 11, Martin of

Tours; 13, Francis Xavier Cabrini; 17, Elizabeth of Hungary; 21, Presentation of Mary; 22, Cecilia.

DECEMBER: 3, Francis Xavier; 7, Ambrose; 12, Our Lady of Guadalupe; 13, Lucy; 14, John of the Cross.

6. MOVABLE FEAST DAYS (Depending upon Easter date)

Sexagesima (60 days before Easter)
Ash Wednesday (40 days before Easter)
Palm Sunday (the Sunday before Easter)
Good Friday (the Friday before Easter)
Ascension (40 days after Easter)
Pentecost (seventh Sunday after Easter)
Trinity Sunday (eighth Sunday after Easter)

7. IMMOVABLE FEAST DAYS

The Annunciation (March 25)
Nativity of John the Baptist (June 24)
Feast of St. Michael (September 29)
All Saints (November 1)
Christmas (December 25)

VII. Appendix C: Facts and Figures

Note that the following facts and figures deal with saints of all types and generations. They are not exclusively limited to the patron saints, although many of these are included here as well.

1. TRIVIA CONCERNING SAINTS:
(Latest figures from various sources through 1990)

Roman Catholic Saints: 4,500 listed in the *Roman Martyrology*.

Most Popular Saint Name: John; some 60 saints bear this name.

First American Saint Canonized: Mother Frances Xavier Cabrini (1850-1917); born on July 15 at Sant' Angelo, Italy, youngest of 13 children; founded the Missionary Sisters of the Sacred Heart (1880); moved to America in 1889 to work with Italian immigrants; founded hospitals, convents, schools, and orphanages; became an American citizen in 1909; first naturalized American citizen saint, canonized by Pope Pius XII in 1946; declared patroness of immigrants by Pope Pius XII on November 13, 1950.

First American-Born Saint Canonized: Elizabeth Ann Seton (1774-1821); born in New York City on August 28; foundress of the Sisters of Charity; pioneer of America's parochial school system; canonized by Pope Paul VI on September 14, 1975.

First Male American Saint Canonized: John Nepomucene Neumann (1811-60); born on March 28 at Prachatiz, Bohemia; immigrated to the United States in 1836; extensive missionary work in New York, Pennsylvania, Maryland, Ohio, and Virginia; first Redemptorist to take vows in the United States (1842); became fourth Bishop of Philadelphia (1852); famous catechisms written for Catholic school systems; canonized by Pope Paul VI in 1977.

First Native American (Indian) Beatified: Kateri Tekakwitha (d. 1680); Cause opened in 1932; pronounced Venerable by Pope Pius II (1943); beatified in 1980 by Pope John Paul II.

Recent Popes and Canonizations: Pope John XXIII canonized 10 saints; Pope Paul VI canonized 83 saints; Pope John Paul II canonized 252 saints and beatified 305.

Canonization Facts and Figures: Between 1588-1978, 82% of the 425 officially canonized saints were male; 679 saints have been officially canonized since 1588; many causes have cost over a million dollars to complete.

The fastest canonizations after death were as follows: St. Anthony of Padua, one year; St. Francis of Assisi, two; St. Thomas of Canterbury, three.

The first canonized non-martyred saint: Martin of Tours (d. 397).

The first officially canonized saint: Ulrich (canonized by Pope John XV in 993).

2. MEANINGS OF FAMOUS SAINTS' NAMES:

Agatha (good)
Agnes (pure one)
Albert (noble; brilliant)
Ambrose (divine; immortal)
Andrew (strong; manly)
Angela (angel; messenger)
Ann (graceful one)
Anne (gracious one)
Anthony (inestimable)
Barbara (stranger)
Basil (kingly)
Benedict (blessed)
Bernadette (brave as a bear)
Catherine (pure one)
Cecilia (blind)
Charles (strong; manly)
Christine (Christian)
Christopher (Christ-bearer)
Clara (brilliant; bright)
Claudia (lame one)
Colette (victorious army)
Conrad (able in counsel)
Constance (firmness)
Cornelius (battle horn)
David (beloved one)
Dominic (belonging to God)

Helen (light; torch)
Henry (ruler of estate)
Hilda (battle-maid)
Howard (chief; guardian)
Hubert (bright mind)
Isabel (consecrated to God)
James (supplanter)
Jerome (sacred name)
Joan (God is gracious)
John (God is gracious)
Joseph (He shall add)
Julia (youthful one)
Justin (just)
Katherine (pure one)
Kevin (gentle; lovable)
Lawrence (laurel-crowned one)
Leo (lion)
Louis (famous warrior)
Lucy (bringer of light)
Luke (bringer of light)
Maria (myrrh)
Marie (myrrh)
Mark (warlike one)
Martin (warlike one)
Mary (myrrh)
Matthew (gift of God)

Dorothy (gift of God)
Edith (rich gift)
Edward (prosperous guardian)
Elizabeth (consecrated to God)
Emily (industrious)
Emma (nurse)
Eric (ever powerful)
Ferdinand (world-daring)
Frances (free one)
Francis (free one)
Frederick (peaceful)
Gabriel (man of God)
George (land worker)
Gerard (spear-brave)
Gertrude (spear-strength)
Gilbert (brilliant pledge)
Giles (shield-bearer)
Gregory (watchman)

Michael (who is like God)
Monica (advise)
Nicholas (victory of the people)
Patrick (noble one)
Paul (little)
Peter (rock)
Philip (lover of horses)
Priscilla (ancient birth)
Richard (powerful ruler)
Rita (a pearl)
Robert (shining with fame)
Rose (a rose)
Sophia (wisdom)
Stephen (crowned one)
Theresa (reaper)
Thomas (a twin)
Timothy (honoring God)
Veronica (true image)

3. HONORIFIC TITLES FOR SAINTS:

Angel of the Schools: St. Thomas Aquinas (1225-74)
Angelic Doctor: St. Thomas Aquinas
Apostle of the Gauls: St. Denis (d. c. 258)
Apostle of Germany: St. Boniface (680-754)
Athanasius of the West: St. Hilary of Poitiers (c. 315-68)
Beloved Disciple: St. John the Evangelist (c. 6-104)
Beloved Physician: St. Luke the Evangelist (first century)
Bishop of Hippo: St. Augustine (354-430)
Christian Demosthenes: St. Gregory of Nazianzen (c. 329-89)
Divine Doctor: John Ruysbroeck (1293-1381)
Doctor Angelicus: St. Thomas Aquinas
Doctor Expertus: St. Albert the Great (c. 1206-80)
Doctor of Grace: St. Augustine
Doctor of Mystical Theology: St. John of the Cross (1542-91)
Doctor Universalis: St. Albert the Great
Dumb Ox: St. Thomas Aquinas
Eagle of Divines: St. Thomas Aquinas
Ecstatic Doctor: St. John Ruysbroeck
Evangelical Doctor: St. Anthony of Padua (1195-1231)
Father of Biblical Science: St. Jerome (c. 342-420)
Father of Church History: St. Eusebius (c. 283-371)

Father of Eastern Monasticism: St. Basil the Great (329-79)
Father of English History: Bede the Venerable (c. 672-735)
Father of Moral Philosophy: St. Thomas Aquinas
Father of Orthodoxy: St. Athanasius (c. 297-373)
Father of Scholasticism: St. Anselm (1036-86)
Golden-Tongued Orator: St. John Chrysostom (347-407)
Great Synthesizer: St. Thomas Aquinas
Greatest of the Greek Fathers: St. John Chrysostom
Hammer of the Arians: St. Hilary of Poitiers
Harp of the Holy Spirit: St. Ephraem (c. 306-73)
Illuminator, The: St. Gregory of Armenia (257-331)
Little Flower, The: St. Thérèse of Lisieux (1873-97)
Maid of Orléans: St. Joan of Arc (1412-31)
Mellifluous Doctor: St. Bernard of Clairvaux (1090-1153)
Most Learned of His Day: St. Isidore of Seville (c. 560-636)
Oracle of the Church: St. Bernard of Clairvaux
Pope of the Eucharist: Pope St. Pius X (1835-1914)
Seraphic Doctor: St. Bonaventure (1221-74)
Spouse of Christ: St. Teresa of Ávila (1515-82)
The Theologian of the East: St. Gregory Nazianzen (c. 329-89)
Weeping Saint: St. Swithin (d. 862)

4. THE FOUR 'GREAT' SAINTS OF THE CHURCH:

Albert the Great (c. 1206-80)
Basil the Great (c. 329-79)
Gregory the Great (c. 540-604)
Leo the Great (c. 400-61)

5. LATIN FATHERS OF THE CHURCH:

St. Ambrose, Bishop of Milan (340-97)
St. Augustine, Bishop of Hippo (354-430)
St. Benedict, father of Western monasticism (480-546)
St. Caesarius, Archbishop of Arles (470-543)
St. Celestine I, Pope (d. 432)
St. Cornelius, Pope (d. 253)
St. Cyprian, Bishop of Carthage (d. 258)
St. Damasus I, Pope (d. 384)
St. Dionysius, Pope (d. 268)
St. Ennodius, Bishop of Pavia (473-521)
St. Eucherius, Bishop of Lyons (d. 449)
St. Fulgentius, Bishop of Ruspe (468-533)

St. Gregory of Elvira (d. 392)
St. Gregory the Great, Pope (540-604)
St. Hilary, Bishop of Poitiers (315-68)
St. Innocent I, Pope (d. 417)
St. Irenaeus, Bishop of Lyons (125-203)
St. Isidore, Archbishop of Seville (560-636)
St. Jerome, transl. of *Vulgate* (343-420)
St. John Cassian, abbot (360-433)
St. Leo the Great, Pope (390-461)
St. Optatus, Bishop of Milevis (d. c. 387)
St. Pacian, Bishop of Barcelona (d. c. 390)
St. Pamphilus, priest (240-309)
St. Paulinus, Bishop of Nola (354-431)
St. Peter Chrysologus, Archbishop of Ravenna (406-50)
St. Phoebadius, Bishop of Agen (d. 395)
St. Prosper of Aquitaine, theologian (390-465)
St. Siricius, Pope (334-99)
St. Vincent of Lerins, monk (d. 450)

6. GREEK FATHERS OF THE CHURCH:
St. Andrew of Crete, Archbishop of Gortyna (660-740)
St. Archelaus, Bishop of Cascar (d. 282)
St. Astanasius Sinaita, monk (d. 700)
St. Athanasius, Archbishop of Alexandria (297-373)
St. Basil the Great, Archbishop of Caesarea (329-79)
St. Caesarius of Nanzianzen (329-69)
St. Clement of Alexandria, theologian (150-215)
St. Clement I of Rome, Pope (30-99)
St. Cyril, Bishop of Jerusalem (315-86)
St. Cyril, Patriarch of Alexandria (376-444)
St. Dionysius the Great, Archbishop of Alexandria (190-265)
St. Epiphanius, Bishop of Salamis (315-403)
St. Eustathius, Bishop of Antioch (d. 340)
St. Firmillian, Bishop of Caesarea (d. 268)
St. Germanus, Patriarch of Constantinople (634-733)
St. Gregory of Nanzianzen, Bishop of Sasima (329-89)
St. Gregory of Nyssa (330-95)
St. Gregory Thaumaturgus, Bishop of Neocaesarea (213-68)
St. Hippolytus, martyr (170-235)
St. Ignatius, Bishop of Antioch (35-107)
St. Isidore of Pelusium, abbot (360-450)

St. John Chrysostom, Patriarch of Constantinople (347-407)
St. John Climacus, monk (579-649)
St. John Damascene, defender of sacred images (675-749)
St. Julius I, Pope (d. 352)
St. Justin Martyr, apologist (100-65)
St. Leontius of Byzantium, theologian (sixth century)
St. Macarius the Great, monk (300-94)
St. Maximus, abbot and confessor (580-662)
St. Melito, Bishop of Sardis (d. 190)
St. Methodius, Bishop of Olympus (d. 311)
St. Nilus the Elder, priest and monk (d. 430)
St. Polycarp, Bishop of Smyrna (69-155)
St. Proclus, Patriarch of Constantinople (d. 446)
St. Serapion, Bishop of Thmuis (d. c. 370)
St. Sophronius, Patriarch of Jerusalem (560-638)
St. Theophilus, Bishop of Antioch (second century)

7. DOCTORS OF THE CHURCH:

Albert the Great (c. 1206-80); Dominican; Doctor Universalis
Alphonsus Liguori (1696-1787); Redemptorist
Ambrose (c. 340-97); Bishop of Milan
Anselm (1033-1109); Archbishop of Canterbury; Father of
  Scholasticism
Anthony of Padua (1195-1231); Franciscan; Evangelical Doctor
Athanasius (c. 297-373); Bishop of Alexandria; Father of Orthodoxy
Augustine (354-430); Bishop of Hippo; Doctor of Grace
Basil the Great (329-79); Cappadocian; Father of Eastern Monasticism
Bede the Venerable (c. 672-735); Benedictine; Father of English
  History
Bernard (1090-1153); Cistercian; Mellifluous Doctor
Bonaventure (1221-74); Franciscan; Seraphic Doctor
Catherine of Siena (1347-80); Dominican; second woman Doctor of
  Church
Cyril of Alexandria (c. 376-444); Patriarch of Alexandria
Cyril of Jerusalem (c. 315-86); Bishop of Jerusalem
Ephraem (c. 306-373); Deacon of Edessa; Harp of the Holy Spirit
Francis de Sales (1567-1622); Bishop of Geneva; Patron of
  Authors/Press
Gregory I, the Great (c. 540-604); Pope; Father of the Fathers
Gregory the Nazianzen (c. 329-89); Cappadocian; Theologian of the
  East

Hilary of Poitiers (c. 315-68); Bishop; Athanasius of the West
Isidore of Seville (560-636); Archbishop of Seville
Jerome (c. 342-420); Father of Biblical Science
John Chrysostom (c. 347-407); Bishop of Constantinople
John Damascene (c. 675-749); Monk; Last of the Greek Fathers
John of the Cross (1542-91); Doctor of Mystical Theology
Lawrence of Brindisi (1559-1619); Franciscan
Leo I, the Great (c. 400-61); Pope; Opposer of Heresy
Peter Canisius (1521-97); Jesuit; Second Apostle of Germany
Peter Chrysologus (c. 406-50); Bishop of Ravenna; Doctor of Homilies
Peter Damian (1001-72); Benedictine; Bishop of Ostia
Robert Bellarmine (1542-1621); Jesuit; Archbishop of Capua
Teresa of Ávila (1515-82); Discalced Carmelite; first woman Doctor
Thomas Aquinas (1125-74); Dominican; Angelic Doctor; Great
  Synthesizer

8. PAPAL SAINTS (According to Reign):

St. Peter (d. 64)

St. Linus (c. 67-76)

St. Cletus (c. 76-91)

St. Clement I (c. 91-100)

St. Evaristus (c. 100-105)

St. Alexander I (c. 105-115)

St. Sixtus (c. 115-125)

St. Telesphorus (c. 125-138)

St. Hyginus (c. 138-140)

St. Pius I (c. 140-154)

St. Anicetus (c. 155-166)

St. Soter (c. 167-175)

St. Eleutherius (c. 175-189)

St. Victor I (c. 189-199)

St. Zephyrinus (c. 199-217)

St. Calixtus I (c. 217-222)

St. Urban (c. 222-230)

St. Pontian (c. 230-235)

St. Anterus (c. 235-236)

St. Fabian (c. 236-250)

St. Cornelius (c. 251-253)

St. Lucius (c. 253-254)

St. Stephen I (c. 254-257)

St. Sixtus II (c. 257-258)

St. Boniface I (c. 418-422)

St. Celestine I (c. 422-432)

St. Sixtus III (c. 432-440)

St. Leo I the Great (c. 440-461)

St. Hilary (c. 461-468)

St. Simplicius (c. 468-483)

St. Felix II (c. 483-492)

St. Gelasius I (c. 492-496)

St. Symmachus (c. 498-514)

St. Hormisdas (c. 514-523)

St. John I (c. 523-526)

St. Felix II (c. 526-530)

St. Agapetus I (c. 535-536)

St. Silverius (c. 536-537)

St. Vigilius (c. 537-555)

St. Benedict I (c. 575-579)

St. Gregory I (c. 590-604)

St. Boniface IV (c. 608-615)

St. Deusdedit (c. 615-618)

St. Martin I (c. 649-654)

St. Eugene I (c. 654-657)

St. Vitalian (c. 657-672)

St. Agatho (c. 678-681)

St. Leo II (c. 682-683)

St. Dionysius (c. 259-268)
St. Felix I (c. 269-274)
St. Eutychian (c. 275-283)
St. Caius (c. 283-296)
St. Marcellinus (c. 296-304)
St. Marcellus I (c. 308-309)
St. Eusebius (c. 309-310)
St. Miltiades (c. 311-314)
St. Sylvester I (c. 314-335)
St. Mark (c. 336)
St. Julius I (c. 337-352)
St. Damasus I (c. 366-384)
St. Siricius (384-99)
St. Anastasius I (c. 399-401)
St. Innocent I (c. 401-417)
St. Zosimus (c. 417-418)

St. Benedict II (c. 684-685)
St. Sergius (c. 687-701)
St. Gregory II (c. 715-731)
St. Gregory III (c. 731-741)
St. Zachary (c. 741-752)
St. Stephen III (c. 752-757)
St. Paul I (c. 757-767)
St. Leo III (c. 795-816)
St. Paschal I (c. 817-824)
St. Leo IV (c. 847-855)
St. Nicholas I (c. 858-867)
St. Hadrian III (c. 884-885)
St. Gregory VII (c.1073-85)
St. Celestine V (c. 1294)
St. Pius V. (1566-72)
St. Pius X (c. 1903-14)

9. RECENT SAINTS (Facts and Figures):

Between 1979-89, the percentage of those who were beatified or canonized according to states of life: Laity, 47.0%; religious and clergy, 53.0%; males, 67.2%; females: 32.8%.

Percentages of those beatified or canonized from different continents (1979-89): Europe, 54.5%; Asia, 41.5%; Africa, 0.6%; North America, 2.0%; South America, 1.5%.

Number of those beatified or canonized from different countries (1979-89): Belgium, 1; Brazil, 1; Canada, 9; Chile, 1; Denmark, 1; Ecuador, 2; Egypt, 1; France, 130; Germany, 9; Great Britain, 85 (half martyrs); Guam, 1; Guatemala, 1; India, 2; Israel, 1; Italy, 55; Japan, 18 (martyrs); Korea, 103 (martyrs); Lithuania, 1; Mexico, 1; Paraguay, 3; Peru, 1; Philippines, 1; Poland, 7; Romania, 1; Spain, 41; Turkey, 8; United States, 4; Vietnam, 118 (martyrs); Zaire, 1; others, 7.

Age breakdowns and percentages for those 1,701 causes being advanced through the Congregation for the Causes of the Saints (1979-89): 9 years old or under, 2 (0.1%); 10 to 19 years, 32 (1.9%); 20 to 29 years, 96 (5.6%); 30 to 39 years, 136 (8.0%); 40 to 49 years, 179 (10.5%); 50 to 59 years, 260 (15.3%); 60 to 69 years, 359 (21.1%); 70 to 79 years, 385 (22.6%); 80 to 89 years, 213 (12.5%); 90 to 99 years, 33 (2.0%); 100 years or older: 6 (0.4%).

The youngest candidates currently under consideration for canonization: Antonietta "Nennolia" Meo (1930-37), 7 years old; Marie of

Mount Carmel (Madrid) (1930-39), 9 years old; Jacinta Marto (Fátima), Venerable (1910-20), 10 years old; Francisco Marto (Fátima), Venerable (1908-19), 11 years old; Anne of Guigne (France) (1911-22), 11 years old.

The oldest persons ever to be beatified or canonized: Felicity Salviati (1612-1737), 125 years old; Blessed Gregory Celli (1225-1343), 118 years old; St. Arthold (1101-1206), 105 years old; Blessed Nicholas of Furca (1349-1449), 100 years old; St. Raymond of Peñafort (1175-1275), 100 years old; St. Christopher of Romagnola (1172-1272), 100 years old.

Total Beatifications and Canonizations of the Twentieth Century: Pope Leo XIII (1878-1903), 119; Pope St. Pius X (1903-14), 69: Pope Benedict XV (1914-22), 20; Pope Pius XI (1922-39), 323; Pope Pius XII (1939-58), 183; Pope John XXIII (1958-63), 14; Pope Paul VI (1963-78), 113; Pope John Paul I (1978), 0; Pope John Paul II (1978-), 555. Total: 1,396.

VIII. Bibliography

Broderick, Robert C., *The Catholic Encyclopedia* (Thomas Nelson Publishers, Nashville, TN, 1976).

Butler, Alban; Herbert J. Thurston, S.J. and Donald Attwater, ed., *Butler's Lives of the Saints:* Volumes I-IV (Christian Classics, Westminster, MD, 1988; originally published in London, 1756-59; revised edition by Herbert J. Thurston, S.J., 1926-38; second edition by Herbert J. Thurston, S.J. and Donald Attwater, 1956; copyright by Burns & Oates: 1956, 1981).

Catholic Truth Society, *The Holy Bible: Revised Standard Version*, Catholic Edition (Division of Christian Education of the National Council of the Churches of Christ in the United States of America; New York, London, 1966).

Cruz, Joan Carroll, *Secular Saints* (TAN Books and Publishers, Inc., Rockford, IL, 1989).

Daughters of St. Paul, *Fifty-Seven Saints* (Daughters of St. Paul, St. Paul Editions, Boston, MA,; original copyright 1963; renewed copyright 1980).

Daughters of St. Paul, *Saints for Young People for Every Day of the Year*: Volumes I and II (Daughters of St. Paul, St. Paul Editions, Boston, MA, 1963 and 1964 respectively; renewed copyright 1984).

Delaney, John J., ed., *Pocket Dictionary of Saints* (Image Books, Doubleday & Company, Inc., Garden City, NY, 1980; revised copyright 1983).

Foy, Felician A., O.F.M., ed., *The Catholic Almanac* (Our Sunday Visitor, Inc., Huntington, IN: 1987-90 editions).

Hartdegen, Fr. Stephen J., O.F.M., L.S.S., gen. ed., *Nelson's Complete Concordance of the New American Bible* (Thomas Nelson Inc., Publishers, Nashville, TN, 1977).

King, Marie Gentert, ed., *Foxe's Book of Martyrs* (Jove Publications, Inc., New York, NY, 1968; reprint 1982).

Lawler, Ronald, O.F.M. Cap., Thomas Comerford Lawler, and Donald W. Wuerl, ed., *The Teaching of Christ* (Our Sunday Visitor, Inc., Huntington, IN, 1976).

Liguori, St. Alphonsus de; Rev. Eugene Grimm, ed., *Victories of the Martyrs* (original copyright by the Very Rev. John Sephton, C.SS.R., 1954).

McCloskey, Fr. Patrick, O.F.M., *Franciscan Saint of the Day* (St. Anthony Messenger Press, Cincinnati, OH, 1981).

IX. Indexes of the Patron Saints

This is a multi-purpose index designed to help the reader find particular names or titles concerning the patron saints. Here you will find a breakdown of the various patrons according to category, with the corresponding page references to the right of each entry. These five categories are: "Patron Names," "Countries and Nations," "Occupations and Vocations," "Special Needs and Conditions," and "Our Lady as Patron." Furthermore, the indexing on Mary is broken down into two methods of reference: 1) under her various titles, which can be found in the "Countries and Nations" category; and 2) under the direct Marian titles themselves.

All page references which mention the various saints in the three appendices are excluded from this index system. Because there are hundreds listed there in alphabetical order, the reader should use these appendices as mini-indexes in themselves to find the various kinds of saints throughout Church history, be they patron or not. Otherwise, to include them in this general index would require a much longer indexing system than is already provided here.

At any rate, only the profiles of patron saints are included in this index. The appendices deal with both patron and non-patron saints.

1. INDEX OF PATRON NAMES

Anastasius the Fuller: fullers, 65; weavers, 115
Andrew the Apostle: fishermen, 63-64; Greece, 23-24; Scotland, 32
Andronicus: silversmiths, 107
Angela of Foligno: widows, 188
Anne: cabinetmakers, 46-47; Canada, 18; housewives, 71; women in labor, 192
Anne Line: childless, 125; converts, 127; widows, 188
Ansgar: Denmark, 20
Ansovinus: protector of crops, 163
Anthony of Padua: Portugal, 30-31; searchers of lost items, 166-167; travelers, 115-176
Antony of Egypt: basketmakers, 42; brushmakers, 44-45; butchers, 45; gravediggers, 67
Apollonia: dentists, 57
Armogastes: poverty, 161; victims of torture, 182-183
Arthelais: kidnap victims, 150
Augustine: brewers, 44; printers, 98; theologians, 114-115
Aurelius: orphans, 155
Basil the Great: hospital administrators, 69
Basilica of Saint Mary Major: Our Lady, 196
Benedict Joseph Labre: bachelors, 121; homeless, 149; mental illness, 152; rejection by religious order, 163
Benedict of Nursia: Europe, 22; speliologists, 22
Benedict the Black: missions, Black, 86-87
Benezet: bachelors, 121
Bernard of Clairvaux: chandlers, 49-50
Bernard of Montjoux: alpinists, 36; mountaineers, 88-89; skiers, 108
Bernardine of Siena: advertisers, 36; communications personnel, 51; public relations, 98-99
Bibiana: single laywomen, 171; victims of torture, 183
Blaesilla: widows, 188 young brides, 192
Blaise: throat diseases, 176
Blandina: falsely accused, 143; victims of torture, 183
Boniface: Germany, 23
Boniface of Tarsus: bachelors, 127; converts, 127
Boris and Gleb: princes, 96-97
Brendan: sailors, 102
Bridget of Ireland: dairy workers, 55; Ireland, 25; scholars, 104
Bridget of Sweden: Sweden, 34
Caesarius: bachelors, 121
Camillus de Lellis: hospital workers, 70; nurses, 91; sickness, 169
Canute: Denmark, 20
Casimir of Poland: bachelors, 121-122; kings, 73; Lithuania, 28; Princes, 97
Cassian: stenographers, 110
Castorius: sculptors, 104
Catherine of Bologna: artists, 38-39

Catherine of Genoa: childless, 125; difficult marriages, 135-136; victims of unfaithfulness, 187; widows, 188; young brides, 192

Catherine of Siena: fire protection, 146; Italy, 26; nursing services, 92

Caedwalla: converts, 127; murderers, 154

Cecilia: musicians, 89; organ builders, 92-93; poets, 95; singers, 107-108

Charles Borromeo: catechists, 48; seminarians, 105

Charles Lwanga and Companions: converts, 128; victims of torture, 183

Charles of Blois: prisoners, 162

Charles the Good: counts, 54; Crusaders, 55

Christopher: motorists, 88; porters, 95-96; sailors, 102; travelers, 176

Clement I: marble workers, 82; stonecutters, 111

Clotilde: adopted children, 120; death of children, 131-132; parents of large families, 157; queens, 99; widows, 188; young brides, 192

Columba: Ireland, 25

Cosmas and Damian: barbers, 41-42; pharmacists, 93; physicians, 94; surgeons, 112

Crispin and Crispinian: saddlers, 101-102; shoemakers, 174; tanners, 182-183

Cuthbert: sailors, 102

Cuthman: bachelors, 121-122; poverty, 151; shepherds, 106-107

Cyril and Methodius: Europe, 22; Moravia, 22

Dagobert II: kidnap victims, 150-151; kings, 74; orphans, 155-156; parents of large families, 158

David: Wales, 34

Delphina: tertiaries, 174; young brides, 192

Devota: Monaco, 29

Dismas: funeral directors, 55-56; prisoners, 162

Dominic: astronomers, 39; Dominican Republic, 20

Dominic Savio: choirboys, 50; falsely accused, 143

Dorothy of Montau: death of children, 132; difficult marriages, 136; parents of large families, 158; widows, 188-189; young brides, 1924

Drogo: mental illness, 152-153; orphans, 156; shepherds, 107; sickness, 169; unattractive people, 177

Dunstan: armorers, 38; blacksmiths, 43; goldsmiths, 67; jewelers, 72; locksmiths, 80-81; musicians, 89

Dymphna: mental illness, 153; princesses, 98; runaways, 165; victims of rape, 181

Edgar: kings, 74; widowers, 191

Edmund: kings, 74; victims of torture, 183

Edward the Confessor: difficult marriages, 136-137; kings, 74-75; separated spouses, 167-168

Edwin: converts, 128; homeless, 149; kings, 75; parents of large families, 158

Eligius: jewelers, 72; metal workers, 85

Elizabeth of Hungary: bakers, 41; countesses, 54; death of children, 132; falsely accused, 143-144; homeless, 149; nursing services, 92; tertiaries, 174; widows, 189; young brides, 192

Elizabeth of Portugal: difficult marriages, 137; falsely accused, 144; queens, 99:

tertiaries, 174-175; victims of jealousy, 179; victims of unfaithfulness, 187; widows, 189; young brides, 192

Elzear: tertiaries, 175

Emiliana: single laywomen, 171-172

Epipodius: bachelors, 122; victims of betrayal, 177; victims of torture, 183

Erasmus: sailors, 102-103

Eric: Sweden, 34

Eulalia of Merida: sailors, 103; runaways, 165; victims of torture, 183-184

Eustachius: hunters, 71; victims of torture, 184

Fabiola: difficult marriages, 137; divorced, 140-141; victims of physical abuse, 180; victims of unfaithfulness, 187; widows, 189

Felicity and Her Seven Sons: death of children, 132; widows, 189

Ferdinand III: engineers, 60-61; parents of large families, 158; tertiaries, 175

Fiacre: cabdrivers, 46; gardeners, 66

Flora: abandoned, 119; converts, 128; single laywomen, 172; victims of betrayal, 177-178

Florian: firemen, 63

Frances of Rome: motorists, 88

Frances Xavier Cabrini: migrants, 141; hospital administrators, 69; orphans, 156

Francis de Sales: authors, 39-40; deafness, 131; journalists, 73; writers, 116-117

Francis of Assisi: ecologists, 58-59; Italy, 26; merchants, 84

Francis Borgia: Portugal, 31

Francis of Paola: seamen, 104-105

Francis Xavier: Borneo, 87; missions, foreign, 87

Gabriel the Archangel: messengers, 85; postal employees, 96; radio workers, 100; telecommunications workers, 114; television workers, 114

Gabriel of the Sorrowful Mother: clerics, 51; youth, 193

Gemma Galgani: pharmacists, 93-94

Genesius: actors, 35-36; comedians, 51; converts, 128; lawyers, 78; secretaries, 105; victims of torture, 184

Geneviève: women's army corps, 116

Gengulphus: difficult marriages, 137; knights, 76-77; separated spouses, 168; victims of unfaithfulness, 187

George: Boy Scouts, 43-44; England (see *Boy Scouts*), 43-44; Portugal, 43-44; soldiers, 109-110

Gerald of Aurillac: bachelors, 122; counts, 54; handicapped, 147

Gerard Majella: expectant mothers, 142

Germaine Cousin: abandoned, 119; shepherdesses, 106; sickness, 169; unattractive people, 177; victims of child abuse, 178-179

Gertrude the Great: West Indies, 34-35

Godelieve: difficult marriages, 137-138; victims of physical abuse, 180

Gorgonia: sickness, 169-170

Gotteschalc: linguists, 80; lost vocations, 151-152; princes, 97

Gregory the Great: musicians, 89-90; singers, 108; teachers, 113; West Indies, 89-90

Gregory the Illuminator: Armenia, 15-16

Gudule: single laywomen, 172

Gummarus: childless, 125; courtiers, 55; difficult marriages, 167; separated spouses, 168

Guntramnus: divorced, 141; guardians, 146; murderers, 154

Guy of Anderlecht: bachelors, 122; sacristans, 101

Hadrian: soldiers, 109

Hedwig, Queen of Poland: duchesses, 57-58; queens, 99-100; death of children, 132; difficult marriages, 138; victims of jealousy, 179-180; widows, 189; young brides, 192

Helen of Sköfde: falsely accused, 128-129; widows, 189

Helena: converts, 128-129; difficult marriages, 138; divorced, 141; empresses, 59-60

Henry II: childless, 125-126; dukes, 57; handicapped, 147; rejected by religious order, 163-164

Henry of Uppsala: Finland, 22

Hermengild: converts, 129

Holy Mountain of Our Lady: Our Lady (Greece), 196

Homobonus: tailors, 112

Hubert: hunters, 71

Hugh the Little: victims of torture, 184

Ida of Herzfeld: widows, 189; young brides, 192-193

Ignatius of Loyola: retreats, 164-165; soldiers, 109

Immaculate Heart of Mary: Our Lady; see Sacred Heart of Mary, 211

Isidore: death of children, 132-133; farmers, 61; laborers, 77

Ivetta of Huy: parents of large families, 158; widows, 189-190; young brides, 193

Ivo of Kermartin: lawyers, 78

James Intercisus: lost vocations, 152; victims of torture, 184

James the Greater: pilgrims, 95; rheumatism, 165

James the Lesser: fullers, 65; hatters, 68-69

Jerome: librarians, 79

Jerome Emiliani: orphans, 156

Joan of Arc: France, 22; soldiers, 110

John of Capistrano: jurists, 73; military chaplains, 86

John of God: booksellers, 43; heart patients, 148-149; hospital workers, 70; printers, 98; sickness, 170

John the Apostle: Asia Minor, 16

John the Baptist: farriers, 61-62

John Baptist de la Salle: teachers, 184

John Berchmans: altar boys, 36-37; youth, 193-194

John Bosco: editors, 59; laborers, 77-78

John Chrysostom: orators, 92

John Gualbert: forest workers, 64-65

John Nepomucene: confessors, 52; Czechoslovakia, 19-20

John Regis: medical social workers, 83

John Rigby: bachelors, 122-123; victims of torture, 184

John Vianney: priests, 96

Joseph: Belgium, 16-17; Canada, 47-48; carpenters, 47-48; China, 47-75; dying, 141; Peru (see *Carpenters*), 47-48; workingmen, 116

Joseph Cafasso: prisoners, 162-163

Joseph Calasanz: students/schools, 111, 166

Joseph Moscati: bachelors, 123; rejected by religious order, 164

Joseph of Arimathea: funeral directors, 65

Joseph of Cupertino: aviators, 40

Joseph of Palestine: converts, 129; guardians, 68, 146

Jude Thaddeus: desperate situations, 135; hospital workers, 70

Julia: poverty, 161; victims of torture, 184

Julian the Hospitaler: childless, 126; ferrymen, 62; hospitalers, 70-71; knights, 77; murderers, 154-155

Julitta: single laywomen, 172; victims of torture, 184; widows, 190

Julitta and Cyriacus: death of children, 133; victims of torture, 184-185

Justin Martyr: philosophers, 94

Lawrence: cooks, 52; Sri Lanka, 33-34

Leonard of Port Maurice: missions, parish, 87

Leonidas: parents of large families, 158

Leopold: death of children, 133: Parents of large families, 158-159; stepparents, 173

Louis IX: Crusaders, 55; death of children, 133; difficult marriages, 138; kings, 75; parents of large families, 158-159; prisoners, 163; sickness, 170; tertiaries, 175; young grooms, 193

Louis Bertran: Colombia, 18-19

Louise de Marillac: social workers, 109

Luchesius: death of children, 133; lost vocations, 152

Lucian and Marcian: converts, 129; possessed, 160

Lucy: eye diseases, 143

Ludmila: Bohemia, 17; converts, 129; duchesses, 58; widows, 190

Lufthild: homeless, 149-150; victims of child abuse, 179

Luke the Evangelist: butchers, 46; glassworkers, 67; notaries, 90; painters, 93; physicians, 94; surgeons, 112

Lydia Pupuraria: dyers, 58

Lydwine of Schiedam: sickness, 170; skaters, 108

Macrine the Elder: poverty, 151; widows, 190

Madonna of St. Luke: see "Our Lady," Italy, 196

Mamas: guardians, 146-147; orphans, 156; victims of torture, 185

Margaret Clitherow: businesswomen, 45; converts, 129-130

Margaret Ward: victims of torture, 185

Margaret of Cortona: falsely accused, 144; homeless, 150; midwives, 86; single laywomen, 172; tertiaries, 175-176

Margaret of Fontana: possessed, 160

Margaret of Scotland: death of children, 133-134; parents of large families, 159; queens, 100; widows, 190

Margaret the Barefooted: difficult marriages, 139; widows, !90; young brides, 193

Maria Goretti: Victims of rape, 181-182

Marina: falsely accused, 144

Marinus (Marinao): bachelors, 123; deacons, 56

Mark the Evangelist: notaries, 90-91

Martha: cooks, 52-53; dieticians, 57; innkeepers, 72; servants, 105-106

Martin de Porres: hairdressers, 68

Martin of Tours: beggars, 42-43; soldiers, 110

Mary: Korea, 27; see unit on "Our Lady."

Mary, Queen of Africa: see "Our Lady," 196

Matilda: death of children, 134; falsely accused, 144-145; parents of large families, 159; queens, 100; second marriages, 167; widows, 190-191

Matthew the Apostle: accountants, 35; bankers, 41; bookkeepers, 43; tax collectors, 113

Maurice: dyers, 58; infantrymen, 72; swordsmiths, 112

Maurus: coppersmiths, 53

Michael: grocers, 67-68; mariners, 82; paratroopers, 93; police, 95; sickness, 170-171

Monica: alcoholism, 120-121; difficult marriages, 139; mothers, 153-154; victims of physical abuse, 180-181; victims of unfaithfulness, 187; widows, 191

Natalia: converts, 130

Nicholas of Flüe: councilmen, 53-54; difficult marriages, 139; magistrates, 81; parents of large families, 159; separated spouses, 168

Nicholas of Myra: brides, 44; children, 126; coopers, 53; Greece, 31-32; merchants, 84-85; pawnbrokers, 93; Russia, 31-32; sailors, 103; travelers, 176; young grooms, 31-32

Nicholas of Tolentino: mariners, 82-83

Nonna: death of children, 134

Notburga: field workers, 62-63

Notre Dame Cathedral of Paris: see "Our Lady," 197

Notre Dame de Chartres: see "Our Lady," 197

Nunilo: single laywomen, 172-173; victims of child abuse, 179

Odilia: Alsace, 15; blindness, 124

Olaf II: carvers, 48; difficult marriages, 139-140; kings, 76; Norway, 29

Olga: converts, 130

Oswin: Victims of betrayal, 178

Pantaleon: bachelors, 123; physicians, 94-95; victims of torture, 185

Patrick: Ireland, 25-26

Paul the Apostle: Malta, 28-29; public relations, 99

Paul the Hermit: weavers, 115-116

Pelagius: abandoned, 119-120; victims of torture, 185

Peregrine Laziosi: cancer patients, 124-25

Perpetua: death of children, 134

Peter Baptist: Japan, 26-27

Peter Claver: Colombia, 19; missions, black, 87

Peter Gonzales: sailors, 103-104

Peter of Alcántara: Brazil, 17-18; watchmen, 115
Pharaïldis: difficult marriages, 140; victims of physical abuse, 181; widows, 191
Philemon: converts, 130; dancers, 56
Philip Howard: difficult marriages, 140; falsely accused, 145; separated spouses, 168-169; victims of betrayal, 178
Phocas: gardeners, 66-67
Pollio: lectors, 78-79
Potamieana: victims of rape, 182
Praxedes: single laywomen, 173
Pulcheria: empresses, 60; orphans, 156; victims of betrayal, 178
Raphael: blindness, 124; happy meetings, 148; nurses, 91-92; physicians, 95; travelers, 176-177
Raymond Nonnatus: expectant mothers, 142-143; falsely accused, 145
Raymond of Peñafort: canonists, 47; medical records librarians, 83
Regina: poverty, 151; shepherdesses, 106; victims of torture, 185-186
René Goupil: anesthetists, 37
Richard Gwyn: parents of large families, 159-160; victims of torture, 186
Rita of Cascia: desperate situations, 135
Robert Bellarmine: catechists, 48-49
Roch: bachelors, 123; falsely accused, 145; invalids, 150
Rose of Lima: Americas, 15
Rose of Viterbo: rejected by religious order, 164; tertiaries, 176
Sabas: lectors, 79; victims of torture, 186
Sacred Heart of Jesus: Ecuador, 21
Sacred Heart of Mary: Philippines, 211
St. Mary of the Hurons: Our Lady, 211
Saturus: poverty, 151-152
Scholastica: convulsive children, 131
Sebastian: archers, 37; athletes, 39; soldiers, 110
Seraphina: handicapped, 147; spinners, 110
Serenus: bachelors, 123-124: falsely accused, 145-146
Servulus: handicapped, 147-148
Simon of Trent: kidnap victims, 151; victims of torture, 186
Solangia: shepherdesses, 106; victims of rape, 155
Solomon: kings, 76; murderers, 253-254
Stanislaus of Krakow: Poland, 30
Stephen of Hungary: bricklayers, 44; death of children, 134-135; Hungary, 24; kings, 76; stonemasons, 111
Syncletica: Sickness, 171; single laywomen, 173
Teresa of Ávila: headache sufferers, 148; Spain, 33
Tharsilla: single laywomen, 173
Theobaldus: bachelors, 124; church cleaners, 50
Theodota: converts, 130; victims of torture, 186
Thérèse of Lisieux: aviators, 40-41; florists, 64; France, 23; missions (foreign), 87; Russia, 23

Thomas Aquinas: students/schools, 111-112, 166
Thomas More: adopted children, 120; difficult marriages, 140; lawyers, 78; parents of large families, 160; stepparents, 174; widowers, 191
Thomas the Apostle: architects, 37-38; East Indies, 21
Thorlac Thorhallsson: Iceland, 24
Venerius: lighthouse keepers, 80
Victor of Marseilles: victims of torture, 186
Vincent de Paul: charitable societies, 125
Vincent Ferrer: builders, 45
Vincent of Saragossa (Zaragoza): Portugal, 31
Vitus: epilepsy, 141
Vladimir: converts, 130-131; murderers, 155; parents of large families, 155
Wenceslaus: Bohemia, 17
Wernher: kidnap victims, 151
William of Norwich: kidnap victims, 151; victims of torture, 187
William of Rochester: adopted children, 120
Willibrord: epilepsy, 141; Holland, 24
Zita: maids, 81-82; servants, 106; Single laywomen, 173

2. INDEX OF COUNTRIES AND NATIONS
Africa: Mary, Queen of Africa, 196
Alsace: Odilia, 15
Algeria: Our Lady of Africa, 197-198
Americas: Rose of Lima, 15
Angola: Immaculate Heart of Mary (see *Sacred Heart of Mary*), 211
Argentina: Our Lady of Lujan, 204
Armenia: Gregory the Illuminator, 15-16
Asia Minor: John the Apostle, 16
Australia: Our Lady Help of Christians, 197
Austria: Our Lady of Mariazell, 204
Belgium: Joseph, 16-17; Our Lady of Banneux, 198; Our Lady of Beauraing, 199
Bohemia: Ludmila, 17; Wenceslaus, 17
Bolivia: Our Lady of Copacabaña, 199
Borneo: Francis Xavier, 87
Brazil: Our Lady of Nazareth, 205; Our Lady Who Appeared, 211; Peter of Alcántara, 17-18
Canada: Anne, 18; Joseph, 47-48; Our Lady of the Cape, 208; Saint Mary of the Hurons, 211
Ceylon: see *Sri Lanka*
China: Joseph, 47-48
Colombia: Louis Bertran, 18-19; Peter Claver, 19
Cuba: Virgin of Charity, 211
Czechoslovakia: John Nepumocene, 19-20
Denmark: Angsar, 20; Canute, 20

Dominican Republic: Dominic, 20; Our Lady of High Grace, 201

East Indies: Thomas the Apostle, 21

Ecuador: Sacred Heart of Jesus, 21

El Salvador: Our Lady of Peace, 205

England: George (see *Boy Scouts*), 43-44; Our Lady of Mount Carmel at Aylesford, 205; Our Lady of Walsingham, 210

Equatorial Guinea: Our Lady of the Immaculate Conception (see unit on "Our Lady"), 208-209

Europe: Benedict of Nursia, 22; Cyril and Methodius, 22

Finland: Henry of Uppsala, 22

France: Joan of Arc, 22; Notre Dame Cathedral of Paris, 197; Notre Dame de Chartres, 197; Our Lady of La Salette, 202; Our Lady of Lourdes, 203-204; Our Lady of Pontmain, 206; Our Lady of the Miraculous Medal, 209; Thérèse of Lisieux, 23

Germany: Boniface, 23; Our Lady of Altötting, 332-33; Our Lady of Kevelaer, 202

Gibraltar: Our Lady of Europe, 199-200

Greece: Andrew the Apostle, 23-24; Nicholas of Myra, 31-32; The Holy Mountain of Our Lady, 196

Holland: Willibrord, 24

Hungary: Our Lady of Hungary, 201-202; Stephen, 24

Iceland: Thorlac Thorhallsson, 24

India: Our Lady of Bandel, 198; Our Lady of Bandra, 198; Our Lady of the Assumption, 24-25, 208

Ireland: Bridget, 25; Columba, 25; Our Lady of Knock, 202; Our Lady of Limerick, 203; Patrick, 25-26

Italy: Basilica of Saint Mary Major, 196; Catherine of Siena, 26; Francis of Assisi, 26; Madonna of St. Luke, 196; Our Lady of Loreto, 203; Our Lady of Perpetual Help, 205; Our Lady of Pompeii, 205-206; Our Lady of Tears, 207; Our Lady of the Snow, 210

Japan: Our Lady of Japan, 202; Peter Baptist, 26-27

Korea: Mary, 27; see unit on "Our Lady."

Lesotho: Immaculate Heart of Mary (see *Sacred Heart of Mary* under "Our Lady"), 211

Lithuania: Casimir of Poland, 28

Luxembourg: Willibrord, 24

Malta: Paul the Apostle, 28-29

Mexico: Our Lady of Guadalupe, 201

Monaco: Devota, 29

Moravia: Cyril and Methodius, 22

New Zealand: Our Lady Help of Christians, 197

Norway: Olaf II, 29

Papua New Guinea: Michael the Archangel (see *Grocers* under "Occupations and Vocations"), 67-68

Paraguay: Our Lady of the Assumption, 208

Peru: Joseph, 47-48

Philippines: Our Lady of Safe Travel, 206: Our Lady of the Turumba, 210; Sacred Heart of Mary, 211

Poland: Our Lady of Czestochowa, 30, 199; Stanislaus of Cracow, 30

Portugal: Anthony of Padua, 30-31; Francis Borgia, 31; George, 31; Our Lady of Fátima, 200; Vincent of Zaragoza, 31

Russia: Nicholas of Myra, 31-32; Thérèse of Lisieux, 23

Scandinavia: Angsar, 20

Scotland: Andrew the Apostle, 32

Silesia: Hedwig, 32-33

South Africa: Our Lady of Shongweni, 206-207

South America: Rose of Lima, 15

Spain: Our Lady of Guadalupe of Estremadura, 201; Our Lady of Montserrat, 204; Our Lady of Ransom, 206; Our Lady of the Pillar of Saragossa, 209; Teresa of Ávila, 33

Sri Lanka: Lawrence, 33-34; Our Lady of Madhu, 204

Sweden: Bridget, 34; Eric, 34

Switzerland: Our Lady of the Hermits, 208

Tanzania: Our Lady of the Immaculate Conception (see unit on "Our Lady"), 208-209

Uganda: Mary, Queen of Africa, 196

United States: National Shrine of the Immaculate Conception (see *Our Lady of the Immaculate Conception*), 208-209; Our Lady of the Milk and Happy Delivery, 204; Our Lady of Victory, 210

Vietnam: Our Lady of La Vang, 203

Wales: David, 34

West Indies: Gertrude the Great, 34-35; Gregory the Great, 89-90

3. INDEX OF OCCUPATIONS AND VOCATIONS

Accountants: Matthew the Apostle, 35

Actors: Genesius, 35-36

Advertisers: Bernard of Siena, 36

Alpinists: Bernard of Montjoux, 36

Altar Boys: John Berchmans, 36-37

Anesthetists: René Goupil, 37

Archers: Sebastian, 37

Architects: Thomas the Apostle, 37-38

Armorers: Dunstan, 38

Artists: Catherine of Bologna, 38-39

Astronomers: Dominic, 39

Athletes: Sebastian, 39

Authors: Frances de Sales, 39-40

Aviators: Joseph of Cupertino, 40; Thérèse of Lisieux, 40-41

Bakers: Elizabeth of Hungary, 41

Bankers: Matthew the Apostle, 41

Barbers: Cosmas and Damian, 41-42
Basketmakers: Antony of Egypt, 42
Beggars: Martin of Tours, 42-43
Blacksmiths: Dunstan, 43
Bookkeepers: Matthew the Apostle, 43
Booksellers: John of God, 43
Boy Scouts: George, 43-44
Brewers: Augustine, 44
Bricklayers: Stephen of Hungary, 44
Brides: Nicholas of Myra, 44
Brushmakers: Antony of Egypt, 44-45
Builders: Vincent Ferrer, 45
Businesswomen: Margaret Clitherow, 45
Butchers: Antony of Egypt, 45; Luke the Evangelist, 46
Cabdrivers: Fiacre, 46
Cabinetmakers: Anne, 46-47
Canonists: Raymond of Peñafort, 47
Carpenters: Joseph, 47-48
Carvers: Olaf II, 48
Catechists: Charles Borromeo, 48; Robert Bellarmine, 48-49
Chandlers: Ambrose, 49; Bernard of Clairvaux, 49-50
Choirboys: Dominic Savio, 50
Church Cleaners: Theobaldus, 50
Clerics: Gabriel of the Sorrowful Mother, 51
Comedians: Genesius, 51
Communications Personnel: Bernardine of Siena, 51
Confessors: Alphonsus de Liguori, 51-52; John Nepomucene, 52
Cooks: Lawrence, 52; Martha, 52-53
Coopers: Nicholas of Myra, 53
Coppersmiths: Maurus, 53
Councilmen: Nicholas of Flüe, 53-54
Countesses: Elizabeth of Hungary, 54
Counts: Charles the Good, 54; Gerald of Aurillac, 54
Courtiers: Gummarus, 55
Crusaders: Charles the Good, 55; Louis IX, 55
Dairy Workers: Bridget of Ireland, 56
Dancers: Philemon, 56
Deacons: Marinus, 56
Dentists: Apollonia, 57
Dieticians: Martha, 57
Duchesses: Hedwig, Queen of Poland, 57-58; Ludmila, 58
Dukes: Henry II, 57
Dyers: Lydia Pupuraria, 58; Maurice, 58
Ecologists: Francis of Assisi, 58-59
Editors: John Bosco, 59

Empresses: Adelaide, 59; Helena, 59-60; Pulcheria, 60
Engineers: Ferdinand III, 60-61
Farmers: Isidore, 61
Farriers: John the Baptist, 61-62
Ferrymen: Julian the Hospitaler, 62
Fieldworkers: Notburga, 62-63
Firemen: Florian, 63
Fishermen: Andrew the Apostle, 63-64
Florists: Thérèse of Lisieux, 64
Forest Workers: John Gualbert, 64-65
Fullers: Anastasius the Fuller, 65; James the Lesser, 65
Funeral Directors: Dismas, 65; Joseph of Arimathea, 65
Gardeners: Adelard, 65-66; Fiacre, 66; Phocas, 66-67
Glassworkers: Luke the Evangelist, 67
Goldsmiths: Dunstan, 67
Gravediggers: Antony of Egypt, 67
Grocers: Michael the Archangel, 67-68
Guardians: Guntramnus, 141; Joseph of Palestine, 68; Mamas, 146-147
Hairdressers: Martin de Porres, 68
Hatters: James the Lesser, 68-69
Hospital Administrators: Basil the Great, 69; Frances Xavier Cabrini, 69
Hospital Workers: Camillus de Lellis, 70; John of God, 70; Jude Thaddeus, 70
Hospitalers: Julian the Hospitaler, 70-71
Hotelkeepers (see *Innkeepers*)
Housewives: Anne, 71
Hunters: Eustachius, 71; Hubert, 71
Infantrymen: Maurice, 72
Innkeepers: Amand, 72; Martha, 72
Jewelers: Dunstan, 72; Eligius, 72
Journalists: Francis de Sales, 73
Jurists: John of Capistrano, 73
Kings: Casimir of Poland, 73; Dagobert II, 74; Edgar, 74; Edmund, 74; Edward the Confessor, 74-75; Edwin, 75; Louis IX, 75; Olaf II, 76; Solomon, 76; Stephen of Hungary, 76
Knights: Gengulphus, 76-77; Julian the Hospitaler, 77
Laborers: Isidore the Farmer, 77; John Bosco, 77-78
Lawyers: Genesius, 78; Ivo of Kermartin, 78; Thomas More, 78
Lectors: Pollio, 78; Sabas, 79
Librarians: Jerome, 79
Lighthouse Keepers: Venerius, 80
Linguists: Gotteschalc, 80
Locksmiths: Dunstan, 80-81
Magistrates: Nicholas of Flüe, 81
Maids: Zita, 81-82
Marble Workers: Clement I, 82

Mariners: Michael, 82; Nicholas of Tolentino, 82-83
Medical Record Librarians: Raymond of Penafort, 83
Medical Social Workers: John Regis, 83
Medical Technicians: Albert the Great, 83-84
Merchants: Francis of Assisi, 84; Nicholas of Myra, 84-85
Messengers: Gabriel the Archangel, 85
Metal Workers: Eligius, 85
Midwives: Margaret of Cortona, 86
Military Chaplains: John of Capistrano, 86
Missions (Black): Benedict the Black, 86-87 Peter Claver, 87
Missions (Foreign): Francis Xavier, 87; Thérèse of Lisieux, 87
Missions (Parish): Leonard of Port Maurice, 87
Mothers: Monica, 88
Motorcyclists: Our Lady of Grace (see "Our Lady"), 201
Motorists: Christopher, 88; Frances of Rome, 88
Mountaineers: Bernard of Montjoux, 88-89
Musicians: Cecilia, 89; Dunstan, 89; Gregory the Great, 89-90
Notaries: Luke the Evangelist, 90; Mark the Evangelist, 90-91
Nurses: Agatha, 91; Camillus de Lellis, 91; John of God, 91; Raphael, 91-92
Nursing Services: Catherine of Siena, 92; Elizabeth of Hungary, 92
Orators: John Chrysostom, 92
Organ Builders: Cecilia, 92-93
Painters: Luke the Evangelist, 93
Paratroopers: Michael the Archangel, 93
Pawnbrokers: Nicholas of Myra, 93
Pharmacists: Cosmas and Damian, 93; Gemma Galgani, 93-94
Philosophers: Justin Martyr, 94
Physicians: Cosmas and Damian, 94; Luke the Evangelist, 94; Pantaleon, 94-95;
Raphael, 95; see also *Surgeons*
Pilgrims: James the Greater, 95
Poets: Cecilia, 95
Policemen: Michael the Archangel, 95
Porters: Christopher, 95-96
Postal Employees: Gabriel, 96
Priests: John Vianney, 96
Princes: Boris and Gleb, 96-97; Casimir of Poland, 97; Gotteschalc, 97
Princesses: Adelaide, 97-98; Dymphna, 98
Printers: Augustine of Hippo, 98; John of God, 98
Public Relations: Bernardine of Siena, 98-99
Public Relations (Hospitals): Paul the Apostle, 99
Queens: Clotilde, 99; Elizabeth of Portugal, 99; Hedwig, Queen of Poland, 99-100;
Margaret of Scotland, 100; Matilda, 100
Radio Workers: Gabriel, 100
Radiologists: Michael the Archangel, 101
Sacristans: Guy of Anderlecht, 101

4. INDEX OF SPECIAL NEEDS AND CONDITIONS

Abandoned: Flora, 119; Germaine Cousin, 119; Pelagius, 119-120

Adopted Children: Clotilde, 120; Thomas More, 120; William of Rochester, 120

Alcoholism: Monica, 120-121

Bachelors: Benedict Joseph Labre, 121; Benezet, 121; Boniface of Tarsus, 121; Caesarius, 121; Casimir of Poland, 121-122; Cuthman, 122; Epipodius, 122; Gerald of Aurillac, 122; Guy of Anderlecht, 122; John Rigby, 122-23; Joseph Moscati, 123; Marinus (Marinao), 123; Pantaleon, 123; Roch, 123; Serenus, 123-124; Theobaldus, 124

Blindness: Odilia, 124; Raphael, 124

Bodily Ills: Our Lady of Lourdes, 203-204

Cancer Patients: Peregrine Laziosi, 124-125

Charitable Societies: Vincent de Paul, 125

Child Abuse: see *Victim of Child Abuse*

Childless: Anne Line, 125; Catherine of Genoa, 125; Gummarus, 125; Henry II, 125-126; Julian the Hospitaler, 126

Children: Nicholas of Myra, 126

Converts: Afra, 126-127; Alban, 127; Anne Line, 127; Boniface of Tarsus, 205-206; Caedwalla, 127; Charles Lwanga and Companions, 127-128; Edwin, 128; Flora, 128; Genesius, 128; Helena, 128-129; Hermengild, 129; Joseph of Palestine, 129; Lucian and Marcian, 129; Ludmila, 129; Margaret Clitherow, 129-130; Natalia, 130; Olga, 130; Philemon, 130; Theodota, 130; Vladimir, 130-131

Convulsive Children: Scholastica, 131

Deafness: Francis de Sales, 131

Death of Children: Clotilde, 131-132; Dorothy of Montau, 132; Elizabeth of Hungary, 132; Felicity and Her Seven Sons, 132; Hedwig, 132; Isidore, 132-133; Julitta and Cyriacus, 133; Leopold, 133; Louis IX, 133; Luchesius, 133; Margaret of Scotland, 133; Matilda, 133-134; Nonna, 134; Perpetua, 134; Stephen of Hungary, 134-135

Desperate Situations: Jude Thaddeus, 135; Rita of Cascia, 135

Difficult Marriages: Catherine of Genoa, 135-136; Dorothy of Montau, 136; Edward the Confessor, 136-137: Elizabeth of Portugal, 137: Fabiola, 137; Gengulphus, 137; Godelième, 137-138; Gummarus, 138; Hedwig, 224; Helena, 138; Louis IX, 138-139; Margaret the Barefooted, 139; Monica, 139; Nicholas of Flüe, 139; Olaf II, 139-140; Pharaildis, 140; Philip Howard, 140; Thomas More, 140

Divorced: Fabiola, 140-141; Guntramnus, 141; Helena, 141

Dying: Joseph, 141

Emigrants: Frances Xavier Cabrini, 141

Epilepsy: Vitus, 142; Willibrord, 142

Expectant Mothers: Gerard Majella, 142; Raymond Nonnatus, 142-143

Eye Diseases: Lucy, 143

Falsely Accused: Blandina, 143; Dominic, 143; Dominic Savio, 143; Elizabeth of

Separated Spouses: Edward the Confessor, 168; Gengulphus, 168; Gummarus, 168; Nicholas of Flüe, 168; Philip Howard, 168-169

Sickness: Camillus de Lellis, 169; Drogo, 169; Germaine Cousin, 169; Gorgonia, 169-170; John of God, 170; Louis IX, 170; Lydwine of Schiedam, 170; Michael, 170-171; Syncletica, 171

Single Laywomen: Agatha, 171; Alodia, 171; Bibiana, 171; Emiliana, 171-172; Flora, 172; Gudule, 172; Julitta, 172; Margaret of Cortona, 172; Nunilo, 172-173; Praxedes, 173; Syncletica, 173; Tharsilla, 173; Zita, 173

Stepparents: Adelaide, 173; Leopold, 173; Thomas More, 174

Tertiaries: Delphina, 1747; Elizabeth of Hungary, 174; Elizabeth (Queen of Portugal), 174-175; Elzear, 175; Ferdinand III, 175; Louis IX, 175; Margaret of Cortona, 175-176; Rose of Viterbo, 176

Throat Disease: Blaise, 176

Travelers: Anthony of Padua, 176; Christopher, 176; Nicholas of Myra, 176; Raphael, 176-177

Unattractive People: Drogo, 177; Germaine Cousin, 177

Victims of Betrayal: Epipodius, 177; Flora, 177-178; Oswin, 178; Philip Howard, 178; Pulcheria, 178

Victims of Child Abuse: Alodia, 178; Germaine Cousin, 178-179; Lufthild, 179; Nunilo, 179

Victims of Jealousy: Elizabeth of Portugal, 179; Hedwig, Queen of Poland, 179-180

Victims of Physical Abuse: Fabiola, 180; Godelième, 180; Margaret the Barefooted, 180; Monica, 180-181; Pharaïldis, 181

Victims of Rape: Agatha, 181; Agnes, 181; Dymphna, 181; Maria Goretti, 181-182; Potamiaena, 182; Solangia, 182

Victims of Torture: Agatha, 182; Alban, 182; Armogastes, 182-183; Bibiana, 183; Blandina, 183; Charles Lwanga and Companions, 183; Edmund, 183; Epipodius, 183; Eulalia of Merida, 183-184; Eustachius, 184; Genesius, 184; Hugh the Little, 184; James Intercisus, 184; John Rigby, 184; Julia, 184; Julitta, 184; Julitta and Cyriacus, 184-185; Mamas, 185; Margaret Ward, 185; Pantaleon, 185; Pelagius, 185; Regina, 185-186; Richard Gwyn, 186; Sabas, 186; Simon of Trent, 186; Theodota, 186; Victor of Marseilles, 186; William of Norwich, 187

Victims of Unfaithfulness: Catherine of Genoa, 187: Elizabeth of Portugal, 187; Fabiola, 187; Gengulphus, 187; Monica, 187

Widows: Adelaide, 187-188; Angela of Foligno, 188; Anne Line, 188; Blaesilla, 188; Catherine of Genoa, 188; Clotilde, 188; Dorothy of Montau, 188-189; Elizabeth of Hungary, 189; Elizabeth of Portugal, 189; Fabiola, 189; Felicity, 189; Hedwig, 189; Helen of Sköfde, 189; Ida of Herzfeld, 189; Ivetta of Huy, 189; Julitta, 190; Ludmilla, 190; Macrina the Elder, 190; Margaret of Scotland, 190; Margaret the Barefooted, 190; Matilda, 190-191; Monica, 191: Olga, 191; Pharaïldis, 191

Widowers: Edgar, 191; Thomas More, 191

Women in Labor: Anne, 192

Young Brides: Adelaide, 192; Blaesilla, 192; Catherine of Genoa, 192; Clotilde, 192; Delphina, 192; Dorothy of Montau, 192; Elizabeth of Hungary, 192; Elizabeth

5. OUR LADY AS PATRON